BEHIND THE SCENES
WITH EDWIN BOOTH

EDWIN BOOTH AS HAMLET
(Act III, Scene i)

BEHIND THE SCENES
WITH
EDWIN BOOTH

BY

KATHERINE GOODALE
(KITTY MOLONY)

WITH A FOREWORD BY
MRS. FISKE

and with illustrations

BENJAMIN BLOM   New York/London

First Published 1931
Reissued 1969 by
Benjamin Blom, Inc., Bronx, New York 10452
and 56 Doughty Street, London, W.C. 1

Library of Congress Catalog Card Number 76-87121

Printed in United States of America
at Westbrook Lithographers, Inc.
Westbury, New York

PREFACE

AFTER the death of Edwin Booth, when loving and
eloquent tributes to his memory appeared in book form,
Mr. Goodale — whose own sorrow had been tenderly
phrased for his column in the Detroit *Free Press*, and
whoever viewed life from the angle of the literati —
suggested that my notes, many of them jotted down in
Mr. Booth's presence, should assume the dignity of pub-
lication. Against this stood, deep-rooted and strong, my
reluctance, born of Mr. Booth's faith. Equally restrain-
ing was a very natural shrinking from even lightly touching with my own brief span of theatre-life the fame that
still blazons its solitary way across the skies of art. That
the manuscript contained nothing that did not glorify
the character of the Master Tragedian; that, with the
passing of Edwin Booth, its very insignificance transmuted my viewpoint into interest and value, did not
shake a refusal in which my husband regretfully if sympathetically concurred.

For our own reading, I did set down a description of
this 'happiest season.' Written in the third person
with all mention of my name painstakingly expurgated,
its only merit was its modesty. A mere ghostly shadow
hovered over my paragraphs. I had drawn an outline
of Edwin Booth, not his portrait.

Todays became yesterdays. Then spoke Mrs. Fiske.
She spoke with the emphasis of finality.

PREFACE

'You owe this pen picture of Edwin Booth to the theatre — to all well-wishers of the theatre — but let us see Edwin Booth as he was seen through the eyes of a young girl member of his company.' With fine scorn the authoritative artist swept aside my disinclination to write in the first person.

So, my original notes, jotted down with such unconcern and so self-unconsciously, but withal so accurately, were again made to serve. Nothing was added but their needed background of *how, when, and where.* Much was omitted to keep the size of the manuscript within bounds, but nothing was left out that in the least affected the integrity of my recollections.

When to Mrs. Fiske's encouragement was added approval of the generous one of whom her great father ever spoke as 'my daughter,' the last lingering fears of disloyalty to our Mr. Booth vanished in the thin air of his own Macbeth witches.

KATHERINE GOODALE

NEW YORK, *January* 1, 1931

CONTENTS

CONTENTS

ILLUSTRATIONS

FOREWORD

A NUMBER of years ago a friend showed me a diary written at the time of a season spent with Edwin Booth — a record of each day's happenings and talks. I then urged that this record be given to the world. I felt that it would be a great pity to lose those intimate stories and that they should be preserved and made public to color the previous Booth reminiscences. But that time did not seem to be the psychological moment for a book based on this material. Its writing has been delayed until the present.

When the eagerly awaited manuscript was finally completed, I was enchanted by its authentic picture of the theatre at its best. I should like to put this book into the hands of every actor, young or seasoned in the theatre. The whole theatre grows large in the genius, the art, and the character of this man. Particularly, the book should be an inspiration to the youth of the stage.

Here we have given us a rare record of a complete season, day by day, picturing our great genius of the theatre in his dressing-room, in the wings, in his private car. One is literally taken back of the curtain of the tragedian's life on tour. And it is delightful to know that one is permitted to share intimately a memory of Edwin Booth's happiest season in the theatre. Not the happiest period of his private life, not the most brilliant in his professional career, but its happiest 'forty weeks' — perhaps owing to the three young girls whom

FOREWORD

Mr. Booth affectionately named 'the Chickens,' one of whom, Katherine Goodale, is the writer of these memories.

This was the outstanding season when Edwin Booth changed from a recluse in his hotel rooms to an habitual sight-seer, and in these pages we can follow his gradual relaxing and his final yielding to youthful and merry companionship. We even see him leading some of the frolics himself.

How happy and at peace it made him that his environment was not marred by professional or other jealousy among 'the Chickens'! They rose to their opportunity, and Mr. Booth gladly filled their hours with pleasure because of their dispositions and attitude to one another before him.

The book reveals the reverence of actors, *born in the theatre*, for the theatre, and their ability to teach by their example this reverence to young actors coming into the theatre from the outside world. Here is also set forth clearly the educational value of acting in a repertoire of classical and poetic dramas, with the usual effect of their sublime thoughts upon characters of actors who are constantly repeating the lines of masterpieces. What wonderful training that was! An enormous repertoire in a few days. When one compares this accomplishment with modern production, it is like comparing a giant with a dwarf!

Then there are such delightful people to be met in these pages. Besides 'the Chickens' — those happy, vivacious, tactful girls — there is Mr. Chase, the manager, ever conscientious and thoughtful for his Star, whose problems become ours as we read; there is Mr. Booth's genial, loyal, and devoted brother-in-law, affectionately dubbed 'Popper' by 'the Chickens'; there are the two grand old ladies of the company, belonging to a still earlier tradition of the stage; and there are hosts of others.

But to return to the central figure of the book — the greatness of Edwin Booth's character is only augmented when he is revealed away from the pedestal high upon which his reputation has placed him, and never is he more to be revered than when one sees him pictured in his everyday life in the theatre. This record makes it clear that Edwin Booth was a product of the theatre — in fact, in himself existed the American Theatre.

The chapter on the San Francisco Fire Boy is deliciously funny, and it almost seems to me I have never read anything more honestly and truly humorous than the story of the proposed reception at the railway station and the street parade.

There is poignant pathos in the last parting between the girl who had understood the man so well and the great tragedian — the last back-look of the gracious, lonely figure. There is much in this book that will live vividly in the memory of those who knew Edwin Booth.

In presenting this unusual picture of our great genius, Mrs. Goodale most happily combines maturity of viewpoint with all the youthful enthusiasm of the young girl who was so fortunate in her contacts with Edwin Booth. And in addition to this, she writes with authority, both because of her own experience as an actress

FOREWORD

and because of inspiration from her husband, the late George P. Goodale, one of America's two outstanding dramatic critics, a man of great heart and clear vision.

MINNIE MADDERN FISKE

BEHIND THE SCENES
WITH EDWIN BOOTH

BEHIND THE SCENES WITH EDWIN BOOTH

. .

CHAPTER I

TEARING UP MY BARRETT CONTRACT

ONE night in the winter of 1885–86, during the Lawrence Barrett production of *Hernani* at the Star Theatre in New York, a young actress of the cast, in the 'Eminent Tragedian's' dressing-room, was tearing up a contract for 'next season,' to make legal the signing of another contract, also for next season, to support Edwin Booth.

It was a sober moment. Might it not mean sundering a strong and on my part a fond tie? Lawrence Barrett had not only placed me in the theatre and trained me in his own company to be his soubrette, but he had woven about me a network of conduct rules. In my impudent moments I liked to tell Mr. Barrett that he lay awake at night thinking up things I was not to do. But he said he should send me back to my mother the very same girl he took from her home.

In his super-happy New Orleans days, Mr. Barrett had danced with my mother, and numbered my planter father among his friends. He had kept his promise to be my friend in the theatre. He gazed now on the little ring my mother had given to me on my sixteenth

3

birthday. It was almost historic, for it had been presented to her in New Orleans for interceding with General Benjamin Butler — her husband's cousin — in behalf of Confederate war prisoners. The ring, set with its wee, perfect diamond, was coined from grateful hearts — for it had been bought in war-time when in the South the cost of jewels was all but prohibitive. Mr. Barrett remembered that my mother had thrown herself heart and soul into the cause of aiding these poor, young prisoners of war — and had he forgotten, there was their common friend General Sherman to remind him. My Star deemed it fitting that it was I who now wore this ring. Was I not a New Orleans baby? — for having been actually born in the North did not count with this New Orleans partisan. He reminded me that between then and now lay my Weimar school-life days with Liszt and my beloved statues of Goethe and Schiller. 'You have been reared in an atmosphere of genius and I am placing you where genius will again be the breath of life for you. There is only one genius on the stage today and he is Edwin Booth.'

Since my 'signing,' weeks before, there had been organized the new management association of Edwin Booth and Lawrence Barrett, and I had been selected for Jessica, Lucretia, Lazarillo, the Prince of Wales, etc. In, fact, I was to be the 'juvenile' at an increased salary, three costumes thrown in (a startling innovation, this), but leaving a dozen more or less for me to pay for. Nothing professionally more dazzlingly brilliant — for my third season on the stage — could have come my way, to everybody's thinking. The profes-

KITTY MOLONY

sion was rich in legitimate actors, and Mr. Barrett was picking a company worthy of his Star. No more of those shocking supports for Mr. Booth that managements had so often martyred him with.

Mr. Barrett had written to my mother: 'Kitty's methods will broaden under the art of Edwin Booth.' That was a dear way of putting it, for my acting art was somewhat too slowly forming to be entitled to be called 'methods.' But I did know by heart — after two years of the legitimate — the acting versions of the Shakespearean plays in our repertoire, and I felt, as my Star felt, that he had directly and indirectly prepared me to 'take in' the art of Edwin Booth. Mr. Barrett had said: 'No one needs to be prepared to take in Edwin Booth's genius.'

Yet this moment, now come, to tear up my Barrett contract was full of qualms. All at once I did not want to be of the personnel of the Booth company. I had seen Edwin Booth act twice, in *Richard III*, and in *The Iron Chest*, supported by the celebrated Boston Museum Company right in its own theatre, but before I had ever seen him on the stage, I had given him my hero-worship. It was in the air to be 'insane on Edwin Booth.' He was on such a high pedestal that I wanted him to stay there — just my ideal; for if I lost it, it were a case of 'This was a Cæsar! Whence comes such another!' So I said to Mr. Barrett: 'I don't want to know Mr. Booth. I don't want to think of him as a man. I just want to think of him as the genius.'

Mr. Barrett understood young girl psychology. He was father of three daughters.

'When next season is over, you'll be wondering which is greater, his genius — or his character. Don't worry about his toppling from any pedestal. Haven't I told you ——?'

'You have made him out perfect; but when you know why an actor is a human being, you don't get so excited standing in front of his posters — you don't shiver so when you read his programs — before the curtain rises. I don't want to lose that something ——'

'What something? Put it into words ——'

'I can't. Of course Edwin Booth is lightning in the clouds! He's the sun in the sky! He's the moon in the night — but it isn't human nature that he won't, in forty weeks, do something I shall be sorry for.'

Mr. Barrett snubbed me by laughing at me, and then saying, earnestly, 'I wish I were as sure you might keep all your ideals as that of Edwin Booth. Come, sign your contract.'

I did.

CHAPTER II

THE first rehearsal was called about ten days before the Buffalo opening, September 13, 1886. It was in New York at the Academy of Music, and for eleven o'clock. Obedient to Mr. Barrett's law, come down from the ancients — ten minutes' grace to allow for difference in watches and town clocks on the first morning, but never afterward — I was prompt. I walked on air to the stage door, one hour ahead of time; but it was the stage door of the Star Theatre where Lawrence Barrett was playing. All at once the thought of the Booth Company over at the Academy made me shy. Here was home — in the Barrett Company — and I *must* touch earth on this stage.

There was some one else walking on air this morning. Mr. Barrett, the veteran, was even earlier than the youngest of his company. He was in high spirits! His dream was come true with this hour! His future was solid! No more worries; big business sure; debts paid. But the happy laugh of his greeting told a story deeper than the business side of his partnership with Edwin Booth. An equally profitable association, with a drawing foreign star, had been of the mind for him; the one with Edwin Booth was of the heart.

It meant something for the 'Eminent Tragedian' to step into second place, which he must do next season in all things, and in some for even this present one. He

7

had been starring a long time. He liked physical comfort. He liked his first choice in everything. And now he was giving up route, dressing-rooms, parts, but chiefly the psychology of audiences. I had told him he would be as a race-horse put in draft-work harness, and he had scolded me for not understanding him. 'The labor we delight in physics pain.' He was doing this for the theatre. It was he, Lawrence Barrett, come into the theatre from the outside, half-starved, uneducated, who today was providing the proper settings for the hereditary Prince. It was he who was easing the nerves of the King, so that the public might again have the King at his best. I was not impressed by the absence of professional jealousy on the second tragedian's part. I never met an actor who did show professional jealousy of Edwin Booth — he was too far above them all for this, but I was impressed by Mr. Barrett's love for the man. It was so at variance with all that was said of him in the theatre.

Mr. Barrett was boyishly teasing me now for my promptness. 'Now that you are going among strangers, you must shed your novice habit of arriving at re-hearsal an hour ahead of time. Don't look so exultant!' He could not keep from studying his own watch — he was as excited, as exultant as I. 'Come! We'll go over together and I'll present you to your new Star.'

On the way to the Academy stage door, I do not know which was diverting the other, for the new partner was nervous, a strange mood at rehearsal time for him. He did so wish that first rehearsal to satisfy Mr. Booth.

The American Opera Management had lent its stage

8

for the Booth rehearsals. Punctuality was in the air, for the Academy stage was already filled by an assembled company and Mr. Booth was standing by the prompt table. It was quite an entrance for me, to be taken down there by Mr. Barrett and 'introduced.'

It had come! I was facing the great Edwin Booth in real life.

He smiled pleasantly at his new partner, yet casually as if they had parted at breakfast — at the remotest at last night's supper. Mr. Barrett was as simple in manner this morning as was Mr. Booth. To my surprise, I heard him say, as if it were the most natural thing in the world and not the most unheard-of — 'I have brought my little girl.' Mr. Booth was gracious enough if he did ignore the personal note of my 'presentation.' He even looked as if he preferred I should 'move on.'

During the short walk over, I had asked Mr. Barrett if he should 'take the rehearsal,' and had been answered he did not know, which surprised me. It was his company. He was the managerial head, but he showed here that everything was bent to 'the genius' — that he took no thought of his own dignity before this new company which he himself had selected and engaged. He was on hand to direct, if —— Then Mr. Booth did the thing to surprise even his lifelong associate — Edwin Booth took the rehearsal himself. Without hesitation he instructed the stage manager to call 'Richelieu, Act One.' The Star went through it thoroughly. He knew every line in the play — no need of a prompter for him. He knew music cues — any cue.

9

BEHIND THE SCENES WITH BOOTH

The Booth business was more elaborate than the Barrett business in the same play. It was easier to do for the reason there was so much more of it. To me it seemed, in this first rehearsal under Mr. Booth, 'the play's the thing' was the keynote of his directing. Nothing suggested he was building up his own scenes to the detriment of the rest of the play. He at once showed that he trusted the experienced actors engaged to support him. His attitude was that these actors knew their business and he took it for granted that they came to rehearsal 'prepared' for their rôles.

When *Hamlet* was called and I took my place for Osric, Mr. Booth gave me an illustration of his tact. He let the scene proceed, but after rehearsal he drew me away upstage and said charmingly: 'Will it break your heart if I take you out of Osric? It's a man's part; I never sympathized with casting girls for boys' parts. I want my boys played by boys. Osric is a young man of the world — and they are always giving him to a delicate little woman ——'

Of course, whether my heart broke or not had nothing to do with it, and when I saw Mr. Charles Abbe's beautiful performance, I was converted to a male Osric. But that didn't pay for my beautiful costume, which was never worn.

After the rehearsal, which Mr. Barrett left early out of respect to Mr. Booth, I was sauntering back to my hotel on Fourteenth Street thinking it over — *it* being my new Star. I passed Tammany Hall, and there he stood. A small crowd was on the sidewalk, and behind it Mr. Booth was trying to take shelter. He was wait-

ing, I thought, for some one — perhaps for his carriage. No one was speaking to him. He recognized me with no hint of a smile, and conveyed somehow that out of regard for my sex, I was to bow first. He returned my own very formal little nod in an impersonal, kindly manner, which nevertheless did not obscure his imploring to be let alone.

I passed by, thinking of him in quite the same way I had been wont to meditate upon the statues of Goethe and Schiller. The geniuses of my childhood's Weimar were no more Olympian to me than was today the figure of Edwin Booth.

Out in the sunshine his face was even more alive — his eyes more glowing — than in the artificial light of the theatre. Mr. Booth was fifty-three, as every one knew, and to a girl in her teens this is almost old. But not once did I think of him except as a young man. No such stuff as maturity or age composed my thoughts. A memory — a very seedling, it was so young — insisted upon being conjured up. It was of the child I had been in Weimar, when one day in an atelier two important artists were saying things above my head, but which I did not forget. Heart to heart they told — I being too little to be heeded — how they struggled to get on canvas that something they saw only in inspired moments, that something that makes a face un-mortal, and its painter immortal. I knew what they meant now. I had seen it this day — in the face of Edwin Booth.

That first morning we rehearsed *Richelieu* and *Hamlet*. The second day we did *Hamlet*, *Richelieu*, and

Macbeth, and were out of the theatre by three o'clock. Many of the company had played together with Mr. Booth and some — Owen Fawcett for one — were of Booth Theatre casts. These veterans did not wait for instructions, but tackled their scenes with the sure touch of knowledge. They were as easy in their parts as Mr. Booth was in his. Three tragedies in a four-hour rehearsal was nothing to them.

The partners must have been in nightly conference. When I came to the theatre on the third day, I was told I must do the Player Queen again. I did not mind giving up parts so much as I did going back to 'baby rôles' like the Player Queen and Marion de Lorme. When I rehearsed Marion, Mr. Booth showed an interest in her that surprised me. He left her on the scene to eavesdrop twice as long as did Mr. Barrett. He was kind about it all. There was no sarcasm in his voice when he said, 'I am sorry to put you back in a part I am told you have graduated from. But the Player Queen lines must be heard across the footlights.'

I suppose Miss Rock, the very pretty dancer who had not had 'lines' before, felt as badly to be taken out of the part as I did to be put back.

Ten days proved enough to get the company letter-perfect in *Richelieu*, *Macbeth*, *Hamlet*, and *Othello*. The repertoire consisted of these four tragedies, and in addition, *Richard III* (Colley Cibber version for the first time in some years), *Katherine and Petruchio*, *Merchant of Venice*, *The Fool's Revenge*, *Brutus*, *Don Cæsar de Bazan*, *King Lear*, and *A New Way to Pay Old Debts*.

These rehearsals revealed a kindly director, but one

on the job every moment. As an actor, Mr. Booth came down to cues. When the scene demanded that the supporting actors have the full speech, Mr. Doud read it.

The personnel included Charles Barron, leading man; John T. Malone, Charles Hanford, Carl Ahrendt, Charles Coleman, John T. Sullivan, Lucius Henderson, Edwin Milton Royle, Charles Abbe, Owen Fawcett, Harry C. Barton, Volney Streamer, Walter Thomas, Francis Bret Harte, John Doud, and Oliver Doud (stage manager), Miss Emma Vaders, Mrs. Augusta Foster, Mrs. Baker, Miss Molony, Miss Ida Rock, and Rosie Milburn (child); besides the stage staff, wardrobe mistress for the supers, etc.; and of course Mr. Arthur Branscomb Chase, manager, Mr. Ormund Butler, advance. The child's mother travelled with her. Behind it all was the mind of Lawrence Barrett and the Star was Edwin Booth.

As a matter of record merely, the parts played were by:

Mr. Barron	— Othello, The Ghost, Edgar, Macduff, Richmond, etc.
Mr. Malone	— The King (*Hamlet*), de Mauprat, Banquo, Duke (*The Fool's Revenge*), Bassanio, Edmund, etc.
Mr. Hanford	— Baradas, Horatio, Lorenzo, etc.
Mr. Ahrendt	— Polonius, Father Joseph, etc.
Mr. Sullivan	— Laertes, Poet (*The Fool's Revenge*), Gratiano, etc.
Mr. Fawcett	— First Gravedigger, Launcelot Gobbo, Grumio, First Witch, etc.
Mr. Abbe	— Osric, Fool (*King Lear*), etc.
Mr. Coleman	— King (*Richelieu*), First Actor, Antonio, etc.

13

Mr. Henderson — Second Gravedigger, Second Witch, Old Gobbo, etc.

Mr. Barton — Duke of Orleans, Rosencrantz, etc.

Mr. Royle — Tubal, Guildenstern, Huguet, etc.

Mr. Streamer — Priest (*Hamlet*), Captain of Guard (*Richelieu*), etc.

Mr. Thomas — François, Second Actor, etc.

Mr. Harte — Bernardo, Clermont, etc.

Mr. John Doud — Call Boy and Utility.

Miss Vaders –– Ophelia, Julie, Cordelia, Katherine, Nerissa, Lady Anne, Desdemona, Maritana, Fiordelisa, etc.

Mrs. Foster — Lady Macbeth, Portia, Queen Elizabeth (*Richard III*), Goneril, Duchess (*The Fool's Revenge*), Queen (*Hamlet*), Amelia, etc.

Mrs. Baker — Third Witch, Regan, Duchess of York, Curtis, etc.

Miss Molony — Jessica, Player Queen, Prince of Wales, Lucretia, Lazarillo, Fleance, etc.

Miss Rock — Gentlewoman, Page (*Richelieu*), Court Lady, etc.

Rosie Milburn — The Duke of York, Child Apparition, etc.

Mr. Magonigle became treasurer soon after the opening and unprofessionally, in the spirit of friendship, assumed the duties of steward of the private car, the 'David Garrick.'

There was a Booth Theatre reunion atmosphere about these rehearsals. Mr. Barrett sauntered over mornings as if coming home again, pleasant, casual, but ready if Mr. Booth should change his mind. But Mr. Booth never did. He directed daily. Lawrence Barrett the autocrat was itching to 'take' these rehearsals. He ached to put some of the big scenes through, to whip up the actors as he did in his own company; but his restraint was perfect. When he could no longer endure it, he left the theatre, always smiling, yet with a wondering, worshipping look for Mr. Booth.

Garry Davidson, the super-property man — the super any sort of a man, when honor, loyalty, service are standard! — Garry, once of Booth's Theatre, but for some seasons past of the Lawrence Barrett Company, said he felt he was in heaven. 'Why! I am seeing Mr. Booth every day again, and in the theatre at rehearsal. What more could I want?'

There was only one Garry ever! He alone won the implicit trust of both these great artists.

The last Saturday rolled around. We were given our trunk labels — 'Theatre' and 'hotel.' Among my trunks, even in 1930, there is one labelled 'Edwin Booth Company Hotel.' Costumes, shoes, wigs, make-up were delivered and packed — including my glittering jewels. Had they been real, they had not been more precious to me, for these were *stage jewels!* That was their glamour! A crown, a headband, the Marion de Lorme 'diamonds'; but the most caressed was the lovely pearl cestus of fine workmanship — a gift from Miss Ellen Terry. With a thrill I folded my Christian-Jessica dress, for it was romance. That very incarnation of Beatrice, the inspiration of all the young legitimate actresses, Miss Terry herself, had gone down on her knees to help pin the paper pattern of her own Portia dress, and had snipped and pinned and 'bossed,' waxing enthusiastic over being able to help on a costume to be worn for Mr. Booth. And she proved that she had kept tabs on Mr. Barrett's company and that she understood perfectly what would most warm the heart of a little juvenile. I hugged that wonderful Jessica dress and wished it were the adorable Miss Terry.

On the last Saturday night, during Antony's oration when Cassius has a long breathing spell in his dressing-room, Mr. Barrett gave to me his parting 'scolding' — one of those understanding scoldings I knew I should miss, for I liked them so well. He said this was really my home-leaving. I was going among strangers, standing on my own feet for the first time.

'I shall not be there to keep you out of difficulties.' I was to heed his warning. 'Do not form friendships during the first weeks. No! None! People who are easy to get acquainted with are hard to drop. I should like to forbid friends altogether, but you must wait until Chicago. Keep by yourself until the company "settles." Hasty friends make enemies. I can advise you upon enemies more than any actor in the theatre.' He spoke this sadly. 'There's Chase. He knows your bringing-up and he's responsible to me. You know I do not sympathize with lonely people. I shall not be there to keep you out of trouble, but' — a sudden softening — 'if there's a real injustice, write to me — you can always come home.'

At last he touched on the theme near his heart, his genius partner.

'You will help me all you can by your own example!

LAWRENCE BARRETT

MY FIRST BOOTH REHEARSAL

One tactful little girl can do much to sweeten the atmosphere for even her star. If Mr. Booth is contented, if his health is excellent, all will go well. Chase will do everything, so will I, and if you will do your part ——— I must leave it to your own tact what to do: but you will help me — if you are not too much in awe of Mr. Booth! Be yourself with him; I have paved the way for you, and Chase understands. Nothing may come of it. I rely on your tact!'

Wasn't there anything special ———?

'No, I have no definite notion of what I want you to do — perhaps nothing at all, only do not be afraid of him. It should not be hard to be a sweet girl and influence the others to be thoughtful. Upon his contented mind my own business future depends. Be yourself with him — if the opportunity comes. It may not ———!'

Everything imagination could conceive of was to be done to make the coming season one of content for his new partner. Might it not lead to Mr. Barrett's dream — his Perfect Theatre? He had told me Edwin Booth was to be its chief attraction; it was to perpetuate the *standard;* eminent artists, prominent actors were to appear there, young talent trained, and he himself — the leading scholar of the American stage — was to direct as well as act and manage. And the best of it was, the money was all pledged.

We travelled to Buffalo, our opening town, in a special day coach. True to my instructions, I flocked by myself. But I bought the Booth Prompt Books and

17

had a wonderful time. Mrs. Baker, Mrs. Foster, and Miss Vaders at once formed a group. Mr. Booth and Mr. Chase sat way up in the front. The leading lady became almost hysterical. She laughed until every one turned to see what it was about. The Star did not seem displeased. Mr. Chase told me afterwards that Mr. Booth said to him: 'This hysteria will come out in her acting. She is facing three big parts for the first time this week. She feels our newness. Let her alone. It's a good sign.'

And Mr. Chase added: 'You see it did come out in her acting.' For from the first, Miss Emma Vaders was a success.

CHAPTER III

THE OPENING NIGHT

WE opened in Buffalo for a three nights' engagement. Mr. Booth did not play Wednesday matinées nor did he play Sundays. I was expecting this schedule, as it was Mr. Barrett's also, and I was glad I could continue to see the 'opposition' Sundays and Wednesdays. I thus saw much of the talent of the theatre. Mr. Booth uncomplainingly played Thanksgiving, Christmas, New Year's, and Washington's Birthday matinées. There were no other holiday afternoon performances then. On Good Friday he refused to appear. On that day his theatre was dark. This was Mr. Barrett's custom, too; but unlike him, Mr. Booth made no reduction in our salaries for the Good Friday closing, neither did he do so when he was ill — which was just once — nor for lost time in travel. He had a way of adjusting those business complications by bearing the pecuniary loss himself.

The opening bills were *Richelieu*, *Macbeth*, *Hamlet*. No Sunday rehearsal! On Monday we were called for eleven, but no Star today. I do not remember another rehearsal the entire season that he attended. No one could help but draw the conclusion that, when Mr. Booth acted at night, he did not intend to tire himself rehearsing.

Mr. Doud was rehearsal authority now, and he put us through this opening day *Richelieu*, *Macbeth*, and *Hamlet*. He for the first time placed in my hands a

19

marked Booth Prompt Book of *Hamlet*, and said in casual tones,

'Just get up those extra lines of the Player Queen and come down to cues this morning. We've no time to waste on those who are "up."'

I was not 'up' in *Macbeth*. Small as Fleance and the Bloody Apparition were, there was the timing to get hold of.

After my dressing-room was put in order, costumes for the three Buffalo plays hung up, the rest of the day flew by. Oh, the joy of being again on the dark stage waiting for the 'lights to be on' — to see to make-up by. Easy as I was, with no chance of a stage-fright, there was the great thrill of the first night of going on with Edwin Booth.

Mr. Booth was in the theatre before seven. He came on the yet dark stage, escorted by Mr. Chase, who was in full evening dress. The lights went on miraculously. Mr. Booth had come in through the stage door, giving me a small surprise shock, as Mr. Barrett invariably entered his theatre from the front. He stopped to say: 'Will you come to my dressing-room around overture? I always look my Marion over.' He walked on, to pause and add: 'I'll send Lodge for you' — real fun in his voice — 'you might come too soon.'

As the Star dressing-room was near my own, it fell to my lot to see the reverence, the ceremoniousness, with which he was received by a little man in a dinner coat, and I began to feel the subtle difference of Mr. Booth of rehearsal and Mr. Booth actually the actor. This little man, who put to shame the hero and valet de chambre canard, turned out to be Lodge. He was so much more than dresser! He was the tenor of our quartette — its leader and trainer. They sang in the *Merchant* and other plays, and never failed to get their 'big hand'; and he was also the one who carried on the trade in Booth Prompt Books and photographs, which boys sold in front.

As my toilette progressed, again I heard 'half-hour,' 'quarter-hour,' and had given Marion her last touch when 'overture' was called, and straightway Lodge appeared. I sighed as I thought of Mr. Barrett's unsatisfactory dressers and wished he might get some one like Lodge, but the next moment I forgot everything except the pith of the moment — I was stepping into the holy of holies of the theatre — into the dressing-room of Edwin Booth.

'Come in,' hastily, businesslike. He gave my piled-up curls, etc., his inspecting glance. My costume, my get-up, was historically correct down to its pearled ruching, and he took this in with a dismissing gesture. There was nothing to be said against it, therefore, nothing at all; but he favored me with the tiniest bit of appreciation as my eyes travelled to a small engraving pinned on the wall near his dressing-table — crowded with make-ups. His eyes followed mine from this picture of the historic Richelieu back to his own face.

As if forgetting me, he gave his face a concentrated scrutiny in his mirror and compared the reflection with the authentic portrait of the Cardinal-statesman. For me there was nothing unfamiliar in a Richelieu make-up, but here was a new touch. It was the 'Frenchiness'

Mr. Booth had put into it. Mr. Booth was a Frenchman now, and a tall one. Of course, I knew that the long robe curled about his feet — ready to trail after him — would give an added effect of height, yet he did surprise me by seeming so tall.

I left hurriedly, for Act First was called, but even as I started to climb the stairs, Mr. Booth came close behind me. I stepped aside for him to pass, but he waved me to precede him, for I was 'discovered.'

This was an early coming to the stage for a Richelieu. I suppose the long vacation did tell even on his nerves. The orchestra was winding up the overture as I took my position. This curtain music sounded like the voice of an old friend, for it was the same Mr. Barrett used for his Richelieu. The curtain rose! The season was begun! —— that season of which Mr. Booth was to say: 'It was the happiest of my life.'

Edwin Booth in *Richelieu* had packed the house. Our front scene was soon over, and I scooted noiselessly to the wings for my peep at Richelieu's first appearance, which came at once, with the change of scene. I listened for the Barrett music to give this cue, and had a special little thrill here, for I heard instead the composition of Louis Treize. All in a split second I was again in Weimar practising the royal tune, but the swelling notes brought me back into the exciting present, for that crescendo could only mean just what it did — the star's entrance. Edwin Booth was 'on.' Then I heard his reception, and it sent shivers up and down my spine!

Tonight each member of the cast who could manage it was in the wings to hear 'his reception.' Proud we

were to be supporting him for forty-two weeks! When
the applause died down, we listened for his voice. Each
one almost stopped breathing in order not to miss the
first notes of Edwin Booth's voice. Like a violin strain
it came, and we cringed, just thinking of how rough our
voices would sound from the same stage.

As I stepped on for my own scene with Richelieu,
I suddenly was numb. What horrible comparisons
every one in front must be making! Here was the greatest of all actors! — the most finished! — and I was by
his side!! How he was showing me up!

When the curtain fell Mr. Booth signalled for François and me to 'hold the picture' for the first curtain
call. He took the others alone.

I whisked into Kitty Molony clothes to be up in time
for Richelieu's great moment — the Curse of Rome.
I have heard people declare with a truculent 'I dare
you not to believe me,' that Mr. Booth grew seven feet
tall as he gave the curse. It was a tremendously startling effect, but to produce it the artist combined stagecraft with his acting. This optical illusion was built up
detail by detail with the assistance of the Star's supporting actors, who carried out his minute instructions.

In the Curse of Rome scene, Richelieu appears for
the first time in his official robes. No costumer's conception of a Cardinal of the Roman Catholic Church
was worn. His robes were *built* abroad by an ecclesiastical tailor — real lace, genuine ermine, heavy corded
silk of a color, of a quality, that clinched for the eye
their authoritative beauty. Here was a composition in
the strongest of color contrasts; the Cardinal Red for

its high-light, while for background there was the black velvet mourning of the assembled courtiers — mourning for his own supposed death. Neither the rope-girdled grey of Father Joseph's person nor Julie's white wedding garment detracted from the primary red spot. Julie was guided by Richelieu below him with a quick, imperious, but not rough gesture. Not for her to obscure the actor from one eye in all that theatre! With the left hand, he snatched away the ermine border — that hindered by falling over his right hand — even as he raised this hand and drew the imaginary circle about Julie, but without taking one step toward her. He faced her, but spoke to Baradas, who stood below him (right).

'Mark where she stands. Around her trembling form, I draw the awful circle of our solemn Church. Set but a foot within that holy bound, and on thy head — yea, though it wore a crown — I'll launch the Curse of Rome!'

As Mr. Booth hurled this speech, he threw his right hand up above his head and raised himself on tiptoes — an unseen movement, for the train of his robe lay stretched out before him on the stage floor. It hid his feet, and that long red line guided the observer's eye to the very tip of his two high-held fingers.

But this was not all. In the same instant that Richelieu rose upon his toes, all the actors on the stage — not one exception — quickly knelt, bowed heads low, and shrank with terror. As they seemed to descend, Mr. Booth appeared to ascend, and the optical illusion that Mr. Booth suddenly became seven feet tall was produced. The supporting actors, literally as well

24

EDWIN BOOTH AS RICHELIEU
The curse of Rome
From the painting by John Collier

as psychologically, dwindled into dwarfs. But out in front no one noticed *them*. All eyes were on Edwin Booth!

But, after all, this carefully planned, smoothly rendered business was a mere outward form — a shell — of that superb climax. Edwin Booth taught me, through observation of him, that he did not spurn 'theatre.' He utilized it. It was his mountain-peak climbing paraphernalia — but it was *no more* than this, and in what 'more' means lay the hypnotic force of his acting.

In this Curse scene his voice held the blasts of Hell. His eyes blazed, in their finality of wrath. His gesture — his posture — was doom to souls! He was not Time; he was Eternity. No one who saw him — heard him — give that curse doubted he could damn a soul.

The audience went wild. I should love to re-live one of those hysterical outbursts of a Booth audience!

Mr. Barrett had not used *Macbeth* in his repertoire after I joined his company; therefore, our first *Macbeth* performance was doubly exciting for me. I did not see Mr. Booth 'made up' until I glimpsed him from the wings. I did not quite like to admit to myself how unsupernatural the witches were, but my pulse quickened enough when one of them shrieked: 'A drum, a drum, Macbeth doth come.'

Enter Banquo — no applause. Enter Macbeth — ah, what a roar out there! He's on now, but 'far up back.' When Mr. Booth came downstage far enough for me to see his Macbeth make-up, I was disappointed. I had taken it for granted that he would be beautiful to the eye tonight, for he was not playing an old man nor a deformed half-monster. I had not the least objection to his being hideous if the character demanded it. I adored my own ugly make-ups. Without giving it a thought, I assumed Macbeth would be 'straight,' and therefore ideal.

In his street clothes Mr. Booth was slender, with not a half-pound overweight perceptible. His Richelieu was a thin, elderly man. Tonight his Macbeth walked on, a muscular fighter, convincing on the instant that he could endure hard knocks, and give them too. He was sure of foot, like the stag. He made one think of 'Leaping from crag to crag.' He held his spear as if his arms were tireless. His face was ruddy with outdoor health, but its poetry was almost obscured. I did not, however, think this during the murder scene, nor in any following scene. Indeed, I thought just the reverse when he gave his line, 'Wake, Duncan, to thy knocking, *I would thou could'st.*'

In his first scene I found myself studying this warrior and forgetting Mr. Booth. His face was but a shade less red than his rough wig. This Macbeth was the sort of man on whose credulity witches could play; for there was in his roving eyes indecision that the pride of his bearing did not hide. He looked ready for the deeds of the play. I didn't like the man I saw on the stage and couldn't tell why. The murders that come later hadn't anything to do with it. I missed something beautiful from Mr. Booth's face. It was all so vague, so slight, yet so insistent that I — goose of a dramatic critic that I was — was troubled. I did not know enough to realize that my disappointment in Mr. Booth's make-up was a tribute to the triumph of his art.

Later in the season, it dawned upon me that Mr. Booth did not 'care a rap' how he *looked*, on the stage, provided the first view of him *put over* the limitations of the character! He let his acting do the rest.

During this performance I came in personal contact with Edwin Booth the director in a way I did not forget, although I hoped *he* might — but doubted it — and prophetically.

I had not seen *Macbeth* from the front. I had pored over the Jenkins 'Mrs. Siddons' Readings' in 'Harper's,' but this did not help me for my parts tonight. My wee rôle of Fleance left me care-free, even enjoying my first red wig. It was the 'Bloody Apparition' which brought responsibilities. Charles Hawthorne had designed my 'ascending-the-trap-through-the-cauldron robe,' in un-bleached cotton with angel sleeves, and he informed me, during fittings, that he would leave the blood-stains for me to put on. He had no blood 'handy,' he said, but I should find 'loads of blood' in the property room — 'They always have a pail of it for Macbeth.'

I dutifully sought instructions of Mr. Doud. He told me to wait until night and then go to the property room — and this seemed to end it. As Fleance is much by Banquo's side, I asked our Banquo (Mr. Malone) if he would teach me how to make up for the 'Bloody Appari-tion.' There were several of our kind, and we repaired to the property room and did find a pail of gore of the loveliest richness. Mr. Malone took the stick and 'did' my wound. Being accustomed to the expert touch of Charlie Collins of the Barrett Company, who always 'did' my face for character parts, I now shrank from Mr. Malone's stroke. But I thought he must know and let him smear up and down and crosswise, after which I myself completed the job on the robe. I made that up to represent a generous dripping from my head wound.

Before I had a chance to inspect myself in the mirror, Mr. Booth entered for his own 'blood.' After one look at me, he exclaimed, 'My God!' — and that base Banquo sneaked away. Left me to bear it alone! After all, it was my face.

'You look as if you had been scalped by Indians. This isn't a border drama.'

'Shall I take it off?'

'I should hope so. Here' — as if he couldn't trust so low an order of intelligence — 'come with me,' and he led me to his dressing-room! He snatched up a towel, dipped it in cold cream, and before I knew it, he was scrubbing my face. He looked at the towel between rubs and seemed to be repressing himself. He told me to use his powder and things. 'Just take the shine off — you are not alive, you know.'

Then he led the way back to the property room and took up the brush, studied my face, and this time I did feel the touch of the artist. He approved his own skill, and for the first time smiled. But not for long.

'You were enough to make the women out there faint away.'

He gave my gown a sarcastic inspection. 'How your wound did bleed!' I hoped a little facetiousness might help, and weakly got out, 'that I was bled white, like the little veals.' But it didn't work; and then, as Mr. Booth started to leave the property room, I remorsefully tried to tell him how sorry I was 'to put you to so much trouble — but I really thought the "Bloody Apparition" meant — well, just that.'

He paused long enough to say that 'there should be enough skin left exposed to prove it was a human being that was slaughtered and *not* a little veal.'

He had rubbed in his lesson and intended I should laugh now. This was my real introduction to Edwin Booth.

I studied my beautiful wound so that I, myself, might reproduce it to his satisfaction; and then I sought out the trap under the stage. The cue came. The 'armed head' went up first; the 'Child Apparition' followed me.

This trap business is a scamper. The first and last apparitions had time for cautious one-way traffic — the first for getting on, the last for getting off — but the middle one to connect with cues, needs to jump lively both ways.

One of the popular greenroom topics for conversations was of the horror Edwin Booth could put in his eyes when he was discoursing with 'ghosts.' He had been the complete undoing of one ghost through its own horror of the horror in his Star's eyes, and of the near undoing of many actors cast for the Ghost to his Hamlet. So, I was prepared for horror as the trap sprang up; yet, when Macbeth's anguished eyes bored into mine and I realized how exposed Mr. Booth's face was in that calcium glare, and how he had to sustain his horror through that long scene — even as I spoke my new lines — there swept through me relief and gratitude that *my* bloody make-up had not been first foisted upon him as he leaned toward the Cauldron. Wouldn't it have been awful if I had startled him into laughing here? I was whisked down with all my grateful fervor gone to waste, for soon I learned the lesson that nothing could 'break up' our Star.

Hamlet was what I was waiting for! To see Edwin Booth as Hamlet from the front was the great thrill the theatre offered. I had all sorts of ecstasies thinking upon his Hamlet, but when the night came I saw little of it. My speeches were three times as long as those in Mr. Barrett's version, and my dressing-room was a very good place to keep my mind on new lines that had been thrust into my memory within two days.

I came face to face with Hamlet for the first time as I stepped onto the stage. I was glad then I did not have lines in this scene and could calmly watch him. I could not conjure up one other face, from life, from paintings, from sculpture — and I had passed my childhood among art treasures — that had his threefold beauty of soul, of mind, of feature. It was the most beautiful face I had ever seen, and the saddest. In this scene he was smiling. I thought of Indian Summer sunshine.

The company was nervous that night, except the Ghost. Mr. Barron was as easy as the Star himself. Miss Vaders was jumpy. When she came off from her mad scene, she had an ovation. It was the longest, the loudest applause any one in the company had won up to now — except Mr. Booth, of course. It established her — behind the scenes. The closet scene went 'strong,' but then this was one of Mr. Booth's big efforts. He carried this scene for the Queen.

Carl Ahrendt, the Polonius, was a valuable actor, so I was the more amazed when he stepped up to me, saying in the nicest manner that he had never before seen an actress give the whole play scene. 'I couldn't believe my ears when you did not stop at the usual cut. *You* have more chance — but I feared Mr. Booth might be thrown out of his arranged business. You gave him a long time to fill in. He listened a long time.'

Not understanding what he meant, I said: 'He used the time to good purpose.'

'You have courage — how did you come to think of doing it?'

'But I did not think — I just carried out orders.'

(Gasping.) 'You were told — to do it?'

How could he imagine that I would 'spring' anything like that on Mr. Booth?

To my further astonishment, the old-timers took it for granted that on my own initiative I had restored these lines. I began to wonder what they thought I was. Such impertinence was 'too much,' and brought back Mr. Barrett's *Yorick's Love*.

In the last act the soubrette (myself) had only one appearance in which she drags off the heroine. But for this short business I might have left the theatre an hour earlier. One matinee, as I sat in the greenroom waiting to go on, Mr. Sturgeon asked:

'Why don't you go home? Why do you come on here?'

'Why do you?'

'It's in my part.'

'It's in my part, too.'

'But if you didn't, you could get out sooner.'

'The management hasn't considered this — yet.'

(Amazed.) 'Oh! You've been instructed to come on — I was thinking you just wanted to.' And this is the very catastrophe of the tragedy — Mr. Barrett's own death scene of Yorick! But this supposition was nothing compared to the inference that without authority I would introduce long-winded speeches right into the heart of Mr. Booth's most telling acting!!! — hold that actor up while I sported myself!!! What of Mr. Booth? Really, even he must be human. Of course, the long play scene of the original text became an old story and its continued repetition was my defence.

We left Buffalo at the close of the performance for Detroit, so that packing prevented my seeing the last act. But I did get up in time to hear the cry, 'Oh, I die, Horatio.'

So pitifully young, that cry!

CHAPTER IV

INVITING MR. BOOTH TO SUPPER

DETROIT, the next stand, closed the opening week. Saturday night Mr. Booth appeared for the first time this season as Iago. The bills were: Thursday, *Richelieu*; Friday, *Macbeth*; Saturday matinee, *Hamlet*; Saturday night, *Othello*.

Detroit was my home. My little niece, scarcely more than a baby, came behind for the first time in her life, and to her mind Hamlet was Hamlet — not Mr. Booth. She gazed so yearningly at Hamlet that I overcame my timidity and presented the mite to him. But I need not have hesitated, for Mr. Booth's face became tender. He impulsively stooped and kissed her, saying, 'You *are* a beautiful little one.' She did not smile, but gazed heavenward, murmuring, 'Hamlet kissed me...' And Mr. Booth again responded to this tribute. It was the first time I saw him out of the actor into the man.

Now came a week of one-night stands, and during these days Opportunity knocked twice at my door.

In Bay City Mr. Chase asked me to 'take a walk' with him early in the afternoon, and during the stroll startled me by a proposition. It was nothing less than that I should become his confidante. Not the confidante of his personal life — far from it: he made this clear at once — but of his business life: not his own business, either — this was emphasized — but of matters pertaining to the management. I had never heard of such a thing and told him so. The great Sphinx is not more secretive than the theatrical manager type. My conviction was that some of them might be in need of air to breathe should they stumble into a vacuum, but of a confidante — never! Mr. Chase said he was different. His temperament required that he tell some one everything, then he was safe from telling others anything. To one person he *must* tell all. He admitted it was a failing — even a weakness... it was not common-sense. It was not custom — 'But I can't help it. I've picked you out. You'll know it all. I'll tell you the "business," then I'll be able to laugh at any of them if they try to pump me. You have no intimates in the company. I watched you, last season. When you know things — you don't look wise.'

Of course I was complimented. I had some slight qualms that I might be thrust into disloyalty to the company, but this was soon laughed down, for it was made plain I was not expected to confide, nor even to comment — only to listen. So official elevation was sealed as my lips were to be, in another sense. I did not expect a personal benefit from the confidences nor ever received it.

That night, after the play at Bay City, Mrs. Foster, Miss Vaders, Mr. Chase, and myself were eating our supper in the ordinary, when Mr. Booth passed slowly by the half-open door. He bowed and went on his solitary way to his own supper. From his half-smiling, half-sad eyes, I thought there shone a wistful little gleam. I knew my imagination could work overtime, but was there in that retreating figure regret for the barrier of his rank — yet with no thought of breaking it down? I was steeped in Mr. Barrett's views. I knew nothing could have induced him to join members of his company at supper, not alone for discipline, but because he could not have enjoyed it. To Mr. Booth, theatre etiquette must have become second nature. He probably took his aloneness for granted; for the most part prized it and would defend it from encroachment, but — here *was* the opportunity to do what Mr. Barrett had asked of me — *be myself with Mr. Booth*. It might not come again, and, even if it did, after passing by this chance, there would be nothing spontaneous about it. It would look too worked up. I should lose my courage. It was too soon, but if — I turned to Mr. Chase:

'Mr. Booth looked fearfully alone. Don't you believe he'd care to eat his supper with us?'

There was a shocked silence. Mrs. Foster looked at me reprovingly; Miss Vaders was non-committal; and Mr. Chase asked dubiously, 'What could be done about it?'

'You go and ask him. You're the one.'

He left the room as if he did not dare give himself time to change his mind. He even squared his shoulders. Mrs. Foster's face was a study. Of course, she hoped Mr. Booth would accept, but if —— I began to feel small; even Miss Vaders would not meet my eye; and then — wonder of wonders! — Mr. Booth came in with Mr. Chase, who pulled out a chair for him, while we all brilliantly exclaimed, 'Oh, Mr. Booth!' Nothing especial happened — apart from the specialness of

Mr. Booth sitting there at all, eating his American-plan cold supper, and sipping his glass of milk.

I said hardly one word. Mrs. Foster had been a society hostess in Chicago before she went on the stage. She now took the chair and filled it with tact. After a while Mr. Booth said he must be at his reading and bade us good-night. I did so want to know what he read, and bashfully asked him, and he said that he was reading himself again into Hamlet. 'I've been opaque in Hamlet — so far — this season.'

Some one said, 'To think of it, after all the study you've given to Hamlet ——' and Mr. Booth broke in with a half-frown, 'I haven't caught more than a glimpse of his soul. Hamlet is a study in the human soul ——' He stopped. He became lighter. 'Who knows what I may do tonight after your hospitality? I thank you all' — and he left with Mr. Chase.

We went to our separate rooms, and I sat down to think it over. I did not believe Mr. Barrett really knew what he wanted me to do. It might be summed up that he dreaded to have Mr. Booth become bored. There was one comfort; no more invitations could in the very nature of things come from me. It was up to the Star from now on. There had been no rebuff. What a nice feeling that was to sleep on!

One-night stands mean packing, but in spite of being busy I hurried to see Mr. Abbe's Osric in Saginaw, and then forgot Osric for the ache in my throat when Mr. Booth gave his line, 'Thou canst not think how ill all's here about my heart.' I watched the skill of his fencing, and when the line 'The rest is silence' came, I forgot to wipe my eyes. Mr. Booth threw a teasing look at me as he passed, but I was too far gone to be retorting when I said that I was coming up every Hamlet night from now on to see him die.

It was on this night Mr. Booth named Miss Vaders and me, 'the Chickens.' Ida Rock was much later admitted to that glorious guild. The Heavy Lead, the Leading Lady, and I were beginning the walk to our hotel when Mr. Booth joined us, offering his arm to Mrs. Foster. Amo — for so I had nicknamed Miss Vaders — and I ran down a slight hill and rather hilariously waited to be overtaken, but when we made effort to become sedate, our dignified Star did not approve. 'Laugh on, chickens, it is joy to hear you.'

During these one-night stands we rehearsed, when possible, the *Merchant of Venice*, *Katherine and Petruchio*, and *The Fool's Revenge*. We did *The Fool* as a full bill. *The Merchant*, however, was cut for a double bill, to be done with *Katherine and Petruchio*. We were busy, but there was time enough for the ladies to fall in love with the Star. Miss Vaders *jumped* in and refused to come out. She made no secret of it. From Mr. Chase down to the wardrobe mistress she acclaimed herself. To only one was she silent — to Mr. Booth. Hers was a curious situation — or rather it was not a situation, it was a state of mind. It set no mark on her, for she was not singular; she was one of so many. Every woman, everywhere, was in love with Edwin Booth. It had not been natural had the young lady playing oppo-

37

site to him escaped. To be in love with him was a vogue. At first the young men watched 'the comedy,' but soon took it as a matter of course. Mr. Chase seemed worried. Perhaps he sensed Mr. Barrett's disapproval, or perhaps he did not want Mr. Booth annoyed. So he talked it over with the Star.

It was 'confided' to me that some one had already spoken about it. But Mr. Booth 'did not see that he was justified in saying anything to her — "for she *does nothing*. She does not waylay me. She writes no notes, sends no tokens. She makes no eyes at me. In fact, she behaves as a nice young lady usually does, and what she may say to others does not concern me."'

So Mr. Chase took his cue; but the elders of my sex were more inclined to be critical. They said 'it was silly.' But Miss Vaders and I were by no means sure that the 'heavies' were not feeling the same way about him, for I had seen their symptoms often in boarding-school.

However, I was too occupied with self-examination for proper observation of others. I had some suspicious symptoms, myself. I was at the cross-roads when Miss Rock came to my room one day and suddenly knelt and hid her face in my lap, and wept, and wept. 'He's so sweet!' Another one! Then and there I made a vow! I would not fall in love with Mr. Booth — for his sake. I tossed my protesting heart overboard, with just a wee sigh for the splash. I soothed Ida, but warned her against letting the company know her feelings; and I begged her to promise that if she must talk, to come to me, alone, reminding her it was 'well enough for Emma Vaders — whose position keeps them all in check — but they'll torment the life out of you.' She said she knew it, had no false hopes. 'I *had* to tell some one.' She admitted she'd die of shame 'if Mr. Booth should become aware of it.'

So the season started. Each lady in love with the Star, who, I suppose, was helped from long habit to take life as it was. Mr. Chase had the 'epidemic' out with me. He 'pitied' Mr. Booth. He said he had never seen anything like it. Was I to be depended upon? I assured him I was.

'Then between us we'll keep the track clear for him.' Poor Mr. Booth! He might well have cried out: 'Deliver me from my friends.'

Ida had been picked for her perfect figure, her divine legs and nimble feet. Apart from this she was a novice in a legitimate company, and they utilized her as a sort of leader of the ballet. She was Chief Court Lady. She saved the stage manager much worry over 'supers.' Once, toward the end of the season, there were no court ladies to be got 'by any indirection,' and Ida went on alone. Just as the curtain was to rise on 'Hamlet Discovered,' Mr. Booth noticed the meagre court, and asked solemnly: 'Is all of the Court Lady here?' As the curtain rose at once on this impromptu, the poor actors had a tussle with themselves to keep their faces straight.

In Kalamazoo, Mr. Booth made me feel so sorry for him. He said he was frightened, and he said it convincingly. He told me that evening, and I heard him repeat this experience on the train next day.

In the afternoon he had lain down to rest, but forgot to lock his door. 'There I lay upon my back on the bed — fully dressed, I am thankful. Then I heard a sound. I opened my eyes. The door was being stealthily opened. I forced myself to accept the idea it was Chase cautiously entering, not to waken me if I were asleep. I tried to believe it — but I knew better. I felt it was a woman. I couldn't move. She came in. She was the most determined woman I ever saw. She was tall — she was gaunt — she was strong. She couldn't help seeing I was trembling. I must have been. She came to the bed at once — looked down upon me. I tried to speak. I couldn't. This did not move her. Without smiling she bent over me — kissed me — on the mouth, too. She did not say a word. She walked out of the room and closed the door. I never was so frightened in my life. I bolted the door, when it was too late, but I'm not over it yet. I've tried to reason it out, but I can't. She was not silly. She looked to be the last woman on earth to care for kissing. I should say she was a hard woman.'

'Perhaps she was a lunatic; there is some sort of an institution in Kalamazoo ——'

'No, I've studied insanity. That belongs to my equipment. She is not insane.'

Mr. Booth needed sympathy. He was appealing for it, and I was ashamed to feel like laughing. He did look so pathetic as he told his grievance. He made me feel a thousand years old. He did not want to drop the subject, so I asked: 'Do you think she was an old maid?'

'No, I saw her wedding ring.'

I tried to soothe him. 'You are Hamlet to her, *not* Mr. Booth at all — just as you are Hamlet to my little niece.' He listened politely, but was not interested in motives. *Why* he had been kissed had nothing to do with it. So I learned, and it was steadily confirmed, that Mr. Booth was afraid of strange women. Be they ugly, beautiful, fascinating, or determined comic valentines, nothing made any difference if they were *strangers*. And strange men he shunned almost as much.

CHAPTER V

A PHOTOGRAPH AT MINNEHAHA FALLS

To break us in for the Chicago engagement, I suppose, we did for the first time the *Merchant of Venice*, *Katherine and Petruchio*, and *The Fool's Revenge* in the Twin Cities.

My dressing-room walls were now decorated with my lovely Jessica costumes, including the boy's dress for the elopement, and the rich costumes for Genevra, wife of Malatesta. But while I shook them out lovingly and gazed at their beauty, Mr. Booth took no notice of them when worn on the stage. He assumed they would be 'right,' with one exception — my Jewish dress for Jessica.

I told him of digging into rare historical costume books; of Charlie Hawthorne, who had left the stage because of his very genius for designing costumes and was an authority. My Star replied mournfully that he had had all sorts of Jessica costumes foisted upon him, from the spangled gypsy — tambourine only omitted — to a complete Goddess of Liberty, wound in tri-color. This seemed a bit stiff, but he said it was so. The gypsy one was the favorite — the more spangles the better — for the daughter of Shylock's sober house. Mr. Booth, however, was far from amused. I tried to assure him that I wore neither spangles nor flags as the young Jewish girl. He dropped the subject with an expression that suggested once he had been hopeful, but — no more.

I knew my Oriental dress was *right*. I was sure he would acknowledge the costume was dignified. And in my heart I pronounced it ravishing — nothing less.

When the overture was called for the first night of the *Merchant*, I was once more summoned to the Star's dressing-room and greeted by a worried Mr. Booth. He turned almost ferociously (his make-up may have given this effect) and gazed upon me. Then he sighed in relief. 'You *are* Shylock's daughter. I am satisfied.'

He kept up his inspection, very earnestly, as if much depended upon my appearance to him. Then, indicating a scarf he wore — 'You should have some of this orange. It was the law. The Jews were compelled to wear it.'

I touched my own striped scarf of deep burnt orange, with its tarnished fringe, of which Charlie Hawthorne had said: 'I hope you don't think I am working off old stuff on you. I've hunted New York over to get this "tone."'

Mr. Booth said, 'It blends too much. Have you anything yellow in your trunk?'

I had a scarf from *Hernani!!* Should I get it?
'Yes.'

I threw out the trays — snatched the yellow silk scarf and rushed back with it. It was 'just the thing!' And it was taken from me and draped and twisted in and out of the scarf I was wearing, and tied in beautiful lines. 'There!'

Act One was called. 'Ready, Mr. Booth?' And he left for the stage.

If on my Christian-Jessica dress designed by Ellen

Terry, my stage father was silent, my stage husband was not. Returning from the stage to their dressing-rooms, as the men passed my door, Mr. Hanford's (Lorenzo) sonorous voice rang out: 'Gosh!! It's lucky I don't have to pay for Jessica's clothes — on my salary!'

Having been placed in a Jewish boarding-school in Weimar, my infant classification was that Jews were human beings who were neither Lutherans nor Roman Catholics. Otherwise, I saw no difference. Mr. Booth's Shylock, I thought, gave out this same human-being-ness, that his Shylock was not intended for a type — not a composite of a race, but just a man who was a Jew. What was *hard* in his Jew was Shylock himself. It was not racial. His make-up showed at once the limitations within which Shylock would reason.

I think Mr. Booth's art of make-up was as ruthless as a modern painter's. It did seem as if he labored to dig out the ugliest traits of his characters and paint them into his face, and that it was in spite of himself, of his own skill, that something bigger than mere wickedness shone through the make-up of his villains; that he couldn't help suggesting that these villains were one with the universe and had eternal souls.

In Minneapolis, Mr. Booth asked if I would enjoy a little excursion to Minnehaha Falls. 'I am ashamed when I realize how little sight-seeing I have done in my own country. Have you seen anything?'

I had only trod the trail that wound from hotel to stage entrance.

'That's a typical actor record. I'll tell Chase to get

up a party. We'll take horses and carriages and drive to the Falls tomorrow. You know your Longfellow, I dare say.'

'We wrote compositions on him and transposed him, in school.'

'Then all is ready. I'll make my début as an American sight-seer,' and, he added, 'I am surprised our little suppers do not tire me.' (I think he had his lips pursed to say 'bored.') I thanked him and he said: 'Indeed, if you get me to crawl from my shell, I shall thank you, for my health needs it.'

'Heroic treatment is sometimes best,' I couldn't help saying.

He was almost merry, and said, 'We'll see.'

He gave his invitation to each lady, personally.

When those invited assembled the next morning, about eleven o'clock, they found Mr. Booth letter-perfect in his new dual rôle of sight-seer and host. He had determined to go through with it regardless of how his heart may have been sinking within him. He threw out such little speeches as: 'I am an intelligent American citizen at last, travelling to see my country's wonders. My bad habits are hoary. I may backslide — it would be like me,' etc., etc. He began the outing in a spirit of responsibility for our pleasure, but Mr. Chase had a quick eye to see and did not intend his Star should tire. Mr. Booth said that the *infant class* was under the manager's care, and he raised his hat to us as his own carriage drove away with Mrs. Baker, Mrs. Foster, and Miss Vaders. Ours contained Miss Rock and, for this drive, the bride of Mr. Doud.

45

For a moment I envied those in the Star's carriage, and I believe the others did. Something in our escort's face made me think he was aware of our regret — and this would never do. Then, too, did I not long to have Mr. Booth *stay up on his pedestal?* So I congratulated myself that rank had dictated the order of our places and, perceiving how bashful Ida was, devoted myself to breaking her in for Mr. Booth's party.

At the Falls carriages were abandoned for a while and we walked about to gaze at Minnehaha. I think each guest was longing to say something 'epic,' but could not think of an epic to quote from. I know I was.

Mr. Booth was an impartial host. To compensate Miss Rock and me for riding in the 'other carriage,' he chatted with us in turn. Thus there came my opportunity to be Hiawatha-ish — alas, I did not rise to it. In one of the pauses, I felt his eyes upon me. He had such control of his expression — when his shyness was thrown off — that even when he was inwardly convulsed — as the supreme tragedian was apt to be at anything amusing — there was no betraying twitch of his lips, nor did his eyes become readable. I did not know all this then, and it was my own blush that told me 'the grave genius' had seen through me, and was dying to laugh; then he reminisced delightfully of the Longfellow he knew best.

When the others joined us, Mr. Booth was asked if he had thought of a play on Hiawatha for himself?

'There are several plays — now'— he gave the Falls a helpless look — 'but they have missed *that!* It would have been pleasant, very pleasant, if ——' Did he

AT MINNEHAHA FALLS, SEPTEMBER 28, 1886

Left to right: Mrs. Baker, Arthur Branscombe Chase (manager), Mrs. Doud, Kitty Molony, Emma Vaders, Ida Rock, Edwin Booth, Mrs. Augusta Foster

mean that he and *his* Longfellow had tried to catch the spirit of those mists for the theatre?

A photographer hunted us up — and oh, joy! — I could scarcely believe my ears when I heard Mr. Booth say merrily, 'Mr. Chase, we must sit for our pictures. It is part of it.'

We had a 'group' taken, and Mr. Booth let the photographer arrange us. I was to learn how very characteristic this was. With the Falls of Minnehaha for background, he posed leaning against one side of a tree while Mr. Chase stood on the other side. Neither was visible to the other. The ladies were seated. To do honor to the Falls, immortalized by Longfellow, Edwin Booth removed his hat. Later when Mr. Chase was confronted by the finished pictures, he was aghast. *He had kept his hat on!*

The day had been windy and chilly. His only thought had been not to take cold, and now the manager was preserved hatted in the presence of his bareheaded Star! 'And,' said Mr. Chase remorsefully, 'Mr. Booth had his voice to think of — yet he risked a cold to honor the poet and his poem!'

We left Mr. Chase to pay the bill. At the end of the trail, Mr. Booth had his hands full of birchbark canoes and sweetgrass baskets, nor would he surrender them when we offered to assist. He carried them proudly, occasionally gazing at them as if amused at himself, yet puzzled withal. We rode back as we came, and reached our hotel about five o'clock. Mr. Chase gallantly escorted Miss Rock and Mrs. Doud to their hotel, after Mr. Booth had distributed the souvenirs. It was an old man, almost dragging his feet, who went down that corridor to his room, and in less than three hours there sprang onto the stage — literally sprang, his step was so light — a beautiful fiend, young as lean saplings swaying in the wind.

Mr. Chase let me sit in front, and I wondered Desdemona did not fall in love with Iago. I was so very sorry for Iago, tied to a wife old enough to be his mother. The audience was with him every moment; gurgled at his diabolical triumphs. The rôle taxed Mr. Booth less than any other; that is why we went sight-seeing on the day of an Iago night!

We left for St. Paul the next day and Mr. Booth said he had slept like a top. On Friday there was a long rehearsal of *King Lear;* two performances Saturday, and then we went to Chicago, a broken-in company, expected to be smoothly efficient. Mr. Booth had not taken cold. His outing proved to be a tonic. He asserted that his health was better than in years.

If I warned myself each night alone in my room, 'He cannot go through another day without doing some little thing I shall be sorry for,' down in my heart of hearts I was beginning not to believe it. Familiarity with Edwin Booth bred reverence for him. To his company as to his public, he was 'King of them all.'

CHAPTER VI

SHYLOCK'S DAUGHTER

IN Chicago haunting memories of Minnehaha Falls not only stubbornly refused to be dead, but coaxed to become entangled with hopes of pleasant futures. But the present held sway. One could not help living in it, for it was one rehearsal after another. We did *King Lear* and prepared *Richard III* for immediate performance. Notice was posted to get letter perfect in *Don Cæsar* and *Brutus*. We had an almost completed repertoire that demanded constant 'keeping smooth.' These rehearsals did not tax Mr. Booth, for he attended none of them. He could not have dropped in for supper now, as the company scattered. Mr. Chase said the weather was too chilly and windy for open carriages. But had skies been sunny, our Star needed no diversion in Chicago, for the 'opposition' was Joseph Jefferson.

Mr. Chase could and did smile in superior fashion at Oppositions. Oppositions did not affect Mr. Booth's business anywhere — but he must have been looking forward to this reunion. It needed no ghost to return to taunt me that the closest of all our Star's friends would not yield him to us — no, not for one hour's outing.

Once on a day journey later on, Mr. Jefferson's car was attached to our train. These friends dined together, but did not seem inclined to waste precious moments on such trifles as mere eating. What pals they

49

were! Each face was alive with complete sympathy of mind and heart. Mr. Jefferson did most of the talking, but he exerted himself to entertain the friend who listened so responsively that he forgot his pipe. That was his supreme compliment.

Chicago welcomed Mr. Booth as if he were a native son. The papers headlined the superlatives I was to become accustomed to that season. Critics congratulated themselves in their columns on being able to compare Booth with Jefferson, Tragedy with Comedy. One writer, in his eulogy, raised the question, which was the greater actor, and answered it himself that, as Tragedy was a higher expression in acting than Comedy, the Tragedian was greater than the Comedian! Ergo! Booth was greater than Jefferson! I rashly emitted an echo of this rating to our authoritative comedienne, the other day, and, in amazement, she exclaimed: 'You don't mean it? You can't!'

There had been no one to pick up the glove when the verdict was given out. I doubt if the writer considered it a challenge. It was too accepted an estimate at the time.

The houses were packed. On my way to rehearsal I often needed to push my way through a long line of people buying tickets for 'Booth.' These lines were there for hours. It made me so proud I was almost late for rehearsal.

It was not pride alone I felt that night I went in front to see *King Lear*. Mr. Booth's Lear exalted and humbled one as does sunrise on the mountain-tops. His

Lear turned us, willy-nilly, into psalmists. One longed to dance and sing in ecstatic praise of that acting. Such thoughts as his acting stirred! What was genius? Where did it come from? What became of it? Would Mr. Booth carry his genius through the grave? How had he mastered it? By what thoughts did he get his Lear clear to himself? Was his solitude nothing but concentration on seething tragedy?

Then I pictured him with his friend this very night, after the play. How easy it was to see them in the mind's eye, both so gently humorous, laughing softly at one another's kindly jests! But I should like to sit beside Joseph Jefferson and watch *him* watching Edwin Booth's King Lear! — And if Mr. Booth would only dissect his art for me! I knew that could never be. He would leave his acting on the stage. I had eyes to see it *there!* But I had to see with my eyes, not *his!* Would the time ever come when I knew enough to see his acting as he saw it himself? He was here and I was here. For weeks I could see him in his great rôles. Was there ever such a fortunate creature? As the audience filed out, I was proud all over again. I fairly revelled in their half-caught words of homage.

There were shake-ups of parts in Chicago, but the change that most affected our fast-forming group was the coming of the new treasurer, Mr. J. H. Magonigle, Mr. Booth's brother-in-law. He was married to the sister of Mary Devlin Booth — the real Mrs. Booth as she was affectionately called.[1] Instinctively Mr. Ma-

[1] Edwin Booth was twice married and twice a widower. As the wife of

gonigle made one feel he would work hard to 'smooth things out.' Here was no tale-bearer. He came; he stayed. He was a little man, too unselfish to be fussy if he did buzz around us; but he saw to it with his bright eyes and wiry manner that we behaved — we younger ones. If Mr. Booth were amused by us, Mr. Magonigle looked elsewhere, but the instant he feared his idol was wearying, he would slip in his hint, none too gently, to vacate the premises — premises being the seat nearest Mr. Booth — in the car. From his arrival he became master of ceremonies on our drives.

An intriguing and revealing little situation contrived itself. It illuminated what Mr. Barrett styled the *vigorous myth* — that the instruction of a newly engaged actor in Mr. Booth's company was limited to being told, 'Walk on, my boy, anywhere; Mr. Booth will find you at night.'

Even without my former Star's warning I should have been sceptical that the hypnotizing art of our supreme actor was built upon haphazard foundations. Neither so far this season had there been visible signs at rehearsals of this supposed carelessness. Yet the legend was too popular to die. I heard it told again and again.

Then came my personal demonstration of Mr. Booth's sensitiveness to the whereabouts of his com-

his maturer years was pitifully afflicted, to his professional associates this later marriage seemed a mournful interlude rather than a part of the great tragedian's actual life. Mary Devlin, the adored bride of his youth, was an exquisite, gentle, self-effacing, and beautiful young girl. Her letters to her fiancé, some of them written in her sixteenth year, not only glow with love for him, but reveal a noble mind precociously developed. She died during the infancy of their only child, Edwina.

pany on the stage with him — how even his own acting was affected by their positions. There was, nevertheless, a reservation; there must be a strong psychological relation of his own characterization to the part or parts *gone on* for by his supporting actors. Were there no *motif tie* to his own rôle, then nothing the members of the company *did* could disturb him. They were out of it.

When *The Merchant* night rolled round, I was again summoned to the Star dressing-room. The piece had been going too smoothly for me to feel apprehensive qualms. Neither did I fear a belated rebuke for my recent dishevelled appearance in *Hamlet* — for Mr. Booth, while not hiding that he *took in* my tied-about-me costume, had not said a word. A veritable chapter of accidents had been responsible. The stage manager rather dubiously comforted me by conceding that 'a careful dresser like you does not willingly make a show of herself.'

Yet without known cause for worry I paused before the door of the tiny room. I dreaded the Shylock make-up. I used to think Mr. Booth could not contrive a gracious expression when made up for Shylock. As I entered, I reproached myself, for his gentle voice belied that ferocious frown. He was asking: 'Will it break your heart ——?' My heart skipped a beat without waiting to break. Was I to lose Jessica? Had Miss Vaders, after all, insisted upon my pet part? But no! Nothing so cruel; it was merely that I stand throughout the scene with my back to the audience.

I was too relieved to notice that Mr. Booth was assuming he was hurting my feelings. He carefully explained that I was to take the centre of the stage upon his exit. He did not say to wait for his applause to die down — my own common-sense instructed me in this. I turned to go, but the Star detained me to dissect the scene. I began to realize the value of my immaturity, for because of it, now, and throughout the season, Mr. Booth was explicit upon much that had been mere orders — if kindly worded — to a more experienced professional.

'This is a quiet scene. Shylock is speaking to his own flesh and blood here. His mask is off. Each glance of mine to you is significant. My facial expression is important here, but I wish to *do nothing*. Any emphasis in this scene is over-emphasis.' He smiled now, or, at least, he thought his smile penetrated his make-up. 'Your costume is more a high-light than a background, but after my exit you may do what you please.'

He might have added that his audience did not come out to see Jessica's costume, but being Edwin Booth — he did not. He even anticipated my dread of being thought silly and vain by him and divined that if I could so serve his art, I did not care how or where I was tucked during the whole of the play. As the actor went forth to the stage, he bade me go to *Centre* on his exit. 'I want them to see your correct costume. I have told you, you are Shylock's daughter.'

I sat me down that very night to write my undying thanks to Charlie Hawthorne for designing a Jewish costume that was neither a gypsy's nor a Goddess of Liberty's. Had not Mr. Booth told me I looked like *his*

54

SHYLOCK'S DAUGHTER

Shylock's daughter? No praise could have elated me more.

I could not help deduce that Mr. Booth overlooked my Player Queen awryness, because the Prince of Denmark is not concerned with the appearance of a strolling player — but Jessica was different. Jessica was his daughter!

I dare say Mr. Booth read me as easily as his morning paper, but young pitiless eyes, ever watching to pounce on some word or look of his I should be sorry for, perturbed him not. I attempted to fortify myself against that coming day by recalling from my Catechism that we are born children of wrath. I retold myself, 'It isn't human nature for him to keep it up.' But stalking Mr. Booth for faults availed nothing. His one change was to unfold gradually to young companionship about him. He himself said this had not been his habit.

We left Chicago for St. Louis on a Sunday by our first special train. Special trains were an old story to me, but riding in the engine cab was novelty, for the indulgent Mr. Chase suggested some 'might like to try it.' The 'Chickens' did, in relays, but the elder ladies declined with thanks. My grimy face so enthused the manager that I was thrust after a struggle into Mr. Booth's drawing-room 'to make him smile.' Mr. Magonigle, who, alas, was present, did more than smile, but not the Star. Between puffs he grimly observed — oh, shades of Bloody Apparition! — that I had a passion for it! He turned the tables on my two baiters;

he evolved a mystery for them, making me his partner against them. I murmured I hoped Mr. Booth had forgotten.

'But you won't let me,' he said.

All that season Mr. Magonigle proved his worth, for he helped on nonsense as we had not dared, and Mr. Booth, outwardly grave, accepted the nonsense and did his part.

Mr. Booth said there were beautiful gardens in St. Louis, and so we drove to Shaw's Gardens. He was more reserved than at Minnehaha Falls. Perhaps his brother-in-law's presence this first time made him a little shyer. Amo was soon calling the new treasurer Papa, and I said it was not fair — and Mr. Magonigle said he 'could do very nicely with another daughter — all brought up and self-supporting.'

'Papa' he became to the three of us, and when we lost our heads in affection for him, we made 'Popper' of it. 'Popper' switched us about today in Shaw's Gardens, not leaving any one long enough with Mr. Booth to bore him, but the treasurer's machinations were so open that the switching in itself made us laugh.

Our host delayed the return signal until we almost missed our dinner. Distinct is that picture of his interceding for us with the head waiter before he went to his rooms to dine alone. No, he said that night, he was not tired. 'It is tonic to think of the outings to come — and this big country of ours has parks and beaches waiting for us everywhere.'

56

CHAPTER VII

MR. BOOTH TAKES HIS CURTAIN CALLS

THE high-light of the St. Louis engagement was our first acting of *Richard*. The management was elated to announce the Colley Cibber version this season, for Mr. Chase, ever with an eye on the box office, fairly crowed over Mr. Barrett's victory in persuading his partner to discard the Shakespeare play. Actors named the Shakespeare Richard dreary. Rachel Noah, of the Boston Theatre, had said to me — here are her own words: 'T. B. Aldrich and some other highbrows have talked Mr. Booth into doing Shakespeare's *Richard III*. Oh, it reads well enough, but Cibber's Richard *acts*.'

In restoring the Cibber version, to judge by the whistling, stamping gallery gods' approval, and for that matter the wild enthusiasm of the entire house, Mr. Booth was giving the public just what it wanted. The applause for his Richard sounded unlike any other he received. It came over the footlights as from one arch-villain to another. His audience was more than *with him* — it was of the same piece. It gloated with him from his first entrance. His reception burst out in the spirit in which 'Dixie' is received, in the North. Every one is moved by it — no one knows just how or why. They simply want it. So they greeted *Richard*.

Mr. Booth had the 'right' entrance for this. The stage was cleared for him. Limping on, he was a figure of evil sure of itself. He might have been the Devil by

57

the cunning triumph in his face. His first line, 'Now is the winter of our discontent,' was as familiar to his audience as the 'Last Rose of Summer,' and was hailed as rapturously as is the song in *Martha*. Here was a villain after their own hearts. They gurgled at his cruel wit. His slight hump and limp were accepted as a sort of cloven foot phosphorescence that lifted him out of the hypocrite class. His costume emphasized his slenderness. It made of him a sculptor's model for the Evil One. But how much more cunning Mr. Booth put into his Richard than is seen in any painting of Satan!

I suppose few scenes have been contrived into which so much pathos can be injected as the Tower Scene in *Richard III*. All the world resents the doom of the poor little princes. These murdered infants are immortal, and if the young actress will only be at pains to make up for an 'angel child,' the Prince of Wales is a grateful rôle to be cast for. Thanks to Mr. Barrett, Mr. Booth set aside his usual quiet business for the Tower scene, and the little princes were forcibly torn from their anguished mother, and I was permitted to indulge in a very orgy of shrieks and screams. There was a *scene in one* to follow the Tower, but after the first night, Mr. Booth had it cut. We deluded chits almost swaggered in the misfaith our great Star was so impressed by our acting that a scene was cut to bring down the curtain for us — to make our calls the surer. Then Mr. Booth blew upon my house of cards and it took its collapsing tumble.

I never lost my interest in Mr. Booth's taking his curtain calls! Here was a transformed Edwin Booth.

KITTY MOLONY AS THE YOUNG PRINCE IN RICHARD THE THIRD

MR. BOOTH'S CURTAIN CALLS

The figure who bowed to his audience when 'taking calls' was haughty of mien, disdainful of glance, supercilious to contemptuousness. Such a contrast it was to the gentle, retiring, lovable, sympathetic, appealing Mr. Booth at any other moment. I could never quite accustom myself to the 'curtain call Edwin Booth.' When the glorious 'David Garrick' days came to pass, I asked him outright why he looked so insulted before the curtain.

'Do I look insulted?'

'You do — to me, at least. You *look* insulted, Mr. Booth, really.'

'I am glad of it. I am insulted.'

'Oh, Mr. Booth!'

(Puff, puff; he makes a smoke-ring, and pauses to admire his skill.) 'Why not? Am I a trick performer? An entertainer?'

(Abashed but stubborn.) 'But no one thinks you are!'

He could, of course, understand why applause was sweet music to some ears, but he became stern: 'How many out there know more than I of *Hamlet* — of any play in my repertoire?'

'None, of course!'

'A possible one here and there: my good friend Furness, for instance! But an audience is not appealed to individually. Collectively — are they authority — out there — or am I?'

'You, Mr. Booth — but ——'

'I have given my life to these great rôles. I do not consider myself an entertainer! I am an interpreter.

59

I reveal the soul of masterpieces. And tyros think it
incumbent upon themselves to let me see they approve
of me! It is impertinent. I instruct! Spattings cannot
elate me!' (His lips twitched as if he knew he was
skating over very thin ice.) 'I'll be moderate. Why
should I be worked up over the approval of unripe judgment? It is I, not they, who know the subject! They
should bow their heads reverently before those poems
I reveal to them.'

'But this is what your audience does do!'

'No, they drag me out to show their approval! — so
I may rejoice that in their good nature I have amused
them. You read me right. I am insulted.'

But I would not have it so. He was misreading his
audiences. I blurted it out with spirit, too. 'If you
could only see yourself act!'

He was amused now. 'I think I do see myself act.'

'It cannot be the same. If you were out there, you'd
be just as hysterical as — as we are. You'd applaud
wildly — if you had sense enough left to applaud with
— for that is what you do to your audiences: you make
them crazy! I sit out there and watch them until you
make me lose my head over your acting. It's like being
whirled around until you're dizzy. They applaud because they can't help it. That's why they stand on their
seats, and yell! That's why the ladies tear off their
flowers and throw them to you! If you would only let
them see the real Mr. Booth ——!'

'My dear child, almost "thou persuadest me" — but
not quite! Keep tabs on me, and if you see me weaken-
ing — changing my spots — throw it up to me!'

MR. BOOTH'S CURTAIN CALLS

I did once see those spots pale, but I forgot to 'throw it up to him.' I was too excited myself, that first night in San Francisco.

Mr. Booth had not yet finished. He smoked on. 'I like your picture of my working on my audience. Wouldn't it be better to say *playing* on them, as if they were a pipe? — But, look on this picture! *If* they were discriminating — *if* their delirium were aroused by art alone —' (puff-puff-puff). 'Oh, yes. There are times when I react to *spattings*' (a dry chuckle), 'and as I bask in their nice perception of art — and agree with them' (a dryer chuckle), 'along comes some little novice with tears in her screams — and they give her the very same calls!'

Down toppled my little gaudy house of cards — but Mr. Booth let the Richard calls go on.

Mr. Booth had so much applause that when it came in the wrong place (to his thinking), he made a grievance of it.

'I never can do anything wrong. Once I thought I had shown myself up. It was in Boston on a *Richard the Third* night. I rushed on with my cry: "A horse! A horse! My Kingdom for a horse!" I caught my foot in a grass mat. I stumbled and fell full length. There I lay — face down! I said to myself, "I've done it now! I've killed the scene!" I waited for the titter — and wondered if I should get up and go on — or walk off and have the curtain rung down. I listened for the laugh, but it did not come. My audience was too polite! It dawned on me it was a sympathetic silence out there —

and then, to my astonishment, I heard applause. What's up now? Who's come on to help me up? I raised my head to peek. There was nothing going on. I was alone on the stage. Well, if they like it, here goes, I thought. I rose and went on with the scene as if nothing had happened — *and* the next morning, to my amazement, I read the headlines "Wonderful Art of Edwin Booth" (or something like that). "This illuminating actor prophesied the end of Richard's reign by falling to the ground as if stumbling accidentally, as he shouted: 'A horse! A horse! My kingdom for a horse!'" Of all the far-fetched psychology — ! It's discouraging!'

I said, 'But, Mr. Booth! You don't know how — persuasive — you are. You really must have covered it up, superbly.'

(A bit contemptuously.) 'Of course, I didn't give myself away before I had to.'

'No — indeed! You are too old an actor.'

This did not *sound* just as I meant it, and I must have blushed, for Mr. Booth (rather reluctantly — I confess) helped me out.

'Oh, to please you — too good an actor. It is the same thing. Gad, I think I must be, when I get a round of applause for nearly breaking my neck.' He smiled, but not enough to hide his grievance, and said, 'Too good an actor not to cover up whatever needs to *be* covered up.'

'You hypnotize your audience. When I'm out there, I feel it.'

Mr. Booth liked to tease me, and so he admitted

62

there might be something in this, but he was soberer as
he added:

'There is much put over the footlights — and goes
well, too — which is as far from *art* as that fall of mine.
Cheap — very cheap! —'

'That's the whole matter with your argument, Mr.
Booth. You can't be cheap. And it isn't cheap to turn
a ridiculous accident into sublime tragedy — either.
If it is not art, then it's genius.'

(Pensively.) 'I might have known it! I cannot do
anything wrong.'

Mr. Chase always referred to these wails by adding,
'A bad notice would do him good.'

This was a business statement. He revered Mr.
Booth too greatly for ill-nature to creep in. But the
manager of many actors saw the humor of this com-
plaint by his great Star.

In almost my first instruction from Mr. Barrett, he
had said, 'Shakespeare is the actor's Bible.' There had
not been such a declaration of faith from Mr. Booth —
declarations were foreign to his lips — but from his
directing of Shakespeare scenes, it was safe to assume
he not only endorsed the actor's Bible idea, but went his
partner one better. Mr. Barrett, who held 'theatre'
sacred; who was steeped in 'traditions' which he fondly
asserted came down from Betterton; who knew which
great actor had originated any standard 'business' of a
legitimate scene; who respected *authority*, not only
repeated words of the Shakespeare plays to make his
point stronger, but permitted his company to do so. As

an example, Ophelia in her mad scene repeated 'dead' for her exit. It was a telling exit, too. Miss Vaders, an experienced actress, at the first rehearsal of her mad scene, gave 'Dead! dead! dead!' on her exit. Mr. Booth stopped her at once. 'The Folio has one "dead"! Please, speak the text as it is written. We cannot approach our immortal plays too reverently. Never change the text of Shakespeare — *to make it easier to act.*'

I remember how impressed by this I was — for it was the first directing of his that conflicted with Mr. Barrett's. Mr. Booth turned to the company. 'You will find you can be effective without interpolating repetitions of the text.' Miss Vaders did find it so. At night, the applause that followed her mad scene, played without the sobbing repetition, made her fellow actors exclaim: 'What a hand!'

I did not try to reconcile reverence for the text with the Colley Cibber version of *Richard*. I doubt if I thought to do it.

In Cleveland, Mr. Booth wondered, and found it difficult to preserve his gravity as he wondered, if it would 'not be the proper thing for such an inveterate sightseer as I have become' to drive up and down Euclid Avenue, 'for it is one of the beautiful streets of the country'; and Mr. Chase added, 'And you may see the palaces Standard Oil fortunes have built.' In a roundabout way this led to the subject of endowed theatres, and I impulsively gave vent to my longing for 'an endowed theatre for Mr. Barrett.' I was conscious at once of a quickened interest in my listener but his eyes were quite unreadable. Of course I had mentally included Mr. Booth but to have said this to him would have choked me. One did not forget he was the great man of the theatre. I decided to keep still but it was not to be. Others sensing Mr. Booth's response led me on. I felt too silly and preposterous for words. I could not quote Mr. Barrett. He was taking care of this theatre idea himself. Mr. Booth soon changed the topic but waited until no one was near, then asked: 'What influenced you to speak of a theatre for Barrett?' There was a flash in my questioner's eyes that boded little good to any theatre project.

I was sure that Mr. Barrett could persuade his friend with time, but it was not for me to *say anything*, and I only knew his general hope, anyway.

'He has spoken of it — as his dream,' I said.

There was no answering smile. 'It is every actor's dream. When we wake up, we know better. Where did you become interested in an endowed theatre?'

'In Weimar. Our school used to visit the Goethe and Schiller Theatre, behind the scenes, once a year when there was no performance going on. We were shown everything. Oh, Mr. Booth, that is the most perspective-creating stage I ever saw! It is three times as deep as the auditorium ——' I checked my exuberant flow of words, remembering he had trod nearly all the famous German stages.

'Oh, Goethe's Theatre!' He mused reverently upon this historic stage, and, as I might have known, gave me more information of it. At length he said with so much meaning, 'Were you in mine?'

'No.' There was a pause, and then Mr. Booth said, more bitterly than I had heard him speak — off the stage: 'When this theatre idea possesses you, come to me and I'll tell you what — *not* to do.'

My inadvertent touch had tortured a wound. Carefully he hid it. I have heard him smilingly answer some question on Booth's Theatre, but he changed the subject as soon as possible. He could make a casual reference to Booth's Theatre; he could tell a Booth's Theatre story, but it hurt him. Later, I understood how deep was his wound.

On my free nights I always went in front — not only to be thrilled, but to get a lesson in acting. To avoid losing myself in a maze, I prepared a question for Mr. Booth's art to answer. In Cleveland, I remember, I asked how much did Mr. Booth rely upon his support to build his scenes up for him to make his points. And his acting this night gave the answer: Were a cyclone to snatch the company from the stage, Mr. Booth could still give a dazzling performance in monologue. He walked on, he acted *with* his company if their ability permitted it. If not, his song became that of the lone lark. He soared to the sun — alone. I tried to question Mr. Booth later upon his artistic pleasure when acting with great artists in joint engagements, but there was never a definite expression upon this theme by him. Yet, he told me often in various ways that he let his characters flood his imagination in the hours of grey dawn, if he could not sleep.

MR. BOOTH'S CURTAIN CALLS.

Next week was New York.

I used to wonder if every one were not a little crazy the week before New York — so many burning hopes depended upon Broadway. But it was different this season. What mischance could befall an attraction whose Star was 'it,' and who was not even bidding for favor for a new play, as was Mr. Barrett's annual custom? The Broadway exhilaration possessed the company, however.

'Oh,' Mr. Chase observed indulgently, 'they expect to make little hits of their own — and I hope they may. We are now going into Mr. Booth's stronghold — and it will surprise me if he is not the only one to get the "notices"! But it's a fine feeling for me to go into New York with no reason whatever to worry.'

'If you were superstitious, Mr. Chase, I should warn you to knock wood.'

'Well, I come of witch-burning ancestors, so there's some fear and dread of spooks left in me yet' — and he did knock wood. 'I suppose Macbeth was not expecting the witches in the day of his success either, but nothing short of something like what happened to Macbeth can prevent New York being *great* — and it's *going* to be great!'

There was occasion to remember that supernatural mischance before we left New York.

I interpreted Mr. Booth's unawed-by-Broadway manner as the gesture of supreme success, and it was intriguing to see what such a gesture was like. Mr. Chase confided to me many of Mr. Booth's out-of-town friends were to be in the city for his engagement at the

Star Theatre, and of course there would be his reunion with his New York intimates. It would be the same in Boston, where, best of all, his daughter awaited him in his own home. Mr. Booth seldom mentioned her name, but his mere allusion to her was revealing of what she meant to him.

No one was curious about Mr. Booth. He inspired trust. If he gave no one the impression of being secretive, he conveyed without effort that to pump him were futile. The 'Chickens' decided the great man was born reticent, and his example taught us not to make of ourselves the topic of our own conversation. Trying to please him was the most fortunate sort of education for young girls.

CHAPTER VIII

THE BROKEN MIRROR

EVER since Mr. Booth had mentioned his own theatre to me, I had been pretending to myself it was Booth's Theatre that was to house him in New York and not the one on Broadway, so I interrupted a confidence with 'Wouldn't it be perfect, Mr. Chase, if instead of the Star, we were returning to Booth's Theatre?'

'The Star's all right. The location is better than Booth's.'

'But think if Mr. Booth were returning to the mechanical stage he originated, and just think of your comfort in those luxurious offices —— !'

The manager capitulated. 'It's a wonder he doesn't grumble all the time — after what that theatre was. Did you ever hear him complain, reminding us of the contrast to the barns he plays in now? No. Nor I. I guess he is making me over. I'd be ashamed to be mean in his presence. Even at the Star — it's going to be great. There won't be a hitch.'

The opening night went as Mr. Chase expected, without a 'hitch,' and it was 'great!' I fancied that I detected a subtle difference in Mr. Booth toward his audience. His manner was as of the heir come home, and the welcome that rushed to him over the footlights was equally possessive. New York audiences were aggressively sympathetic with his enforced absences and did their best to assure him they understood and would

69

again lend him to 'adjacent districts,' but in the happy meantime he was theirs and they were his. Night after night this same proprietary welcome swept to the stage. If any actor desired to be cured of conceit, he had only to support Edwin Booth in New York.

Outside of the theatre, Mr. Booth vanished. In the theatre, he seemed ever to be coming from something pleasant or else going to it. Mr. Chase said that, while all the houses were not sold out, many of them were. There was nothing that was not *couleur de rose* until that fatal night when, hurrying to the stage, I knocked from my dressing-table a large and entirely satisfactory hand-mirror — and it broke. I put down this accident to hard luck, but gave its associated bad fortune no thought whatever. Mr. Booth was so balanced, so calm, that it did not occur to me he would not pooh-pooh omens even as Mr. Barrett did laughingly — his Irish extraction notwithstanding.

After my scene, I met my Star in the wings, and he detained me. On the road, with something daily happening of common interest, I always had small talk on the tip of my tongue for him, but here in New York he had almost become a stranger again, and I could think of nothing to say until my broken mirror came as an evil inspiration.

The curtain was up, the wings were darkened from a twilight stage, but no shadows could have dimmed the flare that leapt into my listener's eyes. I would have given anything — to have unsaid my own words even before he spoke. There was despair in his voice. I should have been grateful to feel I was deceiving myself, but I knew this was not a pretence of teasing play. Alas, I knew Mr. Booth meant every word he was saying.

'It is trouble! Something will happen to me — to the theatre — to you!' He spoke in sharp distress, as if the blow were then and there falling.

'Oh, no! Nothing will happen!'

'You'll see! It has come again — in New York! It's to the theatre! No — it is to *me!*'

I hoped to wipe out this part of his fear, at least. 'No, Mr. Booth, it must be to me! The mirror is mine! I broke it — in my dressing-room. *I* am the one!' Then I tried to be playful, hoping so to exorcise the superstitious fear, but he did not smile. I was heart-broken to be worrying him — yet I could not work myself into a feeling of doom.

The next day I went over to the Star Theatre to replace the broken mirror and get my mail and 'look around.' As I opened the stage door, I felt the chilly desolateness that only a 'darkened' theatre gives out. A sheet was posted: '*Theatre closed until further notice!*' Mr. Booth was ill!

Even now I did not associate my broken mirror with this — the worst thing to frighten a dramatic company, have its Star ill enough to close the theatre 'until further notice.' I went to the front, to the manager's office, to look up Mr. Chase. He was 'worried to death.'

'Mr. Booth has a cold on his lungs. While he is a very sick man, it is not dangerous — yet! But he must be confined to his room ten days, at least. That's out-and-out loss — and here in New York, of all towns! It couldn't be worse, unless ——!' He checked himself.

The word death must not be spoken. 'This is New York, little lady — and it's too bad! But what a man Mr. Booth is! The first thing he said to me was I should pay salaries in full on Saturday. "Pay salaries in full regardless of how long I am sick." That's the sort of Star you have! Can you say anything to cheer me up?'

My firm faith in a speedy and sure recovery was the confidence of youth, but it did cheer our manager.

I did not realize the danger of pneumonia hanging over Mr. Booth. I always threw off my own colds, so Mr. Booth would his, of course. As for salaries, I was not surprised. Day upon day he had not done the thing to topple him from his pedestal, but he was actually building that pedestal into a column. Now, he was paying salaries in full — out of his own pocket, probably.

I used up a few days trying to find one perfect rose that glowed with life and had a tint of heaven in it. I knew what I wanted, and at last a florist understood and promised the rose. I carried it myself to Mr. Booth's hotel, which Mr. Chase had informed me was 'way up' on Fifth Avenue — if I remember, somewhere near the forties. I did not send up my name. I wrote on the card: 'From one who is sorry that she did it.'

The theatre remained 'dark' ten days or more, and then the notice was posted that we would resume the following night.

I was in the cast, and I hid from Mr. Booth when off stage. I hoped he might not observe me, at least until the *closed theatre* wore off. But he espied me. I think he was looking for me. He came toward me, and spoke as if there had been no interruption in our broken-mirror conversation. 'I told you something would happen! To me.' I longed to drop through a trap! — but Mr. Booth was speaking on earnestly: 'It has come and gone! You had nothing to do with it, except to warn me. My life has been filled with tragedies that have been bolts from a clear sky. I have come to expect — the worst. You must not mind — now. It might have been my daughter. It might have been fatal!'

'You are well now, Mr. Booth.'

'Quite! But I am too lazy — yet.'

I spoke impulsively. 'You will not be ill again this season.'

The effect was magical. He dismissed the mirror episode then and there, and not once during the season did he refer to it, nor did he make mention of the 'supernatural cause of his sickness' to any one in the company, not even to Mr. Chase. This was so like Mr. Booth. He knew that many an actor has suffered unjustly for acquiring a reputation for being a hoodoo.

CHAPTER IX

THE ORCHESTRA ON THE STAGE

WHILE making allowance for the element of novelty, it puzzled me that, amid irrepressible Henry Irving burlesques, I did not see one of Edwin Booth. A musical extravaganza that omitted an Irving burlesque would not have sensed public taste. These burlesques were seldom subtle, but nearly always amusing. Usually comedians relied upon a straight Henry Irving make-up with incongruous contrasts of excruciating grammar: *I seen*, *I be*, *you was*, etc., or something equally obvious. It was so easy to recognize the poorest Henry Irving imitation that audiences hailed one with laughter and applause.

The cleverest one in New York — becoming the talk of the town overnight — was that of Henry E. Dixey, which he introduced in *Adonis* of phenomenal run and equally phenomenal delight and mirth. His make-up was straight, and so was his manner; indeed, his art was too subtle for his own imitators to copy.

On the road I had seen Nat Goodwin's screaming farce called *Those Bells*. He gave as straight an imitation of the great English actor as his talents could render. For *fun* he employed a misbehaving spot-light.

I asked prominent actors — among them McKee Rankin — why there was no demand for a Booth burlesque. I was told that there had never been a really *funny* caricature of Edwin Booth. True, the popular

clown George L. Fox had given a successful Booth burlesque, but his art lay in caricaturing the scenes of
Booth plays rather than his acting, and even so the attempt was meaningless to actors who saw the performance. There had never been a Booth burlesque vogue
such as sprang up like mushrooms immediately after
Mr. Henry Irving's American appearance.

I put the question to the king of burlesque imitators,
Mr. Goodwin himself. That comedian — for by this
time he had deserted burlesque for comedy — made this
answer:

'No one can imitate Edwin Booth but another Booth
and an Edwin at that. No one could recognize a
straight imitation of him — it would be — too *different*.
As for burlesquing him — what's there to hang a caricature on? His art's rounded like a ball. He has no rough
knobs sticking out for pegs. In caricature we exaggerate
mannerisms. You can't be funny by exaggerating something that is not in the first place a little overdone by the
one you burlesque. It would be just as easy to caricature the Apollo Belvedere or a Rare Day in June. Mr.
Booth stresses his vowels, they say. Well! What of it?
He says altar, as if it were spelled a-l-t-a-r — which it is
— and he does not pronounce it — altur (like the rest of
us), as if it were spelled a-l-t-u-r, which it isn't. He's
right! and the fool who tries to be funny over the correct
English pronunciation of Edwin Booth just shows himself up. No, I won't tackle Booth! I couldn't be funny
caricaturing perfection. And as for a straight imitation
of him — why let the cat out of the bag on my own acting? It's best to keep them guessing.'

BEHIND THE SCENES WITH BOOTH

En route from New York to Boston, Mr. Chase confided that wild horses couldn't drag him from another boast that 'It was going to be great — not until we are safely on the rails rolling *out* of town.'

'But it *was* great, Mr. Chase!'

'What there was of it, yes! But I'll never get over my fright when Mr. Booth was ill! It's the first time I've had to close my theatre because my Star was ill, and here we are bringing him to Boston in the winter just when everybody is sneezing! Suppose he comes down with another cold —— There is only one hope: he will be so happy in 29 Chestnut Street, with his daughter and her little one, he'll throw off colds. Isn't it nice to think of him surrounded by all his trophies and laurel wreaths and things — if he kept them —— Would you think, from talking with him, he'd had the adulation of the "smooth world" as the cowboy puts it?'

As for myself, I was swearing in secrecy that 'wild horses' should not drag a word from my lips if I broke a hundred looking-glasses.

On the opening night there swept to the stage a welcome to Edwin Booth and response for his 'points' as if those in front were gathered at a shrine. 'Back' the same reverence was active. 'Old actors' were reminiscing and condescendingly instructing novices that it was in Boston Mr. Booth had made his début — even on the Museum stage. It was small wonder Boston was so proud of him! Didn't he win his spurs here — literally wearing his father's when he went on for Tressel! It was

EDWIN BOOTH'S HOUSE, CHESTNUT STREET, BOSTON

Boston and not that 'Broadway town' that first crowned his genius.

Even on the train from New York, Mr. Chase had complained that the Boston Theatre was 'too big except for what it was built for — ballet spectacles and sensational scenic productions' — but a memory prompted me to differ with him.

'It's not too big for Mr. Booth's audiences. They had to have the orchestra play on the stage, to make room ——'

'In what bill?'

'*Hamlet!*'

'You know this for a fact?'

'Ask Mr. Booth.'

'He's never mentioned it to me, and I shouldn't like to — unless we repeat the miracle. Who told you?'

'The orchestra leader himself!'

'Lothian? — And they actually put the orchestra on the stage — In the Boston Theatre!!!'

'They had to, to make room.'

'If it has been done, it can be again! This is his home town! Little lady, it's going to be great.' But Mr. Chase asked for the story.

I had been won by the popular orchestra leader with this very story of Edwin Booth's drawing power. Mr. Lothian had greeted me, by asking how did I like Boston's tiny Madison Square Theatre, and then had laughed uproariously at his own jest. The size of the Boston was visualized for one by the constantly made statement that an audience considered 'good business' in the usual auditorium looked like 'poor business' in the Boston Theatre, while when it was indeed poor business the picture the auditorium presented was something a supporting company is not supposed to notice. One of my first stage instructions was to forbear remarks on fine houses, no matter how crowded or brilliant, lest my silence imply I had also taken note of a poor house — should there be one. True to form, not once this season did I mention the capacity business. But to return to the Booth story.

'Yes,' Mr. Lothian was saying, 'it's a big place for most of them to fill, but Edwin Booth gets away with it. We had the orchestra up on the stage. And didn't I let Barry Sullivan know about it!'

It seems that when Barry Sullivan was playing his engagement at the Boston Theatre — long before my time — he found fault right and left. He rubbed up the wrong way all who came in contact with him behind the curtain. One morning at rehearsal he 'went for' the scenery. He lost his temper, and the leader lost his. 'Barry Sullivan took the centre of the stage and "got off": "How do you expect an artist to act Hamlet with this scenery? It's rags!!! Rags!!!"' continued Mr. Lothian.

'But I couldn't stand it longer. I got even with him for all he'd put on me! I chortled back: "Edwin Booth did it this season, and he packed the house so we had to put the orchestra on the stage. They were mobbing for seats."'

I (in high glee): 'What did he say then?'

'Nothing! He was floored.'

THE ORCHESTRA ON THE STAGE

'Was the orchestra ever put on the stage for Barry Sullivan?'

'Ha! Ha! That's good! We could have found room for every orchestra in town out there after his biggest audience was in. But what did he expect? Challenging Edwin Booth in his own line! But you've got to be reasonable! They can't all be Booths.'

There it was again — the poetic loyalty for him behind the curtain, extending to the musicians playing his incidental music.

Most vivid of my Lothian memories is the one of a Friday night when he rushed 'behind' that I might get the good news first of all from his lips. He could scarcely breathe, he was so excited. 'It's going to be again! I was hoping you could see it! Tomorrow for the matinee they'll have to put the orchestra on the stage!'

'Oh!!!!!'

'You'll see it for yourself!' Then, contemptuously: 'That "barn" as they like to call it is sold out again — for *Hamlet*! All that's needed to crowd the Boston — is stars like Edwin Booth.' We both laughed as if he had said something uniquely dazzling.

Mr. Chase, too, sought me out during the performance. While not excited, he did not try to hide his gratification. 'Your miracle is going to be repeated.'

I hoped he might be willing to 'mention' it to Mr. Booth *now*.

'You bet I will. I should have the audience photographed — if it were left to me. But there's no use in suggesting that line of publicity to Mr. Booth.'

BEHIND THE SCENES WITH BOOTH

Even our Star was not calm that matinee. His eyes told his story. He hurried past me, yet with a half-smile that expressed his realization that we all shared his response to Boston's love for him. His face was tender as he 'peeked out' at that audience-filled orchestra space. He murmured, as if it troubled him, 'They cannot see when we're up stage,' and then and there he disregarded his rehearsed business and played down where those dear faithful people could see him better.

We did our full repertoire in Boston, and charmed I was when *Richard* was billed, for the tragedy was not put on in New York — so much time being lost through Mr. Booth's illness. The big Boston Theatre stage and its wide wings lent themselves enticingly for watching Mr. Booth act.

I never could get enough of his Hamlet. Any rôle of his lifted me off of the earth. I was thrilled at my own privilege to hear and speak the great lines of masterpieces. I was glad I was alive to have my imagination filled with poetry on honor, sacrifice, immortal love, patriotism — any of the noble sentiments I heard expounded constantly.

An older actress of the Palmy Days came behind and congratulated me upon being engaged for the 'legitimate.'

'I long to get back,' she said. 'Seeing your costumes hanging up makes me homesick enough to cry. Child, your character can't help being formed by these great women — by the heroes of Mr. Booth's repertoire. Of course, he makes his villains fascinating, but don't

80

they get come up with every time? They poke fun at
the wrong things in most of the modern plays — and
it's fearfully wearying to speak the same trash, night
after night!'

CHAPTER X

'SHE SPOILED HIS SCENE'

In the *Merchant of Venice*, Mr. Edwin Royle's line rang out to stir his listeners on both sides of the curtain, 'But Antonio is certainly undone,' and in this scene of conflicting emotions Mr. Booth's unforgettable notes floated or crashed to one by turns. The voice which could be so hauntingly mournful, when charged with agony, also mounted to orchestral rhapsody. His line, 'I thank God! I thank God! Is it true?' made me turn cold, and his 'I had it of Leah when I was a bachelor' was so pitiful it started the tears.

Until Boston I had only *heard* the 'Tubal scene': — now I resolved to take advantage of the spacious first entrance and *see* the acting. Necessarily I was wearing my Jessica elopement dress. That this costume might react upon Mr. Booth did not occur to me nor to our stage manager, who made room for me by his side. None amongst us would do a thing to upset Mr. Booth for reasons more potent far than conforming to stage etiquette. In the theatre sense, I had been formed by Mr. Barrett, and he would have thought nothing at all of glimpsing a character off stage while yet in the costume of — any scene whatever. With him it was the unforeseen on the stage that made him nervous; nor had Mr. Booth at any time protested when actors watched his scenes from the wings. Then, too, there was the ever-reiterated 'Be anywhere, my boy, Mr. Booth will

82

find you,' that drove from my memory the one thing that I should not have forgotten — my own experience of Mr. Booth's Shylock sensitiveness to Jessica.

I made no effort to conceal my presence from the Star during this scene. At its close, as he was taking his thundering calls, even as I was hurrying to my dressing-room to 'change,' I grew all out of conceit with the callous Jessica. Her father's heartbreak had undone my sympathetic conception of her. In order to regain my 'manner' for the next act, I grappled to my heart all Shylock's speeches of his daughter and his gloating fury of soul over Antonio's misfortunes. But I should see this powerful acting every time the piece was done from now on. This I determined on. What if I did have to rush my change! However, in spite of desire, I could not manage it.

There was a sequel to tread upon the heels of this Tubal scene. There comes back the picture of Mr. Booth, in the 'David Garrick,' [1] leaning over a table examining some magazines, when, without changing his position and speaking so lightly that his words would have seemed to come inadvertently, if he had not directly addressed me, 'Would you mind keeping out of the first entrance during my Tubal scene?' He was so casual and friendly that listeners were forced to follow his lead, but, even so, general conversation ceased.

'We have done *The Merchant* several times since Boston, so I dare say there is no need to warn you, but in case — if you will keep out of my line of sight after the elopement scene ——?'

[1] Edwin Booth's private car, in which he travelled later in the season.

This I promised, yet I was puzzled.

He gave me a quick, sympathetic look. 'You would like to know why. I go on in that scene with a clear picture of Jessica. My own flesh and blood has betrayed me — betrayed her race. I am deserted. This gadabout is spending my money having a good time on it, and I am hopeless — alone. I charge my voice with Shylock's agony and then look up and see you — my daughter — standing before me, come back to me. My picture breaks up! I lose my scene.'

This was the worst yet! And then somebody gave one of those stage whispers that are projected to reach the last row in the gallery: 'She spoiled his scene.'

Quietly, without a flicker of his eyelashes, Mr. Booth continued: 'Don't feel too sorry now. You did no harm. The scene did not suffer, only — you jerked my mind.'

He smiled with real mischief, for between Mr. Booth's *spoiling* a scene and *losing* one lay the difference of the wide world. I inwardly gloated over that 'spoiled his scene.'

My attempted apology was waived, but he listened sympathetically when I told him I had not realized he *could* be affected by seeing me in the wings in costume.

'I am sure of it, and I dare say the older members of the company have told you that nothing upsets me on the stage.'

'If you lost that scene' (very mild emphasis on 'lost') 'in Boston, I really think your audience should be congratulated — for they wouldn't want their hearts broken any more than you shattered them that night.'

'Perhaps the shock was good for me, after all.' Genially: 'I exerted myself to cover up.'

'I don't know how you usually play the scene, Mr. Booth, but I could not sleep all that night.' It was so hard to praise him that I was elated to get this in.

Mr. Chase asked was it the character of Shylock which made him sensitive to unexpected influences?

'No! I should not care to see Miss Vaders down under the stage through Ophelia's grave; although when she is on the stage with me, I am equal to any mischance that may arise!'

Here was a fascinating how-de-do! The theatre accorded Mr. Booth a poise as fixed as the North Star. I did not know what to make of it! All was law and order in this actor's art. Comets did not seem native to his horizon.

After Mr. Booth left us, Mr. Chase added that for his part he didn't see anything to that chestnut they told, 'Don't worry, my boy, Mr. Booth will find you at night,' because any actor engaged to support Mr. Booth would know enough to drop below him and not take the centre of the stage unless he was instructed to. And how could Mr. Booth help finding an actor on a small stage if he takes the position his training tells him he should?

Later, I said to Mr. Booth, I hoped I was the only one who made him lose his scenes. He laughed — gently as always.

'Wait till you can say you spoiled my scene! But you'll not forget — keeping out of the first entrance for Tubal ——'

CHAPTER XI

'SANTA CLAUS' PLAYS MARION DE LORME IN
PHILADELPHIA

THE train carrying us out of Boston was taking us to Philadelphia, via 'One Night Stands.' There were two weeks of these, with Christmas and New Year matinees thrown in, for good measure of discomfort for our Star.

December 20, Worcester, Massachusetts.
December 21, Holyoke, Massachusetts.
December 22, Albany, New York.
December 23, Utica, New York.
December 24, Oswego, New York.
December 25, Syracuse, New York.
December 27, Rochester, New York.
December 28, Bradford, Pennsylvania.
December 29, Elmira, New York.
December 30, Scranton, Pennsylvania.
December 31, Wilmington, Delaware.
January 1, Lancaster, Pennsylvania.

If ever a harnessed artist was justified in looking glum, surely it was Mr. Booth, as he walked unobtrusively into the Boston Station. He knew what lay ahead of him. Apart from theatre routine, it meant getting up in the dark, gulping his breakfast, a different bed each night. All this on top of having been ill enough in New York to close his theatre, and of leaving his sickroom before regaining his normal strength. And as if this were not enough, the management sentenced him to the tortures of Tantalus, letting him taste the joys of family reunion, the comfort of home, only to pull him

86

out of it five days before Christmas. He would have been justified in being the picture of the disgruntled — but here is his picture! He was genial and smiled in amusement as Miss Vaders and I giggled our affectionate how-de-do's to one another. He sensed that to me these 'one-night stands' were a lark, and that I was in fine holiday fettle; his feelings were not injured that an unthinking girl ignored his own physical strain, and he mildly — yes, I admit it was mildly — entered into our gladness. Reserve among the 'Chickens' evaporated that morning in the Boston Station when we started out on a renewed journey with the same hotels to shelter us again.

During the next two weeks, Mr. Booth did not join us for supper, but he bade us bundle ourselves into his carriage when he drove to the hotel from the theatre or he walked with us were the distance short enough. He was always sympathetic, and once he said to Amo and me that as a diet the 'Chickens' agreed with him, because there was not poison of envy in our flesh.

In despite of the unsentimental appeal of an actor's Christmas — for to those of my association this day and all other holidays meant only an extra matinée — when Mr. Chase informed us that we should pass through Syracuse the day before Christmas and return to the same city to play the holiday itself, I asked to be let off the train in Syracuse and there await the coming of the company, for I had suddenly conceived the holiday notion of trimming a Christmas tree for Mr. Booth. Late that night I sat on the floor gazing at the disappointing

87

tree which I had tramped through the slush of a strange city to find. Shopping the day before Christmas is not easy even when one knows the shops, and my money had given out all too soon. I sighed as it came over me that the little tree was too personal to thrust on Mr. Booth. There was that Kalamazoo woman who frightened Mr. Booth so with her kiss! A skimpy Christmas tree was not exactly a kiss, but suppose he thought it something worse, that he read in its tiny flaming candles a sign I was losing my cool head and spoiling everything. Mr. Booth never heard of that poor little tree. Amo had it with her breakfast.

Our Star did not pass this Christmas Day by as the idle wind, for his ladies one and all found gold-handled umbrellas in their rooms upon return from the matinée with cards from *the management*.

In Philadelphia was a house with a room which, Mr. Booth told us, was the most interesting one he had entered — in all his life.

'When dining with the owners — necessarily on a Sunday — my hostess, on rising from the table, without giving a hint of the unusual in her manner, said: "We'll have our coffee in the back woods!" She guided me through the stately hall to a door that looked like a rough cabin of the far west mountains! There was a fireplace — just the sort a man might jumble up for himself! Unsorted sticks — not evenly cut city cordwood — were burning in it. A black kettle hanging on a crane steamed away; a bearskin was underfoot. Oh, everything that should have been there was. And the roof had a hole in it. I was so taken aback that I gazed at the leaky roof and asked like a fool, "What do you do when it rains?" There was a triumphant laugh. That was the line I should have spoken on the cue they gave me. That was what they were hoping I might ask. Every newcomer asked about the rain. There was no need for explanation. The leaky roof was sheltered from the elements, for it was underneath an upper story of the house proper. I congratulated my hosts upon their achievement of a "real thing." It was adventure. Even the citified coffee could not destroy my illusion. Days came galloping back, that were quite as rough, with the coffee not so civilized and — when I had to wash the dishes.'

'Do you mean your California days, Mr. Booth? When you were a boy there?'

'I do. But if you had come upon me then and treated me as a boy, I should have been humiliated. I am satisfied now to rough it in a log cabin that's hidden away in a Philadelphia mansion. Yes! It is the most interesting room I have seen in all my life.'

The repertoire was given to two weeks' heavy business, with *Richelieu* for the opening. Then *it happened.* It could hardly have been more ridiculous, yet, thanks to Mr. Booth, the fatal titter was averted.

The local stage manager of the Chestnut Street Opera House had filled the position of chief property man in Booth's Theatre with 'Garry' serving under him. He knew, to a flat or border or a bunch-light, what Booth settings required. No puzzling over 'advance plots' for him, and he gloried in having new scenes painted and old ones touched up. Everything must be spick and span — glorified, if left to him — for this red-letter engagement of the local season. I had been accustomed to join his confabs with Garry and many a Booth Theatre yarn so came my way. On the opening day he displayed with pride a complicated 'entrance' — the secret door Marion de Lorme uses. But because he was he, Mr. Doud did not, according to habit, test the elaborated panel. Marion's tender fingers were supposed to give three knocks — her signal to Richelieu — that she was come. But, so the gallery gods might hear the three knocks, the stage manager pounded loudly with a wooden mallet upon a small board nailed to the floor.

On the opening night, Mr. Doud pounded and I pulled, but the door did not budge. It is a fearful thing to make a stage wait, and when this involves the Star, it takes on criminal proportions. I pulled, yanked, shook. The door stayed closed. Mr. Doud tried his skill. No use, the holding button was on the inside.

We could do no more, for already the walls were wobbling too perilously for illusion. With Mr. Booth waiting on the stage, any slit through which I could crawl must serve. I took the only one there was, after Mr. Doud had nodded consent. I squeezed through and was grateful enough to see the open stage. On 'entering,' I was not surprised to find Richelieu standing, instead of the regular business of sitting until long after Marion kneels and kisses the ecclesiastical ring — for, of course, Mr. Booth had covered up my wait.

The house was still as a church, and when he was reseated and the scene under way, Mr. Booth got in something, *sotto voce*, about 'Santa Claus.' For that's what I had done — walked *out of the chimney*, flouncing my long and delicate lace scarf about in the fireplace, dragging my full rose silk train over the glowing coals. And, thanks to Mr. Booth, there had not been a giggle!

When the curtain fell, I waited until after his 'calls' to apologize — a rite Mr. Barrett insisted upon when an actor went wrong in a scene, but I could not wedge in my contrite speech, for Mr. Booth was only interested in my elaborate sleeves. From their immaculate surface he brushed with the airiest touch flecks of imaginary soot, and seemed to be condoling with me upon my chimney sweep appearance. I even expected him to say again I had 'a passion for it' — the fun in his eyes told me he was thinking backward to my 'Bloody Apparition.'

Mr. Chase had a letter from Mr. Barrett, who was playing *Rienzi* in Brooklyn that week, instructing him to bring me to New York. He was staying at the Fifth Avenue Hotel. We went over on a *Lear* day. Mr. Barrett asked me to dine with him, and then broke the news. I was to be transferred at once to the Barrett Company. 'I am making a change, and I thought you might as well come home.' Nothing could have softened the blow so much as the balm that Mr. Barrett's Company was yet *home* for me, but the blue waters of the Pacific glistened, for Mr. Chase had let hints fall about California.

The day was valuable, for in Mr. Barrett's presence

the hard labor of the stage again sank into my conscious-ness; while in Mr. Booth's atmosphere, life in the theatre was all ripe plums begging one to eat them. Mr. Barrett took me down cellar with him and let me see him stoke the furnace!

Soon Mr. Chase appeared and favored caution in making changes, for Mr. Booth had become accus-tomed to his company. Of course, then, Mr. Barrett sent me back. I was glad — I was sorry.

After the play, when his carriage left me at the *Arnold* door, Mr. Barrett inspected the modest exterior of the building from his carriage window. 'I am proud, my child, that you live so economically' — and then he sob-ered and spoke as he had done so many times before — as my own father might have spoken, 'Don't put up with any nonsense from them. If you are troubled, write to me — and I'll send for you to come home.'

'Do you mean Mr. Doud? He's really very nice, this season.'

'Then I suppose I shall not hear from you.'

For all the humor in his voice, he was giving his orders. Letters, except on business, were not desired. 'Good-bye! I saw through your politeness. I am sending back one perfectly happy little bodkin. God keep you.'

This was the Lawrence Barrett whom more than I of his company knew — interested in our expenditures, generous, humorously jesting upon us and himself — the one to obey, yet always reverent. His 'God keep you' was not empty form — he charged it with prayer.

If Mr. Booth heard of my New York trip, he made no sign. I brought back fresh and vital memories of Mr.

Barrett's friendship for his partner. I had believed him when he said, 'If Ned should be disappointed in our association, it would break my heart.' I harped on this friendship to Mr. Chase, who had a habit of putting his convictions into questions, so he asked: 'Which do you think is the nobler friend — the one who inspires or the one who serves?'

CHAPTER XII

WE came to Baltimore, and a wonderful thing happened. It was something like an unveiling of Mr. Booth. Here were moments when he let us see how happy he *could* be — might have been all his life but for his dogging tragedies.

From the beginning of his confidences, Mr. Chase had lingered upon the renewed effort that was being made this season to induce Mr. Booth to be booked for Washington. The refusal was followed by a flood of letters — letters composed by men skilled in argument, diplomacy, eloquence. It was made clear that his reception, while not official, would assume proportions of a welcome from the Nation, but Mr. Booth's purpose was fixed — and the Great World came to him. No human being could have missed the meaning of his ovation. Official, Diplomatic, Social Washington were in front night after night. It was not hard to 'feel' these audiences. They had planned to send in floral tributes and had been denied. Mr. Chase said his Star turned pale when he heard of it. There was no need of the outward form. Invisible laurels were piled at his feet. One sensed them. 'Forget! We crown your genius with your character! You are free of your bitter shadow!'

Among Mr. Booth's trophies were two golden wreaths: one given to him in Germany and one in New York; but what must have been his thoughts when his own charac-

ter was transmuted into laurel leaves for him in Baltimore! His perfect taste had kept him from acting in
Washington and Washington came to him.

Calmly one reads of special trains that for years had
been run from Washington to Baltimore to carry Mr.
Booth's admirers for each performance. But one was not
so composed when facing those electric audiences. It
sent the blood coursing — thinking upon what it meant.
Was not the Nation's own tragedy back of all this homage? Mr. Chase 'kept me up' on the celebrities. 'Front-
page stuff,' every one of them, he said, and added, his
voice husky: 'Such a calamity would have ruined any
other actor — but it has done him good.' This was the
box-office tribute. It puzzled the manager to the last
how this miracle of an Edwin Booth had happened.

Once in 'David Garrick' days — yet to come — Mr.
Booth, in telling of the Booth children, was so carried
away that his eyes filled with tears — merry ones, too.
I, alas, forgot, and asked: 'How many brothers and
sisters did you have, Mr. Booth?' I hated myself for my
thoughtlessness. Any word of mine now could not but
make the situation worse. I left it to him — and Mr.
Booth took care of it. It made my throat ache that
many another forgetful one may have schooled him for
such handling. He smoked on a bit, then said unemo-
tionally: 'I forget the lot of us. I'll name them — you
count them for me! Junius Brutus — after my father, of
course — Rosalie, Henry, Mary, Frederick, Elizabeth
— I come in here — Asia, Joe — how many is that?'

'Nine, Mr. Booth.'

'What big families they used to raise!'—he smoked on.

BEHIND THE SCENES WITH BOOTH

There were ten Booth children, and the name of Wilkes was not spoken. Indeed, I well knew it would not be. It was his manner of avoidance, rather than the avoidance itself, that I thanked him for within my heart — for sparing me as I had not spared him. Here was drama! He had no brother by the name of John Wilkes Booth.

He did not get up and leave soon either, but helped us to steer free of our rocks. But there had leapt from his eyes such a flash of appeal, so beseechingly humble, that told of stirred-up dregs, that I prayed he might think on Baltimore.

Without the least spread-eagleism Mr. Booth was vitally patriotic. Once he had been boyishly so, he said this himself. It was his pet story. I used to coax it from him by marshalling listeners one by one — never two at a time. Two listeners meant one less telling of the story.

He was playing in London an engagement upon which much depended. It could not be shortened. His wife was with him, and they were awaiting the birth of their first child.

Always he began it with 'I couldn't get over it that my child was to be born under a foreign flag. I worried over it to myself, and all at once I had it! I saw my way to outwit that imp called Fate. I had Old Glory draped over my wife's bed. Under her country's flag she lay and our child was, literally, born under the Stars and Stripes.' His eyes always snapped here with pride at his own ingenuity in outwitting that 'imp of Fate,' but almost at once softened in their glow of gratitude — his child was an American — for all that imp's perverseness.

It did seem to me, from write-ups in local papers, and from *special* welcomes of audiences, as if Mr. Booth were always returning to his home town. I liked to think this out, for several cities had valid claims. New York's was based upon Booth's Theatre; in memory and imagination this achievement stood, if vanished in concrete form. Boston put forward his Museum record, his first appearance here on any stage and his early triumph as a star on its boards, and the indisputable fact of his present residence in Chestnut Street. Baltimore rejoiced in his ancestry; the house where he was born; the nearness of the homestead, Tudor Hall, Bellair. But San Francisco — they told me — boasted theirs was the town of his struggling youth; that in the City of the Golden Gate had come the first recognition that he was true son of his father.

In other towns the evidence was there to put one's finger on. Here one needed to let the claim lie fallow in one's mind, before it bloomed — all at once — into a wonderful story.

Forrest and the Elder Booth were dead. Across a continent — literal and metaphorical — a kingless kingdom was calling to its heir. A vacant throne! an unworn crown! — were waiting.

The son was urged to answer that call. Faint-heartedly, he drew on seven-league boots, with no inkling they were not common everyday shoes. Only one step, and he reached the Gate, and quietly knocked. But ——!

BEHIND THE SCENES WITH BOOTH

The throne knew its heir. The crown suspended in mid-air, the better to elude the grasp of all pretenders, tumbled itself down to rest upon that youthful head. Crowned and sceptred, his slender shoulders even now shrank in doubt. 'It couldn't last!' But New York sat up and took notice of what was going on in Boston, and soon the 'heir' came to Gotham; his startled eyes beholding his own bills all over the town — 'Edwin Booth — The Hope of The American Stage.'

Mr. Chase wound up the Baltimore engagement for me with his open confidence that no dead heart would have not been warmed to life by the audiences that week. He was thankful that his Star had held out. 'Mr. Booth would not go to Washington, and Washington came to him.'

'Mayday creatures — sporting bright wings in golden sunshine.' Mr. Chase did not intend to be poetical nor complimentary. 'That's what you feel like — you three! Now, isn't it? You can't help being happy. It comes natural to you.'

I supposed so. I hadn't thought about it. It would have been difficult not to ring down the curtain on a past however tragic — the present was too monopolizingly attractive. I believed Mr. Booth had turned a sharp corner after Baltimore. The deeps of his solitary self were hidden as ever, but he smiled at fantastic interludes that might have distressed him in the beginning of the season, even in New York — Boston — Philadelphia. Through thinning shadows we travelled into spring and on his journey through the South to West and East again, Mr. Booth took little walks on Cherry Street, Fun Street, and once he even turned down Prank Street. *164698*

In Pittsburgh the Opposition was Frank Mayo, and amid thrills that never did quite run down, the Mayo engagement opened for me another door on the art of Edwin Booth. Mine was a mere peek through a narrow crack but slits can reveal vistas. In Pittsburgh I saw Edwin Booth act a scene as he was not expecting to act it; and had no warning of the necessity for a change in his long-established routine for this scene. I heard his audience respond to his unpremeditated acting with demands for six calls instead of this curtain's usual three. It was said that Edwin Booth could do on the stage whatever he chose to do in instantaneous perfection. I had the proof. Mr. Mayo who in actor phrase 'made it possible' gloried beforehand in the ease *our genius* would rise to the occasion. 'He will treat your new readings as a little encounter with a suddenly risen wind. A swift spread of his wings and the wind will not only be pierced but left way below him. He is the only actor I know who needs no rehearsing, no slow building up or trying out effects. Put him to the test.'

Mr. Mayo was a Booth's Theatre star. Bless him for his temptation and my fall. It was his plot. He devised not only the change in interpretation of a many times acted scene but he drilled me in new readings. He was sure Mr. Booth would enjoy the surprise. Mr. Booth's sense of humor kept me guessing about this to the end of the season, but in any case he forgave, if favoring me now and then with a gimlet look and some 'Ah's' for me to apply to myself.

But, nothing could take from me my elation of those moments when on the stage with Edwin Booth I felt I was seeing the very essence of his art. The triumphant Mr. Mayo said I had had the rare chance of watching Mr. Booth apply his technique. The warm-hearted actor wished that he himself had been in front to see what I saw that night.

The lesson I learned from Mr. Booth's instant and complete response to the unforeseen was that he kept his wits at work while he was acting; that he was ready to take advantage of the least opening; that he caught the faintest gleam of light and threw it upon his own characterization, and above all that *surprise* was a veritable match to set off his genius. Anything that startled this actor out of his routine was enough to let loose the divine fire within his art.

Mr. Chase confided a bomb, fused and lighted, and it did not fail to explode. It seems Ido,[1] without the least desire to violate formidable etiquette, had asked for a big part 'just for once, so I can show managers the program with my name on it and secure a better engagement next season' — and whether he knew the circumstances or not, Mr. Booth had said Ido might go on for Regan in *Lear* for Cincinnati. So much for Ido. But Mrs. Baker did not suffer the loss of her Regan in silence. Although her King could do no wrong, it did seem to her past comprehension that Mr. Booth, who had not let Ido do the Player Queen because her lines

[1] Ido was our nickname for Ida Rock.

must be heard across the footlights, should select this heavy, cursing Regan for her. Every one blamed Mr. Chase and Ido, while they absolved Mr. Booth. He had somehow been *hoodwinked*. I really pitied Mama Baker. As our call boy said, 'she took on dreadfully.' When the mystery was on full blast, our urbane manager inveigled me apart and confided: 'Well, unless she gets a costume, Miss Rock can't go on for Regan, after all, because she says she has no money. Will Mrs. Baker object to lending hers, do you think?'

Oh, innocent, *untheatre* Mr. Chase! 'Of course she will! And how would Ido look in mama's costume! It's four times too big! Are you hinting I am to lend one of mine? I have no *Lear* costumes.'

He only chuckled. He had sown the seed, and knew it.

When the proper time was come when one might venture to speak of it to Mr. Booth — since this seemed to be *his* Regan — my spirit had chastened itself. I meekly put forth that Ido might wear my Player Queen dress — if he didn't mind.

It was between acts. He was at leisure, and he looked at me brightly.

'That solves her problem, I should say.'

'But it's too finicky for *Lear* — that is, my crown is. Perhaps one of the men will fake her out.'

'Would you approve of my Macbeth crown and mantle?'

'Your crown —! Your —! over my Player Queen dress!! — Oh, Mr. Booth!'

He was beseechingly enquiring this of me. At times

I forgot — off the stage — that Mr. Booth was the greatest of actors. He was so very natural I accepted the unnaturalness of his Macbeth crown offer as natural enough when I once landed on my feet through the Looking Glass into Wonderland. I felt so Alice-y that I couldn't help gurgling at the delicious preposterousness of it all.

My responsive laugh to his suggestion brought Mr. Booth's smile, but he did not take the pleading from his eyes. His eyes were wordlessly telling me he did so want — to pretend to play with us. It could be no more than pretence. He did not want to pretend to play that he was young — but if *we* could pretend that he had not grown up! And here was his crown! Here was Regan! His crown was his symbol! If — while he remained Edwin Booth in every sense — we could pretend *for* him —! It was for such a little while! Only until the end of the season when we would scatter, perhaps not to meet again! He would have the rest of his life to be sensible in and forget he had pretended to pretend he was at play.

There had been racing through my mind all he had said of himself. He had not *grown up*, he was *born up;* his boyhood had been filled with such responsibilities to his father — Mr. Barrett had told me more of this than had Mr. Booth — his youth had been so unyouthful!

There was but one way to answer his silent appeal, and that was to begin the game at once. Many a mickle of his own speeches during train-ride conversations had gone to make this muckle of understanding, and many a muckle of his speeches in the near future was to prove that I was right.

He asked me to send Ido to him when he came off, giving me a worried look.

'She doesn't know much about getting herself up for the stage — does she?'

'Oh, I'll do all that.' We laughed a tiny bit. Mr. Booth's laugh at all times seemed to well from his soul and had little need of his body to give it expression. It was such a contagious, merry laugh, one did not notice it was often soundless. My sole instruction from him for Regan's get-up was that I fasten his Macbeth crown securely on Ido's head, for the crown was heavy 'and I do not want my Regan to look tipsy.' I promised his crown should not wobble.

Ido did not trip in her giant's robes, but Fate can do the meanest things. So on Ido's great night, especially arranged that her name might be on a program opposite a big part, what did 'Popper' do but forget to instruct the printer, and the program had Mrs. Baker's name down for Regan — and poor Ido's was not there to be shown — ever. Hot was the resentment of the regular Regan, who was heard to complain, 'If a novice has a reputation to make, I have one to lose.' But for all this, cues were taken from Mr. Booth, who shook hands with Ido when the last curtain fell on her sole performance in *King Lear*. This was the only time all this season that one of his company was thus honored.

CHAPTER XIII

THE 'DAVID GARRICK'

On the way to New Orleans, Mr. Chase confided the plan of the 'David Garrick.' It was his first private car — and mine. It was to cost three thousand dollars — without meals! — to run between New Orleans and San Francisco. Mr. Booth was paying for the car himself. Any mode of travel (private cars included) was an old story to him. Of all Mr. Chase's confidences, this one was the most suggestive of possibilities. Did it mean that Mr. Booth, wearying of companionship, was arranging for royal seclusion? I pictured him sequestered in that private car. Progressive confidences revealed that Mr. Magonigle and Mr. Chase were to invade the 'David Garrick.' I wondered why Mr. Booth had not travelled in a private car all the season. Suppose he had! What a different season it would have been for us! Yet if he were bent on escaping us — if we had become pestiferous! — in spite of Regan — or worse, if because of it! — Whatever it was, end or beginning — it had come! When I touched bottom, the sun shone through the troubled waters, for I heard Mr. Booth asking me to be his guest in the 'David Garrick.' He gave his invitation as if begging a favor. How like him! How very like him!

'Will you save me from indigestion? My solitary meals are become a nightmare. Come and liven me up while I eat. Then I'll lean back in my armchair — there is to be one — and smoke — for a change!'

Of course, we laughed at this. 'You chickens may fly at one another and peck out your eyes. Oh, mine have been on you —! Will you accept?'

Mr. Booth invited Mrs. Foster, Mrs. Baker, Amo and Ido. It was our custom not to repeat the Star's little speeches to one another, but it goes without saying he made each feel her welcome. With the 'David Garrick' in the offing, had New Orleans been the Dismal Swamp, it had put on rosy hues. Mr. Booth chose to become our host for weeks ahead after weeks of us in the past. Here was assurance that he was not bored, and with this comfort self-consciousness melted into thin air. We were three perfectly natural young persons in his presence ever after.

I have always congratulated myself that fascinating New Orleans was the scene of my babyhood years. Here were the offices of my father's Louisiana plantations, and here my mother led her gay and brilliant life and danced at balls with Lawrence Barrett. I could not help but wonder this week, if I should be now with Mr. Booth had not his partner danced with my mother.

Almost without preliminaries we gathered for another sight-seeing drive. Mr. Magonigle broke the ice by saying such sunshine was good for one's bones. Mr. Chase agreeably added: 'Speaking of bones, our first stop is the cemetery.' In that luscious air, no one even thought of dirges, but Mr. Booth often paused that morning, to speak on in a few moments, as if there had been no pause. After a reference to the monument he had had erected in Baltimore for his father and mother, he told us of his wife's memorial window in the little church near Newport close to Boothden.[1] He said feelingly, 'My daughter came to me telling me of her wish to place this window in memory of her mother. It is a beautiful window.'

My own brief saunter with Mr. Booth did not break his mood. He was silent a long while before he spoke. 'My daughter and I were there' — another pause. I thought he referred to the unveiling. He said much of the window and the artist and the picture, and then he sighed and smiled: 'There! Enough for today. You are too sober for even our surroundings.'

Might I ask something, a question on acting? 'Mr. Barrett insists that the place to learn to die is a hospital; the place to learn to play Ophelia's mad scene is an insane asylum.'

Mr. Booth agreed with insane asylums and art galleries, but was emphatically against watching death-beds. 'It is the psychology of the dying you should capture. You miss this when watching death-beds of strangers, and you are too stunned to be instructed by death struggles of those you love. Study animals. No! I have tried hospital deaths. I learned so little from them I gave the study up. In my personal life I have watched two women die. One was an angel — the other a devil. The angel did not want to die. She loved too well the one she was being torn from — the one who needed her. She was rebellious. She died shrieking. It is so we act a

[1] Mr. Booth's summer residence in Newport.

death of the hardened criminal. Shrieks — terror —
defiance — and this woman was an angel.'

After a while I ventured: 'And the devil?'

He asked bitterly: 'Have you watched a kitten
purring itself to sleep? It did not hurt her to part from
loved ones, for — she had not loved any one but herself.
Insanity is another question. Learn mad scenes from
life.' Death's opposite pole, birth, must have held
Mr. Booth's thoughts, for suddenly he said, as if it
meant much to him, that he was born with a caul —
then, assuming ignorance of cauls on my part, added
impressively: 'That is a thin tissue over the face when
one is born.'

I made haste to assure him I was familiar with cauls
and their portent. They meant the gift of second
sight.

He evaded this, but emphasized his conviction it was
good luck to be born with one — 'That is, if you keep
it by you constantly.'

I told him I credited any phenomenon signifying good
fortune — at *his* birth.

He thanked me without smiling. He accorded cauls
the respect which was their due. He told me of an accident connected with his Australian tour when he was
very young. He was sure he owed his life to his talis-
man, for his escape from drowning, while fording a
stream on horseback, had been miraculous. Afterwards, it was lent to a friend going into danger and who
begged for it. 'I knew better than to part with my caul,
but I could not refuse him. He kept it so long that I
wrote demanding it back, and he admitted that it was

lost — gone! I knew my luck would turn. Misfortunes came. I think few have had more.' [1]

It seemed unsympathetic to refer to his compensations in good fortunes — and surely few have had more — so I was silent.

As we sauntered among those lovely, tiny houses of the dead, the air was so sweet and Mr. Booth radiated such energy even of spirit that I could not help telling him how glad I was he did not drown, that he was alive and would be alive, oh, for ever so long!

'If Mark Grey had not died, I should not be alive this morning.'

Mr. Booth had previously told us most of the story of the attempt to shoot him from the audience in McVicker's Theatre in Chicago. The play was *Richard II* and Mr. Booth was giving the soliloquy when his murder was attempted.

This morning he was more personal in relating the details. It was the psychology rather than the facts that moved him. I was expressing little of my horror as I said: 'What a target an actor on the stage is! How easy it is to shoot him down.'

'Yes, and if that lunatic had not died, he would have kept on making me his target until he hit me.'

'He really was crazy ——?'

'I had not seen the man, nor heard of him. He must have been crazy. He had not a ghost of a motive to kill me. He sat in the balcony. I saw the smoke from his pistol when he fired. I knew then exactly where to

[1] 'My grandmother showed this caul to me when I was a little girl.' — Extract from letter to author by Edwina Booth Crossman.

point him out. My caul saved me. Second sight — premonition — warning! I do not account for what I did — but there is no other explanation. My Richard business is to be seated in the soliloquy. My head is always in the same position for certain lines — so many feet from the stage. But on this night, without premeditation, I suddenly rose from my chair, and did something I never do; I leaned over to steady myself as I rose.' He glanced toward me for confirmation that he could not be so awkward as to rise in this manner.

'When my head was bent low, the bullet passed over my head and not into it. The aim was true. That lunatic was a dead shot. Grey had spaced me and timed me. But for my bending over, he had killed me. Do you know what I did — when I heard the shot and saw the smoke? I was as calm as I am now. It seemed not to be happening to me. It was like a scene I was directing! I came down to the footlights and pointed out the man who had the pistol in his hand. I said, without excitement, "Arrest that man!" He was seized, and when the audience would let me, I went on with the play.'

'What became of him?'

'He was sent to an insane asylum. He had but one mania — to shoot me. There was a man who did not rest until he freed the one whose mania was to murder me.' Mr. Booth's eyes held his hurt wonder. 'You would not think he — any man — would have done this to me ——' I never saw Mr. Booth so sad in real life.

BEHIND THE SCENES WITH BOOTH

All the season it had escaped me how Mr. Booth made his great Iago point when he set his jaws after his line, 'From now on I never shall speak word.'

There was more to his acting here than vigorously snapping his teeth, even if everything this actor did, snapping of teeth included, *told*. Why was it so effective? In New Orleans I watched for my answer each moment he was on the stage, for Edwin Booth's art had at least taught me he scorned the element of surprise. When he bounded on at the rising of the curtain, he put over such physical vitality that I wondered if Mr. Booth did not intend it for a symbol of his mental vitality. Right here the audience accepted an Iago *who could not be broken*. It did seem as if Mr. Booth were guarding, in all he did, against scepticism when he came to his supreme line — 'From now on I never shall speak word.' Tonight he made me realize that the shuddering admiration he aroused here depended upon his *audience's faith in Iago's will force*. No one doubted that even under torture that jaw would stay shut. Had there been a doubt of this, the point would have been ruined.

Over forty times I saw that self-imposed lockjaw, and not once did it seem studied, and I never failed to catch Iago's unspoken gloating over those who would try to open his jaw, and fail. Mr. Booth could not miss this effect with any audience, for his art had been building toward it throughout the play.

It is an exhilarating experience to laugh with an audience, applaud with an audience, be stirred by any emotion with an audience that is swayed by genius! I knew every word of the play; I knew the business, the music, and all the cues. I knew when the curtain would fall. I knew the performance so well that I could lean back and let the psychology of Mr. Booth's Iago possess me. I did not name it psychology — I did not know enough. But during the curtain calls, when the Star looked 'insulted,' my thoughts leapt with glee to a recent Hamlet night when I stood by during these same calls. After one he saw me and hurried to me, with a grievance in his eyes. It was a real grievance, too, and he longed to share it.

'See what they have done to me! I am shorn. That imbecile of a barber — I warned him — and look at my hair! Cropped hair for Hamlet! I cannot act Hamlet with cropped hair!'

Mr. Booth had before this often voiced his loathing for long hair. He said it was 'one of the disagreeable tolls our profession takes of legitimate actors. My first vacation luxury is to have my hair cut.' By no means was his hair worn freakishly long, but neither was it *cropped*. He said that he always turned his overcoat collar up as far as it would go, to hide his hair. I had not forgotten Mr. Booth's many little speeches upon his business of running his fingers through his hair as Hamlet.

'It will take weeks for it to grow. I am lost without my business. I am giving the poorest Hamlet of my career tonight!'

'Oh, Mr. Booth, why, I am quivering yet!'

He turned upon me sharply, 'You are moved!'

'My hands are like ice.'

He was thinking of something with which I was unconnected. Then he became sarcastic, but at himself. 'My Hamlet was cold enough to turn my sympathetic friends to ice.' He changed his mood without smiling. 'I am convinced an actor cannot gauge his own acting. I *feel* I am giving a metallic Hamlet — and you are quivering. This reverses my Bertuccio. You remember my daughter's verdict?'

I did remember. In this performance of *The Fool's Revenge* in Boston some seasons ago, Mr. Booth had actually suffered with his Fool, and was so stricken with the hunchback's mental and spiritual agonies that he decided when the curtain fell that he had just given his greatest impersonation of Bertuccio; but when his daughter came from her box at the close of the play, she was worried. She feared her father was ill. To her his acting this day was listless. Mr. Booth always spoke of this contrast between his own feeling in the rôle and the effect he produced on his daughter as the very keynote for acting.

CHAPTER XIV

ROLLING WESTWARD

Over the Southern Pacific the 'David Garrick' rolled to Galveston, and so began those days that seem even now too good to be true. In this private car Mr. Booth became host, and I much fear at first he found his position trying. He endured our enthusiasms over the car's fascinating comforts, but warnings were in the air to beware of open gratitude. It was Mr. Chase who vouchsafed that Mr. Booth was *paying for everything*, meals included, and that Mr. Booth would do the tipping.

Mr. Magonigle had the office of steward thrust upon him. He ransacked local markets for delicacies. The breakfast hour was eleven, dinner came at three, and supper after midnight — unless it was Sunday, then supper was more of a tea to be followed by what Mr. Booth styled 'a collation of milk and crackers' with a bit of cheese and Apollinaris.

At one table our host presided, and across the aisle Mr. Chase was head of the table. Two ladies faced Mr. Booth and two Mr. Chase, while the remaining ones sat at either side the Star or manager. The last vacant seat was 'Popper's,' who pretended his feelings were thus hurt.

At first, three times a day, we stood in line waiting for our host to assign our places at table. He desired to be impartial. After repetitions of this little ceremony, I fancied it bothered Mr. Booth, so I went into conference with Mr. Chase. My scheme was laid before the Star, who jumped at it. *We drew lots.* Popper concocted the mechanism. Before each meal, in Mr. Booth's presence, the lottery was held. These drawings accumulated excitement as a rolling snowball. The longest slip meant the honor seat next to the host, of course, and so on down to what was left. Mr. Chase held the hat from which the slips were drawn, while Mr. Booth watched the proceedings; winners and losers were greeted hilariously, and he was thus relieved of an apparent show of favoritism and ate his meals in the high spirits the drawing had worked up.

My luck became too good for dark suspicions not to form deep within my mind, and I accused Mr. Chase to his very face — when none was by.

'It's not for you to object. Leave it to the others.'

'But ——'

He pretended to be angry, and said never before had his honor been impugned; neither had Popper's, neither were they in the prestidigitator line, but — anyway, Mr. Booth was at heavy expense for this car and we were his guests — not paying out one cent; and he deemed it unguest-like for us to criticise the management's efforts to make the Star comfortable, and, besides, didn't I want Mr. Booth to have all the aids to good digestion available?

I did.

'Why, of course!'

As no one else complained, it seemed as if mine might be an overly suspicious nature, so ever after I held my peace. The drawings went merrily on. Tea, coffee, chocolate, and milk were served and Apollinaris abundantly, but not a drink with alcohol — not wine nor beer. Neither were they permitted to be brought aboard the car. This rule was enforced. I remember how surprised I was, for every one I knew anywhere served wine as a matter of course. Mr. Booth's temperance table was my first exception, and Mr. Chase confided to me that never in hotels, nor at any place or time, did he see his Star's glass filled with any drink save milk or Apollinaris.

One day at dinner, Mr. Chase said that handling so many of Mr. Booth's checks signed Edwin T. Booth, made him curious to know what the 'T' stood for.

'My name is Edwin Thomas Booth. But I dropped the Thomas except for checks and legal papers. There are some secret flourishes to my legal signature.' Mr. Booth's hand wafted those flourishes on the air as he asked: 'Did you catch those curlicues?' No one had. 'It saves many a forgery. You remember Thomas Flynn, Mrs. Baker?'

'I do, Mr. Booth. I knew at the time you were named for Mr. Flynn and for Mr. Forrest.'

Edwin Forrest! Why, of course! I got out my pencil.

Edwin For̸rest   Ju̸ius Br̸tus Booth

Subtracting the middle names left Edwin Booth. What a heritage of a name! 'Edwin Booth' was the one name in all this world for him. Suppose it had been something excruciating like Peter! Oh, well, it wasn't! Edwin Booth was glamorous prophecy. As I scribbled, Mr. Chase leaned over my shoulder to say: 'You couldn't get up a better name for posters and signs. Just the right number of letters.'

Mr. Booth recalled a Richelieu memory. In Toronto there once had visited him a Frenchman fresh from Paris who dissected the Booth impersonation from a Frenchman's viewpoint. 'When you came upon the stage — amazement! It was Richelieu! His portrait animated! When you moved — it was the Frenchman! Your hands, your shoulders, your eyebrows, your lips in their twists — were French. The French aristocrat was before me! But when you spoke — pardon — you were no longer French!'

We coaxed for more. Mr. Booth said he was interested, but that he did not consider that a question in acting had been raised.

'This critic's shrinking from listening to an American actor in a French character is shared by an English-speaking audience witnessing French-speaking actors in Shakespeare. Dramatic critics should rise above dialect. Dialect is local, but speech — language — is not, any more than passion or emotion is local. Ask yourselves what language does God speak to your hearts. The answer gives you the key of the approach to great plays. If Richelieu were the only Frenchman in the play, I should speak as a Frenchman. It is *feeling* in a voice that tells the story. If the voice rings true, any language will do to act in. In Germany, I spoke

English to German support. At the Metropolitan, last spring, Salvini spoke Italian to our English — but we told our story. There may have been carpers ——!'

Any voice beside Edwin Booth's sounded rough or flat or thin or shouty. His seemed to range from molten note to thunderclap; from the faint echo of the swish of a flower to discords of passion. How it carried! People sitting way back told me they caught his lowest tone. I never heard him going through vocal exercises. Perhaps he did in his hotel solitude, but I doubt it. He smoked enough, according to authorities, to ruin his voice! He did not coddle it! It did not seem to be on his mind, but whenever his speech was of acting, Mr. Booth laid stress on the voice!

Mr. Booth recalled his dream of another Frenchman for the stage! A dream that was not to come true.

'My ambition has been to create Napoleon! I was in the market for a Napoleon play. I thought something would come of it. Napoleon should be a great — a very great play: but you know my repertoire.'

'Did no one write a Napoleon play for you?'

'Oh, yes! Several! More than several, but none were "theatre"! They missed Napoleon! There was no psychology — no flesh and blood either. They were Napoleons in name only. They stalked through the acts like spouting statues — or petty men — by turns! None of the dramatists caught that one thing which made Bonaparte, Napoleon. It is too soon. No historical character is ready for drama — until a hundred years have passed. Before a hundred years there can be no perspective for Napoleon. Now, we see this of him and that of him, but we do not see the man. Here is a master drama awaiting the dramatist — when the hundred years are up. I've crammed for him, but — there was not a Napoleon play for me.'

Mr. Booth sighed for this might-have-been. He returned to Napoleon often. He said to me, 'I have longed to act "Bonaparte." The play is quivering in my mind asking to be written. Once I could not understand why my authors did not see what was clamoring to be seen.'

CHAPTER XV

CIPHERS WITHOUT RIMS

ONE day Mr. Booth told of a letter newly come from his friend Mrs. Thomas Bailey Aldrich. After a little he waxed so amused that he fetched the letter and read bits of it aloud. Mrs. Aldrich described a recent experience that had embarrassed her frightfully — so she penned; but Mr. Booth was unchivalrous enough to doubt her written word, for he laughed almost heartily at the notion of Mrs. Aldrich not rising to any occasion in unconcern. And then, too, there was her qualifying talent of rendering ridiculous whatever she elected to be absurd. From her lively description of her humiliation, Mr. Booth drew an even livelier pleasure. He laid down his pipe the better to chuckle, and his compliment could go no further.

Two Frenchmen of distinction touring the country called at the Aldrich home to pay their respects. The famous American author was not at home. Mrs. Aldrich was reluctant that the French travellers should be turned from her door. It did not seem appreciative of their courtesy. She decided to explain her husband's absence.

The house was in the throes of being closed for vacation months. Curtains were down from windows, but the parlor was yet presentable — that is, if the servants had not executed her orders to remove all upholstered seats from chair frames and cover up with

cotton cloths everything in the room. She came downstairs to dismayed admiration for her expeditious
domestics. She had not conceived it possible they could
make such headway — there hadn't been time. But
the Frenchmen were already in that shrouded room,
and — they did not speak English and she did not
speak French! In her reckless haste she had not
weighed the possibility of this dilemma. All the
Frenchmen she had met spoke English fluently. By
a gesture she bade the callers be seated, but in her
confusion she forgot about the seatless chairs; sat down
herself in the nearest one and immediately doubled up
like a closed jack-knife. Although she was touching
the floor, her feet were on a level with her face. Unsmilingly, the polite Frenchmen extricated her. One
clung to the chair frame and the other pulled the
lady — until their faces were red. Out she came, and
then Mrs. Aldrich conveyed to the distressed foreigners
that they had her permission to vocalize their amusement by setting them her own contagious example. It
was followed. She wound up her letter with a finale
that sent Mr. Booth off into his merriest laugh.

Of the Aldriches he told this tale: He said 'Tom'
was using it in his next book, then being written. But
that's another story. This one is of Mr. Booth's relish
of the tale. The Aldriches were travelling in Egypt. A
slight misadventure halted their cavalcade to the outraged remonstrances of a wayside character. Mr. Aldrich was fascinated with what he conjectured were
insults heaped on himself. Here was opportunity to

enlarge his vocabulary. Literature might even be enriched. He requested of his interpreter an unexpurgated translation. This magnificent being, who could, in Mr. Aldrich's eyes, have sat for a portrait of Mohammed to the Prophet's credit, gave the curser a look of scorn ineffable. He bowed low to Mr. Aldrich, and said majestically: 'Give him no attention! He speaks nothing! He *is* nothing! He is *a cipher without a rim.*' This epithet — 'a cipher without a rim' — tickled Mr. Booth's fancy. He used it upon very special occasions.

Once, in Mr. Booth's absence, there was a discussion upon the relative values of the five senses; what it meant to be deprived of one of them, especially of the sense of sight or hearing. We were rather serious over it. Some held blindness was preferable — some deafness.

Mr. Chase said: 'You are groping! Let me help you. Put it this way. Would you rather *hear* Mr. Booth's voice on the stage — or *see* him act?'

And then Mr. Booth returned, and we told him the matter of our argument. He thought it illuminating that the blind usually seemed cheerful and the deaf unhappy. Some one said the question before the house was if we had to choose between the two senses needed to perceive his acting, would we choose to hear him or see him?

'Now I dub you all ciphers without rims!' — and one of us rose to the occasion. 'You make your supporting actors feel like ciphers without rims when they are on the stage with you.'

Mr. Booth asked me if I could keep my face straight

under any condition. ' I have decided to risk you. I see in the audience such Hogarth-y — such Dickens-y faces, that it is all I can do, sometimes, not to point them out. But then comes the fear — suppose my actor should laugh in spite of himself! I must put you on your honor!'

There were two sorts of honor in my election, and I thanked him for them both.

'You won't thank me when you are choking on the stage — and I shan't be a bit sorry for you. I shall be enjoying myself.'

After this he did point out the queerest faces, but he did not see me laugh — that is, not until the curtain fell and he had come from his calls.

One drowsy day, when Mr. Booth had retired to the seclusion of his drawing-room and shut the door upon himself, I tucked myself into a chair and soon was sound asleep. Then!... I dreamed that I awoke. Something was happening. I was too dazed to do more than blink, but it was at Mr. Booth I was blinking. He seemed to be merry over a victory — and was demanding a pair of gloves of me.

'Whose gloves? What gloves' — and I realized I was not dreaming, but very wide awake.

'I have won my gloves,' from Mr. Booth. 'I kissed you while you were asleep — before witnesses, and you must pay your forfeit.'

He had begun his play-lines bravely enough, but when he reached the kiss, he faltered, and embarrassment was fast overtaking him. I swung to his side to help him out. Such noble efforts at play must be encouraged.

'I don't think it's fair! All I did was to be asleep ——'

'That's it,' from Popper, 'and got kissed before witnesses.'

Giggles from the witnesses.

Mr. Booth's manner was a plea for an honorable outlet from a situation he had rashly let himself in for.

But my own teasing blood was up now, so I said that I would buy the gloves; the kiss was worth it; and then Mr. Booth blushed, and I was ashamed and blushed, too — and so furiously that even Mr. Booth rejoined in laughter. But he did not yield those gloves. In each city I was reminded by him of gloves, until I went shopping for a pair. I had doubted his sincerity, even fearing he might object to the forfeit — but those were the days when he placed his Macbeth crown upon a little page's head! 'No, indeed, you must pay your just debts.' Mr. Booth was gracious enough to say he had 'won' these gloves, but long before the forfeit was paid, I am sure he convinced himself the gloves were earned.

Despite my Lord Cardinal, or even the melancholy Dane, Mr. Booth was a tease if one may use so harsh a word for his gentle gibes. He would group us about him and prod Popper into telling us of the time that he (Popper) acted Solon Shingle. This performance had been a benefit in Baltimore some years before, and the unsuspicious one would innocently warm to the memory of his laurels. He had made a hit, and his brother-in-law was proud of that success, but all of a sudden Mr. Booth would be saying dryly — 'You imitated Owens.'

'Of course, I did,' his brother-in-law would boast. 'That's why I am so proud of my hit. I copied Owens's voice; his walk; gestures; facial expression — and they were good enough to say I was such a perfect imitation of John E. Owens they thought they were seeing him. They had to pinch themselves to remember it was I.'

When Popper left us, perhaps to look out for the comfort of the remainder of the company in their Pullman, Mr. Booth would surrender to his relish of this Solon Shingle acting.

'Owens told me that he himself took Magonigle for his own model when he studied his Solon Shingle. He attributed his great hit largely to the fact that he reproduced Magonigle. Along comes this benefit — and they cast that dear man for Solon Shingle — because he was Owens's model in the first place. But the point is that Magonigle had not recognized himself in Owens's acting nor has he a suspicion now that he inspired Owens. It is curious — and interests me. Do we never see ourselves as others see us?'

Mr. Booth remarked one day that he was reconciled that there was not a son to bear his name. 'I dare say I should be as partial a father as the rest of them. I might even think my son could *act!*' He chuckled over a recollection. 'One of these mistaken fathers judicially informed me his son was playing with a prominent actress and was "startlingly successful." Mind you —

this father thought he knew what good acting was — and so did I. I went to see the son of a great man, and waited for his appearance expectantly — and lo — he was the puniest of the lot!'

The puniest of the lot! Shades of supporting actors! Was this Mr. Booth's summing-up of us?

Mr. Booth smoked on as if he had not said anything in particular, and I realized what a rare opening he had given me to compliment him on his acting.

'Are you sure, Mr. Booth, your judgment on acting is authority?'

Every one stopped what he was about, and listened.

Mr. Chase was worried. The dowagers had an 'I told you so' expression; Amo and Ido looked as if they thought I had lost my mind. Mr. Booth's sense of humor helped him to recover. He said a bit ominously: 'I hoped — there are those — well — I acknowledge I am a judge of acting.'

'Oh, indeed, Mr. Booth, yes, but you must admit you cannot know as much about acting — as I do!'

He stopped smoking, and said politely — a bit too politely for comfort, if I didn't make good soon — 'I am the elder!' — and waited.

'What makes me a better judge of acting has nothing to do with age. It is acting, alone! And you know yourself, Mr. Booth, I have seen the perfection of acting — and you never have!'

Again I had a long look from his unreadable eyes. He puffed away once or twice, and then said, without the ghost of a smile, 'You have squirmed out of it.'

CHAPTER XVI

DARNING MR. BOOTH'S SOCKS

ONE picture of Mr. Booth is domestic. His door opened and he came out into the car, his arms filled with rolled-up socks. He gazed upon us beseechingly, as if he hardly knew how to ask the favor he had come for. Mr. Booth wanted his socks darned!

In the 'David Garrick,' expense never lifted its intrusive head. Carriages were kept waiting for us until the time Mr. Booth was over his chatting mood. Mr. Chase might groan, but his Star disregarded any hints that the bill was mounting, and now incongruously stood the host of the 'David Garrick' with eyes imploring us to darn his socks.

Too many half-holidays in Germany had I been kept at my darning lessons under the suspicious eye of a merciless teacher, who watched each separate stitch and ripped out one thread gone askew, for me not to tackle those socks with confidence. I was so eager to darn those socks, I ran for them. Mr. Booth clung to his burden until he reached my chair, where he impressively deposited his armful. The holes were not bad as holes go. Ido was yearning for some socks, so I magnanimously permitted her to assist. She sewed better than I, but when it came to darning, hers was only a common-garden variety, while my stitch imitated the weave. Amo gazed enviously upon us, but we informed

126

her that darning socks was out of the line of dashing leading ladies. Mr. Booth settled down to watch our progress. He was such a stickler for skill that the German stitch at once caught his fancy. I told him I was giving him a genuine German darn. He said he liked everything German but the kissing, and that once in Germany during his recent tour — and the story-telling was on.

After a daytime performance in Germany, when the theatre had been crowded with women, Mr. Booth thought the entire audience must have rushed behind to greet him on the stage. He was still in his costume of Hamlet, and he said that each of these hundreds of women kissed him. As he told of it, his face resumed the heroic expression it must have worn during those moments of fortitude. It was the custom of the country; he would not wound the feelings of these appreciative women. Then, too, he realized this osculation was a form of politeness. 'I did not mistake the impersonality of those kisses and went through with it until I became mechanical.' He stood on the stage; grasped an extended hand, leaned forward, was kissed; kissed back; pushed her down the line, sixty to a minute, he reckoned. It might be less, but not much. Then he smiled at a memory. The line of kissers passed by rapidly, but there approached one who smiled with a different mode of attack. 'Perhaps I had met her before? There was not time for speculation or questions. She extended her hand; I took it; leaned forward; but she drew back! "I am an American" — rather haughtily —

"Oh! I beg your pardon and thank you so very much" — shoved her down the line, and studied the next face, hoping *it* might be American, but it wasn't.'

I did not want to cast 'aspersions' on my country-women, especially those of my profession, but Amo and I had seen him kissed right here in the United States. Many a time, as we hurried from our trains, we ran into theatrical companies whose actresses — (the middle-aged ones to be sure) — caught Mr. Booth and kissed him hard. He submitted, but afterwards, his face would wear a puzzled expression as if he were asking why? Then there were even older ones — mothers — who had known him from a baby! Each of these actresses upon encountering him claimed a kiss. But *their* eyes held the expression of seeing glory!

When all the socks were darned, Mr. Booth made an orderly pile of them and carried them off. Upon his return he was asked if he would blow his wonderful smoke rings for us. And would he blow more stories through the rings?

He would and did.

There were many 'London Assurances' for Mr. Booth, but today his memory clung to his mishaps.

The one he resented most seemed to be accusations of doubling a dummy with Fiordelisa — while she was being carried down the ladder — in *The Fool's Revenge*! He said the papers harped upon the use of a dummy in this scene. He was severely criticised for it! No dummy was made use of in London at any time by him.

DARNING MR. BOOTH'S SOCKS

His leading lady was carried down in the arms of the proper actor, but the papers continued their scoring. The management in print denied the substitution repeatedly. To no purpose! The criticisms continued. He asked his Fiordelisa if she could not do something to prove she was a live human girl.

She was almost in tears over it. She blamed herself. 'I risk my life on that ladder to let them see I am real. I toss about as much as I dare. I kick my legs! If I squirm any more, Mr. Booth, it will be suicide and murder, for we shall both topple from the ladder.'

Mr. Booth made a little pout. 'I rehearsed the scene myself. Of course, her face could not be exposed for an instant. If Bertuccio is given a chance to suspect it is his own daughter he is helping abduct, the play stops then and there. We had all this written up — by writers of standing; but it wasn't of the slightest use. The papers continued to abuse me for cheap tricks, and very poor cheapness at that. It was a case of *won't see*.'

This injustice to his stage directing rankled. There was so much of the other side for him in London — there were so many delightful tributes to him — but I suppose it is human nature to nurse a thorn-prick even while inhaling perfume from gardens of roses.

Once, I asked Mr. Booth if he were ever nervous before going on. Something he had said made my question timely. He gave what might be named a refined chortle to express his disgust at himself.

'Never in my life! It's been my ambition to have a

stage fright. It has become an obsession with me. I have listened to actors describing chills running up and down their spines, dry throats, cracking lips, gonenesses about their middles, and I heard for myself the flatness of their voices, and I resolved to coquette with those tremulous agonies. I, too, would have a stage fright — if only for once. London was the best place to develop one I could think of. Any normal actor deserves his stage fright on his opening night in London. I went at it as intelligently as I could. All that was necessary was to keep my mind on the importance — the significance — of my London engagement, and what a disastrous reception, here, in the heart of the world, would mean to my career. When the overture was called, I believed I had at last worked up a *bona fide* stage fright. I should soon be facing the choice and master spirits of this age and probably they would be hostile — and I'd be done for. As I stood waiting for my cue, I thought I felt a tremor — I was not sure — and then the cue came and I walked on as calm as an oyster. I am hopeless. If London could not throw me into a stage fright, nothing can! But I should like the experience — once.'

I told Mr. Booth I knew all about it.

'But, my child! What for? It does not help you — does it?'

We tried to induce Mr. Booth to tell us of his London triumphs, but he evaded them. I had read of them. Perhaps Mr. Chase was right. A bad notice might do him good.

DARNING MR. BOOTH'S SOCKS

Mr. Booth's German tour was too recent not to be in his thoughts.

'I love Germany,' he said to me many times. And so I was freer to speak of my own German life to him. It interested him that for five years I had forgotten my English and that now — even in the 'David Garrick' — I often dreamed in German. I think my understanding of much that was under and over Germany's homage of him broke through his habit of reserve. With eyes aglow, lips smiling, and with voice so tender that it hinted of a tremble, our greatest actor shared with me his response to Germany's tribute to him. He told me of his laurel wreaths thrown over the footlights and of one wreath fashioned in leaves of pure gold. He said it was the golden symbol of a golden spirit.

He had grappled to his own soul with hooks of steel the soul of the German Theatre. He wandered among mazes of German thought without losing his way. The German Theatre had been resident in his mind long before his German tour. But there was one grudge he owed Germany!

'They made me act there for all I was worth. Germany got the better of me on Iago.' He pouted at himself over this. 'There was no lazy avoidance of Othello for me on that tour. I tried to put Iago in my contracts — but they would not have it! It meant nothing to German managers that Iago was one of my reputation builders. I even — knowing of their fondness for the word — told them Iago was my *masterpiece*.' He chuckled over masterpiece. It was so 'German-ish.'

'But it didn't work. A visiting star must act the leading rôle! Iago was not the leading one.'

Mr. Booth spoke of his being worsted over Iago again and again. He relished this 'joke' on himself. He said Othello taxed him strenuously, while Iago sat upon him as a thistledown. But Iago remained his German grievance, and the only one!

I told him I longed to see him as Othello, and he said quite devilishly: 'You never shall.' To tantalize me he described the picturesque Othello costumes that were designed for him in London for this German tour.

I asked: 'Have you them with you?'

'I suppose so! Now, do not conspire! I shall not be inveigled into acting Othello.' Yet in San Francisco — for man's proposing is not disposing, as we all know.

There was a German tribute Mr. Booth could not speak of without emotion, and it required much cunning contrivance for it to be told at all. The proper mood — the proper hour — the proper listener.

When he reached Berlin, he was received behind the scenes by the stage manager-director. This personage was an autocrat! At rehearsal he yielded the American actor cold courtesy.

'He embarrassed me,' Mr. Booth admitted. 'His punctiliousness was harder to endure than contempt and rudeness. I should not have noticed these, I dare say — but his over-accentuated formal politeness could not be ignored. His directing let me see at once he was a student of Shakespeare and an authority on stagecraft.

DARNING MR. BOOTH'S SOCKS

He knew his business. I realized I could trust the artist in him.

'I had no fear of his working against me. He was attentive to my suggestions. I should have what I was entitled to; but not one jot more did he intend me to get out of him.

'The rehearsal ended and the performance began. I was busy and so was he! I had not given him a thought — the scenes ran too smoothly for that — but — when the final curtain fell, it occurred to me there might be something pleasanter in life than running against this hostile stage manager again, so I turned to leave the stage. Something solemn charged the atmosphere. It arrested me. The actors stood as statues — but — the stage manager came to me. He bent over my hand — he seemed to be kneeling — he kissed my hand and said, "Herr Meister!" It was done so simply — with such sincerity — I wanted to cry.'

'Perhaps there were tears in your eyes, Mr. Booth.'

'Perhaps!'

I always cried a hidden bit here. It was so a part of the Germany of those days. A Germany of genius and worship of genius!

CHAPTER XVII

THE SAN ANTONIO MATINÉE

WE started out gayly for the famous Galveston Beach, but Mr. Booth did not seem in a holiday mood. I fancied there were moments when he forgot we were there. In this he was encouraged, for this was our part. He detained me once to gaze with him out upon the rolling ocean demanding to know if I were breathing deep. 'Hold the breath longer. Then the rest of the exercise is involuntary.' But the cloud upon his brow darkened, and he spoke of his daughter. He did his best to conceal an anxiety that was making his heart ache, but he could not do it, great actor as he was.

Was he worried — was she ill?

'I fear so. I am selfish about her. I do not rise above any physical pain of hers. There will be another baby — soon. I shall be different when it is over. Her mother died young! You appeared to be so fragile when I first saw you, I told Barrett you would not last the season. But he laughed at me. "She'll be the freshest in the company when the season closes." It means much to me to see a delicate little woman with powers of endurance — just now.'

I told him of a New York *Cæsar* night — in the Star Theatre — when the mercury dropped lower than in forty years, they said. It was claimed the thermometer stood twenty below.

'I know the pranks Cæsar plays with thermometers.'

134

KITTY MOLONY
'A picture Mr. Booth named "No." He said
I seemed to be saying "No!"'

THE SAN ANTONIO MATINÉE

Even Mr. Booth smiled at Cæsar weather jests, for it did seem that when we were shorn of our proper clothing to go on in the scanty Cæsar raiment, the weather-man's name was Puck.

I was the boy, Lucius. Mr. Frank Millet was behind that night shivering in his heavy overcoat, and when he greeted me, the artist groaned. He turned to Mr. Barrett. 'I hope she doesn't come down with pneumonia.' An unsympathetic Mr. Barrett replied: 'Oh, these delicate little women are the toughest things in creation.'

My story hit the bull's-eye. This was precisely what Mr. Booth was yearning to hear — that delicate little women lived through anything. He seemed to be comparing my vitality with his precious daughter's, and was satisfied. His daughter must be as 'tough' as I was. Later by weeks, he felt the need to show us the telegram with its great news. It was not until we saw his anxiety lift that one could realize how heavy a heart he had been hiding for so many days during which he had been planning pleasures for us. In after years I understood what a diversion the 'Chickens' truly were to Mr. Booth in an anxious time.

Whenever I read of Mr. Booth's habit of melancholy, his wan smile, shrinking manner, cold dignity, austere seclusion; the blithe-of-heart Edwin Booth in the 'David Garrick' seems more a dream than a reality. Perhaps he was a dream, a day-dream, that he himself made of the boy he coaxed from his soul. In balder words, Mr. Booth was eternally young; younger than we, when at play.

135

We soon learned to keep our wits upon the rules of the game. Commonplaces were 'not fair'! Airy fancies were tossed back and forth over an equator line that was not to be crossed by the players in person. In watching our fledgling effort to spread our clumsy wings and follow him in his straight flight up to the sky — and yet keeping our own side of the line — lay Mr. Booth's delight. I will not wrong his memory by a notion that he set up these invisible barriers for taboo, for had there been need to restrain us, Mr. Booth had not played with us at all.

On the Galveston Beach Mr. Booth had declared that because of the tonic in that sea air, he would repeat the outing in San Antonio and had then and there assumed an old school stage manner — as persuasive as it was grand — and asked me to do him the honor to drive with him in San Antonio. Not for me to respond to a grand manner; rather it was my stern duty to remind him that San Antonio was a one-night stand, and that he had a confirmed habit of resting upon those afternoons.

'Don't ever discourage one trying to reform. It is of yourself you are thinking.'

I protested, and with warmth accepted the invitation. Of its prankish sequel I had no suspicion — nor did any one. At one station Mr. Chase received a telegram. When he approached Mr. Booth, who was entertaining the older ladies, he begged his pardon for interrupting, but the reply should be sent from the next station. The telegram was carefully read by the serene smoker and as serenely returned to the manager.

'Tell him I'm not free.' He puffed away for a little longer; finished his story; withdrew and closed his door.

Mr. Chase sighed and followed.

After a half-hour or so, he came out again with a manner all forlorn. He gazed out of the window awhile, then opened his 'Monthly' and seemed to be reading. Soon he crossed to me, offering the magazine, and between its leaves lay the telegram. It was worded something like this:

'House sold out. Will you play *Hamlet* matinée? Offer three thousand dollars for your share. Guaranteed. Wire at once.'

It was dated at San Antonio. There were but three one-night stands between San Antonio and us — Houston, Dallas, Austin.

'Well ——?'

'Not well at all! It's too bad! He won't play that matinée — and he must. Mr. Booth says he asked you to drive in San Antonio for that afternoon, and that you accepted. I'm depending on you. You do see that three thousand dollars is too much to pay for any drive with any young lady. Don't you?'

Of course I was not indifferent to this sportiveness. I behaved badly enough to crow, but Mr. Chase sat gloomily by threatening 'wires' to Mr. Barrett. He was so distressed that I offered to help him out. What was I to do?

'Persuade Mr. Booth to give the matinée.'

I tried to convince Mr. Chase I had nothing to do with Mr. Booth's decision. If he didn't want to play that matinée, it was because San Antonio was a one-night stand, and he couldn't appear twice in one day there! It would kill him! Mr. Barrett had never done such a thing: no wonder Mr. Booth wouldn't listen to it!

'If I believed this was his reason, I should be back of him, but he said himself, just now, he was feeling great. He says it's you!'

'Mr. Booth is poking fun at you. You know I do not drive out alone with him. What about the others?'

'He says you are the only one he has invited — yet. He refuses, out and out, to break his promise to you for any three thousand dollars. But, look here! That will pay for the "David Garrick" to San Francisco! That's what this car costs and that matinée will pay the bill. I must wire from the next station. This is business, little lady, it's not fun!'

'Of course not, Mr. Chase. Will you ask Mr. Booth if I might speak with him?'

Mr. Chase rose as if he had been shot. He gave me a grateful look, yet felt it incumbent to add that if I should weaken, Mr. Barrett wouldn't like it. The manager did not seem any happier when he reappeared to send me to Mr. Booth.

I skipped into the drawing-room, and there sat the tragedian posing as a little spoiled boy — determined to have his own way, yet somehow realizing that circumstances must eventually prove too much for him. I must have grinned, but the eyes before me warned me to play my hand with finesse. No blunt 'business' would be accepted by him for my excuse. So I became most society-ish.

THE SAN ANTONIO MATINÉE

'I am so sorry, Mr. Booth, but I forgot a — previous engagement for San Antonio. If — another time — please ask me again, will you not — when I am free?'

'What did Chase tell you?'

'Why — the facts, I suppose. But Mr. Booth, my unfortunate, unbreakable engagement will prevent my acceptance even if you take the others. I am so sorry I have a previous engagement.'

'We might have Chase in' — and soon the manager was in.

'I may as well act as sit in a stuffy hotel, Mr. Chase. She says she won't!'

'I'll wire from the next station, Mr. Booth' — and the manager kept out of his Star's sight until that station was left behind.

Mr. Chase could not believe it was all play, but it was. From the first that telegram might have been safely sent. I liked the complexion of this bit of the game far too well to want it over. I need not have feared. It had just begun. There were pathetic complaints of my lack of moral courage. There was not a change Mr. Booth could think up he failed to foist upon me. In Dallas, in Houston, in Austin, he did not come near me on the stage without mumbling, 'Unfeeling female'; or 'I only asked for air, and she denied me that.' These are mild samples of all he made me endure when he had me helpless and on my honor to keep my face straight. Even during that packed matinée in San Antonio, he contrived asides for my torment. 'But for you I should be enjoying myself on that drive. You have no regard for my health.'

CHAPTER XVIII

A LESSON IN SMOKE RINGS

In Galveston a five-pound box of fruit glacé was sent to me and I reserved the candy to share in the 'David Garrick.' I came to the car alive with importance, but was confronted by a large barrel of apples that Amo had had donated and was nobly contributing. How insignificant that mite of a box of mine now looked. I had not the courage to proffer it — till there came one of those happy surprises. Mr. Booth said he did not know of a salad he enjoyed more than fruit glacé served on lettuce with French dressing. So the salad was served for dinner and held its own on the menu until long after San Francisco. Mr. Chase began to hint that but for the certainty of it, he would like to bet that candy weighed a ton. Popper held to the original five pounds, but then he had not weighed the box. Had any one? None had. Then bets were permissible. At last even Mr. Booth suggested a spring salad was seasonable, and not until then did our false steward confess to marketing for candied fruit in about each stop we made. 'But, Mr. Booth, it wouldn't have tasted half so good if you had known it came out of a prosaic market-basket. Now would it?'

One day he asked, 'In what town did you ask me about insane asylums?'

'In New Orleans, Mr. Booth.'

That he had not forgotten my question did not surprise me. Did he not nightly demonstrate his remarkable memory? He carried a library in his mind.

'Have you visited insane asylums — yourself?'

'Oh, yes, Mr. Booth, many!'

'Did you find your Ophelia in one of them?'

'N-o —! But I saw enough to color my voice — to know what to do with my eyes — in the mad scene!'

'I suppose I have been in most of them. For years I studied insanity. They took me to patients that are as a rule kept out of sight. My New York physician used to arrange for my visits all over the country. I was never more embarrassed than one day — in the private room of a woman patient. They had told me she was an interesting case. I saw at once she was a woman of gentle blood. She was eating her dinner when I entered, and I took my seat to observe her. It did not occur to me to apologize for intruding upon a crazed patient. I fixed my eyes upon her to watch her every expression. She kept her own eyes upon her plate. She grew glummer and glummer. I became absorbed in her. Suddenly she stopped eating, and looked at me, her face full of contempt, and said scathingly, "How would you like to be stared at by a stranger while you are eating?" I rose hastily and said: "Madam, I am ashamed. Please pardon me!" She only sniffed, so I bowed and left the room with an opinion of my breeding as poor as that abused and outraged woman's.'

'Was she sane?'

'Sane enough to know good manners from bad. Oh, they told me afterwards she had *spells* — but when I saw her she was as sane as I am now.'

BEHIND THE SCENES WITH BOOTH

I could not persuade Mr. Booth to describe his violent cases. He said he had studied each of his mad scenes from life, and also for 'antic dispositions put on.' He smiled a wee bit. Well we knew what character he was referring to. Lear he had built from life. 'I began by imitating my father, but as fast as I could, I replaced his characterizations with my own studies — out of asylums — and in.'

After a *Hamlet* bill at one supper our topic was fencing — how important fencing was in developing grace. I always saw the Mercury when Mr. Booth fenced. His was the same lean, graceful, vital figure. I have heard his fencing raved over by West Pointers. I believe Mr. Booth indulged in a vanity for his skill in fencing and a bit for the number of smoke rings he could blow in succession. This latter accomplishment seemed to give him more pleasure than any other of his talents. He permitted compliments to be given freely for his smoke rings if he did have underneath his acceptance a manner of laughing at himself — for this very vanity. I asked him if he had met his superior in making his rings of smoke. He said: 'No, and if you wish to acquire this accomplishment I will be your teacher!'

Mercy! How Continental Mr. Booth was! Ladies did not smoke in the United States. Instead of being shocked, here he was saying that he 'rather fancied the posture of a charming woman fastidiously fingering a cigarette. But smoking should be skilful. I'll teach you to make rings if you will practice for finesse.'

Mr. Booth devoted so much of his time to the elder

women on this long jump that I hesitated to bring out my package of cigarettes. But all at once he said across the car, 'This is an ideal time for a smoking lesson.' I should have preferred not to have spectators, but — every one was anticipating my apprenticeship and egging me on. There was no chance of rivalling my teacher, probably. He could form four rings while Mr. Chase was limited to one.

Mr. Booth asked to see the brand and I gave him the package. Never shall I forget his consternation when he beheld those *cubeb* cigarettes. Gamely he resigned himself to their odor. My little finger was disciplined. With an airy grace he showed me by example how to flick the ashes. This much was easy, but rings! How I envied him for those lovely smoke rings! They were tortures of Tantalus. The lessons were drawn out over many weeks, for San Francisco interrupted them. I had become almost expert when Mr. Booth revolted and pronounced his ultimatum. Either I smoke tobacco — or the lessons stopped; he regretted to be disobliging, 'but my nose is to blame — and by all that's reasonable why not regular cigarettes?'

I felt rather priggish when I confessed a promise to Mr. Barrett that I would not smoke — oh, and lots of things — for a certain number of years. Mr. Booth approved, however, but soon he became lighter and said: 'Should I lose my sense of smell — or something parallel — we will continue your lessons with cubebs. Your little finger is doing very well.'

There had grown up a partition between the 'David

Garrick' guests and the remainder of the company, akin to the thorn wall around the Sleeping Beauty Palace in the fairy tale. I used to think of this when from my window, so snug in the private car, with a tempting dinner ahead of me, I would watch our actors rushing by to eat their twenty-minutes-for-refreshments meal in the station restaurant.

Cliques will form in any company. We of the royal circle found life pleasant, as I suppose any chosen few do everywhere. I should not have known of the feelings of the unchosen, but for Ido. She shed tears when she was dubbed 'stuck up' by a few of her former meal-mates.

Mr. Chase always went into the station dining-rooms 'to look out for the company.' We would hear the gong clanging as the train pulled into the station, and then, during these twenty minutes for refreshments on this long jump to Los Angeles, Mr. Booth took his constitutional — reluctantly — up and down the platform.

One night it was dark before the poor actors had a bite to eat. I walked briskly on the platform, and after a while Mr. Booth joined me — and he was smiling. 'Chase will be along soon to pour my misdemeanor in your ears' — and Mr. Chase did do that very thing. Mr. Booth, he said, had gone to the lunch counter — not even the dining-room — and sat on a stool and eaten 'one ham sandwich, two hard-boiled eggs, two cups of thick coffee in thicker cups, one doughnut, and one piece of apple pie with cheese.'

'Oh, Mr. Booth!!'

144

A LESSON IN SMOKE RINGS

'He asked for *mince*,' Mr. Chase put in, 'but fortunately they were out of it.'

Mr. Booth was proud of himself. There was a swagger of triumph about him for overruling the laws laid down for him by his Medes and Persians doctors. His was a case of rebellion — for a night! Why shouldn't he glory in doing what he knew better than to do?

I said I was glad of it, if I did wonder how he could swallow that awful stuff. He threatened to do it again, but there is no record of it — not that season.

Although Mr. Chase and Popper worried, the Star himself anticipated a good night — and in the morning blandly announced he had not slept as well in years.

The gratitude of his supporting company may have overtoned his sleep that night, for this very day Mr. Chase had let it be known Mr. Booth was paying salaries in full this week. He refused to make deductions for time lost in travel from San Antonio to Los Angeles. He had said to Mr. Chase: 'Why should my company lose part of their salaries for something the management is responsible for?' We all expected to be docked. When one tried to thank him, Mr. Booth waved off further speech. Once he was heard to say, 'Please discuss business with my manager.' But his smile revealed he was putting himself in the company's place. No wonder he slept soundly on the way to Los Angeles.

Mr. Chase attracted my attention to Mr. Booth's efforts to distribute impartially his favors among the ladies. He said: 'I did not know there was a man alive whom it so hurt to hurt any one else. He's a lesson to me.'

CHAPTER XIX

THE SAN FRANCISCO FIRE BOY

In those boyhood struggle days in California, when indigestion was incomprehensible, when something good to eat was more hope than custom, the tide turned and left Edwin Booth safe upon a shore of affluence of regular meals. He was engaged in San Francisco and soon he was cast for the leading rôle in the play *The San Francisco Fire Boy*. Mr. Booth had not forgotten the Fire Boy's lines, and one evening, after leaving San Antonio, he gave us his big scene — at least its curtain. If others could not burlesque Edwin Booth, he could burlesque himself, and on this night, he did.

The big moment came in the kitchen. In old-time theatre parlance, kitchen does not mean a place to cook in, but is a set that is not a palace, not a prison, not a cathedral. The Fire Boy's kitchen had one wall with a door and a window. The sides were 'flats' which did not need doors because an actor could enter through any part of the wall. In melodrama it was considered that the effect was heightened if whenever a window was thrown open a snowstorm raged outside. This locale being California, the storm may have been merely a typhoon, but you never can tell about stage climates.

The hurtling elements worry the Fire Boy's poor old white-haired mother. She confides her fears to the audience. Her only son, so rash, so young, so reckless, so brave, is out there fighting flames and smoke this fearsome night! She is taken with a chill; she pauses to listen; she screams: 'It is he! It is he!' (incidental music, soft, crescendo to forte) — and — enter the San Francisco Fire Boy.

The fluttering mother assists him to remove his dripping fire coat and helmet. His face is scorched, she wails. He is half dead, he admits. He is fresh come from a devastating fire and has saved lives this night. He's 'used up,' he says, every now and then. He's hungry! He's wet! He's cold! He has not slept o' nights — had there not been a fire raging night upon night for weeks?

He's everything uncomfortable, and the poor, old mother, *so* tender, *so* affectionate, lends her feeble strength in guiding to his chair the fainting Fire Boy. Is he not her one ewe lamb, her joy, her pride, her sole support? She hangs up his soggy coat and starts to pull off his wet boots — but no! Spent as he is, the noble youth will not permit a menial task be done for him by his dear loved mother! He takes off his own boots! The steaming supper is dished up, set before him on a red-and-white checked tablecloth, and the weary, grateful, sweetly smiling lad drags himself over to sink into his chair. Fumes of food revive him and he falls upon his 'vittles.' He raises his knife! His fork! — Hark! What sound is that? Can it be? It is! — The Fire Bells!! They sound dangerously close by, too, and the fire must be next door, for the red light flares through the window. The heroic youth pushes back his chair, scorns his untasted supper, shouts: 'Mother, give me my coat! My helmet!'

Mother (frantic agony): 'No, no, my son! My only son!' (Tries to foil him with embraces.) 'Not again this dreadful night! Your weary eyelids droop for loss of sleep. Rest this night at home! Pity a mother's aching heart!' etc., etc.!!! (Business of mother clinging to her son.)

Fire Boy: 'Away, mother! Hold me not! Or ever after, your cheek shall blush in shame when not whitened by remorse! Hinder you me!! — on this night of nights?' (Struggle.) Still the fire bells ring! 'My boots! My coat! My helmet! Mother, let go! The fire bells!!!' (Red light rages outside window so fiercely the walls become transparent.) 'Unhand me! I will go! What matters that I be spent? Do you not hear the fire bells? Let go! I shall to the fire! Duty calls! I will away! I go to quench holocausts! I go to save the city from conflagration!! What is my death if I save the city? — for, mother!!! A San Francisco Fire Boy is the noblest work of God!!!!!' (Rushes off centre door.) Picture of swooning mother. Curtain! Yells, whistles, stamps in front. Mrs. Fiske said they were to be heard 'down to the wharves.'

Aye, over in Oakland!

Mr. Booth's acting of this bit in the 'David Garrick' was sketchy, but in spite of his 'holding-in' it was the funniest thing I had ever seen or heard. He was poking fun at himself! There was a hint of pathos underneath the surface! After all, those were the days when *Excelsior* was just around the corner! He had thrown his very being into the San Francisco Fire Boy. It was the prophecy of the future! He 'got them' that night! Applause had thrilled him then. He was not yet the actor whom a bad notice would do good! And now he was on his way again to that city of San Francisco after an absence of ten years. He was to open there in *Hamlet*, and — his thoughts were running back to the San Francisco Fire Boy!

Apologies are due the author of *The San Francisco Fire Boy*. I have set down *probable* lines. I heard the scene only once and in snatches with my own mind functioning for burlesque. The spirit of the scene has been caught. There is one line that is the author's own. 'A San Francisco Fire Boy is the noblest work of God,' is here given as the original script has it. No one who has once heard this line could forget it! Mr. Booth's pose and voice, as he hurled the speech at the world, is equally unforgettable. A merry star danced somewhere when he was born, but the storm-clouds gathered and the night was soon black!

During the years, a habit had formed to clutch Mr. Booth in relentless grip. It was the habit of wakefulness at night, and sometimes insomnia robbed him of all sleep. As an actor's day begins when he goes on the stage to act, Mr. Booth was, of course, wide awake when he left the theatre near midnight. After his light supper, and 'just one more smoke,' he retired to his drawing-room to write letters, sometimes he said, but always to read through long, restless hours or until he was exhausted. Then perhaps — if his 'vulture thoughts' had not been too rampant — in the cold dawn he might fall asleep; if so, he did not wake until ten or after. 'If those weary vulture hours,' he once said, 'could only be annihilated, I might go to sleep sooner.'

I think Mr. Booth's idea of supreme luxury was to go to sleep at night promptly and stay asleep until late the next morning. The Chickens were 'good sleepers,' and Mr. Booth would make his wistful good-night to us as if to say, You poor little deluded chits, thinking of me as the most fortunate of men, and here you are about to drop into sweet, soothing, strengthening sleep as easily as you turn off the gas, while I go to fight my vultures through wasting hours. Memories with their flapping wings keep me awake.

Oh, it was plain to see, Mr. Booth was not ready to retire when his sandy-eyed guests one by one said their good-nights. He accepted these departures as natural, and assumed that my own vanishing would soon come. But in me he found his match in owlishness. At first Mr. Booth remonstrated — a bit feebly — that a young girl should get her beauty sleep, but he admitted he was charmed to remain out in the open car a little longer, for 'Memories are hard upon one in lonely hours.'

In my German album was written by my French teacher, a quotation from Jean Paul Richter: 'Memory is the only paradise from which man may not be driven.'

'But, one is already outside the Gates of Paradise when one lives in memories. Not all of mine are vultures. There is one that is my guardian angel! There is another! I must not let it get hold of me — late at night!'

150

I thought I knew of whom both these memories were.

He told me of his mother! There were many anecdotes of her. During the last quiet years of her life he made his habitual call upon her. He was expected, and received in state. I think Mr. Booth said this visit belonged to his mother's Long Branch home.

'Mother was wearing a concoction on her head that looked far from comfortable. It was a counterpart of that fearsome headpiece of the Duchess in "Alice in Wonderland." "Why, mother, what is this on your head?" She was seated and plaintively answered: "It is a cap Agnes [Agnes Booth] sent to me. It *is* heating for the head." I had been giving that head-dress closer inspection. "Why, mother! That is not a cap! It is a tea cosy!"' [1]

Into Mr. Booth's face came such affectionate amusement! He let his thoughts linger on that dear woman sitting in her parlor, so uncomfortable about her head — all because she did not want to hurt the feelings of an absent daughter-in-law. He smoked on; his thoughts were turned inward; even when he said his pleasant good-night, I knew he was thinking of his mother and I hoped the memory might croon him to sleep.

Often in these annihilating hours Mr. Booth spoke of his daughter. There were no direct anecdotes of his beloved and only child, but by circumlocution he did tell much of her. There was the story of 'Edwina the Last of her Race.' Such a thin little tale as it was, and yet Mr. Booth lingered upon it many times, all because in a

[1] 'I was with my father on this visit to my grandmother.' — Extract from letter to author by Edwina Booth Crossman.

roundabout way he so could speak of his daughter to me. Some years before, when this daughter was a very young girl, a stranger made herself known to him, for she had written a novel whose title was 'Edwina the Last of her Race.' It abounded in coincidences with the Booth family history, but Mr. Booth insisted the author's integrity was assured. 'She was not informed upon our private lives.' Among other similarities was a Mammy. Mr. Booth gave this touch tenderly, for he, too, had had a faithful and cherished Mammy. The author believed she herself had coined the feminine form of Edwin and she had named her heroine Edwina for a celebrated father. 'Of course my daughter is not the last of her race now, but she was when we read this story, and her babies bear another name than Booth. I am glad I have not sons. When a name becomes important — it had better die with the one who makes it distinguished.' Did he mean his own father and one of his father's sons? This must be a vulture hour for him. I did not speak.

Mr. Booth's words in these stilly nights were often of his dead, yet graves were not conjured up to yawn before us. He made this witching hour a boon for me. His speech descended upon my crude fears softly as the gentle dusk. Under the influence of his quiet belief in life eternal, I too thought on graves as bridges.

I have not a recollection of telling Mr. Booth of my dead or of my living ones. It amazes me a young girl could have been so impersonal. Tales of myself, with nothing to them, I did unfold, as of the time I saw my own shadow gigantically cast upon a fog. I added, I

thought 'The Shadow on the Fog' would be a fascinating title for a mystery play, the fog to reveal the very
murder it was utilized to hide. The detective element
Mr. Booth passed by, but he favored me with one of his
most Boothian looks as he said: 'Shadows on fogs —
ciphers without rims — we are metaphysical.'

In Los Angeles, life was out-of-doors by day and
crowded houses by night. We drove to Pasadena, to the
Villa, and to all the show places. We wandered in orange
groves and wondered if Heaven could be more beautiful
than this mass of flowers. In my own special little paradise I ran into the serpent. Mr. Chase insisted he was
merely poking a flea in my ear. It was a mean flea, but
one is not a confidante for nothing, even to the most
unselfish of managers.

CHAPTER XX

In Los Angeles, it had been evident something was on Mr. Chase's mind. Not calla lily hedges, nor heliotrope, vine-covered roofs of little sheds that snuggled down in all this wondrous beauty forgetting their own ugliness, nor the fascination of picking oranges from trees and eating them then and there, diverted our erstwhile triumphant manager from his new-found worry. He brightened only when addressed directly by his Star. I had forebodings. There was a dark secret wriggling toward me. It would soon strike. Too recent was San Antonio, with the three-thousand-dollar drive for me not to be suspicious. I was warned but not armed. Do what I might to avoid duets with the manager, he pounced upon me for another 'confidence.' It was worse even than I believed it possible to be. He revealed his diabolical scheme, but this time he realized the enormity of what he was asking and looked ashamed — almost — yet hardened his heart.

'Miss Kitty, I — we — Mr. Barrett is trusting you with a responsibility that will tax all your tact. You are to be our diplomat. There is something you must do for us before the opening night in San Francisco ——'

I think I awaited his further words wide-eyed and speechless. There are moments for which any expression is inadequate. What could it be? Why was Mr. Chase so grave? Wildest imaginings did not point to a disaster hanging heavy over our heads — rather over Mr. Booth's head, for it could only be the Star, since diplomacy was to be requisitioned. For lesser beings managerial orders had sufficed.

It came out bluntly. To understand properly the niceties involved, I was requested to read a portion of Mr. Barrett's last letter. Boiled down, my plight lay in my selection to *persuade Mr. Booth to wear a wig in Hamlet*. Straightway all sunshine faded from my life.

Mr. Barrett, with his fingers ever on the public pulse, had hearkened to those who suggested Mr. Booth looked too old in *Hamlet* — that is, his grey hair did. It was not his beautiful face, genius flitting, playing, fighting, caressing made his face eternally young. It was not his walk, for he skimmed the stage even as Ellen Terry, their difference in grace being one of gender. It was nothing but that greying hair. Again I gave my homage to the generous spirit of Lawrence Barrett. He was doing his best to accentuate the allure of his overshadowing rival. How simple it would have been to keep still and do nothing! There was no sinister Iago cunning in this friend, but he knew the public to a 'T.' The wig must somehow be contrived.

It was easy to bring it into existence. Meyer, the greatest wig-maker in the country, close to the stage entrance of the Star Theatre near Fourth Avenue, had made all Mr. Booth's wigs. He had the Booth head measurements on his books. He knew precisely how to twine a curl to shade the Prince of Denmark's brow — had he not seen his Hamlet when he was billed all over New York: 'Edwin Booth, the hope of the American stage'? 'I know his *young Hamlet*'; and so he had guaranteed a counterfeit counterpart of Mr. Booth's own hair. The finished product had been expressed to Mr. Chase only after Mr. Barrett was satisfied with it. This much was routine, but to get it worn by the Royal Dane — herein lay a need for diplomacy of a higher order than had been employed so far.

There had been guarded 'allusions' in Mr. Barrett's more recent letters to his partner: 'I find my grey hair cramps me' — 'I wear a wig because,' etc. Lately everything had been written to Mr. Booth and said to him why he should wear a wig in *Hamlet*, except *accusing him of looking too old*. And when one came down to it and faced it, this was the sole reason. No one had a hope of deceiving him, for vanity had no part in him. And yet, telling any one he looks too old ——!

That was what was put up to me. To say this very thing. All too well I realized I was a last resort, selected after all else had failed. Would this be taken into account? No, indeed! Go and accomplish the impossible! The wig cast its horrid spell upon me! I began to dream of wigs!

Mr. Chase regarded the San Francisco opening as the logical and psychological moment for 'the wig's initial appearance.'

'They have not seen him for ten years in San Francisco. Mr. Booth is returning to those who not only adore his art, but claim him as their own prodigy. He is their boy who has made good. Tell Mr. Booth it will sadden them here to see his greying hair — in *Hamlet!*'

Mercy! Was this his notion of diplomacy? I sat me

down to think it out. Had I not heard Mr. Booth say many times his Hamlet was an intellectual interpretation for scholars? How he would shudder at his hair being made *the thing!* Besides, Mr. Booth was the artist complete. He knew each value of his body as he knew the values of the notes in his voice. Just thinking upon raising the question of a Hamlet value to Mr. Booth made me weak. To play upon him as if he were a pipe? It couldn't be done! Didn't I know the keenness of his mind and how he saw through everything? Didn't he always put two and two together? Had he not been reading Mr. Barrett's letters for the last months and listening to Mr. Chase's talking at him and willy-nilly continued to appear in *Hamlet* unmindful of his greying hair? Never did I go at any enforced duty so reluctantly. Misgivings haunted me. I watched his Hamlet again. The very soul shone through the body of the actor. Yet it was true. According to the text he was too old to be Gertrude's son.

Once Mr. Booth asked me why I was so sad. Oh, to confess all — throw myself — the wig rather — upon his mercy! But that would never do. I did not fear that under any blundering approach of mine, my Star might turn upon me and remind me that I was an undisciplined minx; an ingrate of a little pig before whom he had cast the pearls of his boy-play; and that I was now rending him with my effrontery on wigs when he had himself told me Hamlet was the study of his own soul. No, Mr. Booth would not be brutal. He would *think* his reproach in gentlest form, but this ameliorated nothing; any sort of deserved reproach from him — well, I didn't

believe I could live through it. I could not betray
Mr. Barrett and I could not betray Mr. Chase. I was
completely at sea what to say about that wig.

Intuitively I knew why Mr. Booth resented being
asked to wear one in *Hamlet*. There was no comparison in his mind of Hamlet with any other character
he portrayed. *Hamlet was Hamlet!* Macbeth wigs,
Bertuccio wigs, Richelieu wigs — any character of his
that required one had it as a matter of course. They
were tools in trade. But these characters were not
Hamlet! I never heard him say that splendid line

> How infinite in faculty,
> In action how like an angel,
> In apprehension how like a god,

without seeing the ideal man Mr. Booth himself saw at
this very moment. I believe he carried this ideal man
from the theatre with him and saw him always in his
own encounters with Life. He had become accustomed
to the notion that in his Hamlet, audiences saw this
same ideal. And then, out of a clear sky, came the bolt
— they advised him to wear a wig to look younger.
Suddenly up sprang those milestones along the highway
of his art. He had not even read their mileage before,
but now he notices them, studies them, and behold —
they were casting shadows from the west and the shadows must lengthen as he travels on.

There were no illusions left for him in his personal
life. He had no pleasures, no tastes, incompatible with
greying hair; but I believe that wig came as something of a shock. Did I hear sighs over the briefness of
life? Far from it! I think but for his sense of humor the

artist would have stood out against a wig for Hamlet. But he could not take himself so seriously as a man. I think he forced himself into donning 'the d——d thing' with a good laugh at himself. I always felt my own part was the outward form of Mr. Booth's inward spiritual grace of humor. I never really knew what he *thought*. I only know the antic disposition he put on for my benefit, and there were times when I think he hoped all he said of that wig might be repeated to Mr. Chase — and to one other.

My 'attacks' were as *rounds*, between which I went to my corner to rest. I could think of no diplomatic invention, no polite fib that Mr. Booth would listen to. On a saunter back to our carriages from the Villa, I heard myself grumbling: 'Why must people be so literal that they forget audiences see with the mind's eye?'

'See what?'

'Why — the characters of the play — if they are acted — as you act them!'

Mr. Booth gáve me a searching look, but his smile was amused. 'I think I understand!' Suddenly he seemed angry and then shrugged this mood off. But he said grimly: 'So you know all about it?'

'I do, but, but ——'

'You think a wig may please those — I entertain?' Scorn ineffable!

'Only a few!'

'Hamlet! It's diabolical, a wig for Hamlet! If they do not like my Hamlet — let them stay away!'

'You know they will not do that. It's not that, Mr.

Barrett means, I am sure it is not! I am not doing this very well, Mr. Booth. I am blundering fearfully. I think I know how you feel, and every one feels the same way who has any sense of artistic perception at all ——! I am furious! I can't think up one reason why you should — except — please forgive me ——! Could you stoop to them?'

'And wear the *thing?*'

That is what I meant, but then I went wild and begged him not to yield.

'Let me hear your arguments in favor of it. Why did you undertake to persuade me?'

'I didn't know how outrageous it would sound to me.'

'But there is one truthful reason. Let us have it.'

'You would look younger, wouldn't you, with hair like your own?'

'Before it turned grey? Undoubtedly! Suppose we take you as a fair representative of average intelligence, out there. Now, do *you* want me to wear this wig?'

'I do, Mr. Booth.'

Then he looked at me quite a while. His eyes became mirthful. He gave his silent laugh. 'I am not a clown to amuse in *Hamlet* — yet I will try it on. Mind, I do not promise to wear it. I will think about it from your viewpoint! I will consider the audience's feelings.'

But I had to make surer now that there was a possibility.

'Will you try it on, Mr. Booth, for the opening night in San Francisco?'

'Now, I will not be pinned down. A wig weakens a face. It lessens its sensitiveness. There's something to be lost for Hamlet more important than youth. But we shall see!'

Victory was not won, nor was it defeat.

I poured out my grievance to Mr. Chase. He had brought this punishment on his own head. Wasn't Hamlet's beauty in the eye of the beholder? Were there not enough intelligent people left on earth who wanted pure art and knew that art takes time? Wasn't the world full of stupid little young things? Youth —! Bosh! It wasn't as if everybody hadn't been young once! And Mr. Booth knows a wig will obscure his soul. Wasn't it far greater to see Hamlet in the mind's eyes through Mr. Booth's mind's eye? 'He hypnotized us into seeing a mere boy as Hamlet, and now you are spoiling everything ——'

'He's going to wear it?'

'He's going to try it on.'

'Good for you! Now, to keep it on his head — if you can.'

'I'm on Mr. Booth's side! I think it is hateful — even to mention such a thing to him.'

'You don't see Hamlet from the front, little lady. It is important and is so easy to do.'

'Easy!! I think you are the most ungrateful man I ever heard of.'

'What did you say to Mr. Booth?'

'I don't know. He saw through me at once.'

'Keep your mind on that hair — won't you?'

CHAPTER XXI

'BOOTH OPENS TONIGHT'

THE run from Los Angeles was to be the last for five weeks and so the comradeship of the 'David Garrick' was broken up. I could not eat that last desperate morning's breakfast when it was now or never, for the opening night would wait for no man. Mr. Chase seasoned my eggs by saying with mailed-fist tones under his velvet smile: 'Mr. Barrett is confident you will persuade Mr. Booth to wear the wig tomorrow night. It will be an opera audience. You realize it must be worn.'

There were to be two weeks of *Hamlet*. Mr. Chase told us the engagement was creating wild excitement. We all realized that we were on the eve of gala nights, and every one but myself was happy, although even I responded to Mr. Booth's spirits. Hour by hour as we neared Oakland, he became more and more care-free. It did seem as if since touching California earth he had drawn from the soil its strength and warmth.

I love to think back on that happy actor who answered the call of California; where once he had dreamed dreams he dared not hope might come true. Of course, Mr. Booth had played here over and over in his maturity, but he said the last time he had brought his cloud with him; while now he was in the best of health and having the happiest season of his career. I knew he did not mean the most brilliant nor even the most significant.

BOOTH OPENS TONIGHT

'It is not the happiest year of my *life*. That peak belongs to other years. But in the theatre these days are my happiest.'

It was good to see Mr. Booth take down the shutters of his house and find it merry within. He was so full of fun this last 'David Garrick' breakfast that I told him I should not be surprised to see posters all over town for *The San Francisco Fire Boy* in place of *Hamlet*.

There were a few moments for me alone, during which he said might he hope I had forgotten my engagement with him?

'Is there an engagement, Mr. Booth?'

'For a trying-on.'

'No, I had not forgotten — but there was no time set.'

'Come to my dressing-room when overture is called.'

I longed to fling myself at his feet dramatically in the fashion of Camille to Armand's father, and weep out: 'Over my brightest moment there was hung a cloud. It is the shadow of — that wig. *Won't* you please wear it?' But all I said was, 'That wig has cast a pall over San Francisco for me!' This delighted him, but he did not lift that pall.

The train pulled into Oakland. We took our belongings from the car that morning. It might even be a farewell to the 'David Garrick.' The Star had not yet expressed his pleasure upon retaining the car, Mr. Chase said. Out on the platform Mr. Booth was bowed low to by his advance man, Ormund Butler.

I wandered to the front of the ferry. Back in San Francisco! Soon to hear the call of the Golden Gate!

As the ferry moved across the bay, it dawned afresh upon me what this San Francisco engagement meant to Mr. Booth. He was going to the Palace, as were Mr. Chase, Mrs. Foster, Mrs. Baker, and Miss Vaders. I was returning to the Baldwin Hotel. It was under the same roof as the Baldwin Theatre, and I should not need an escort late at night.

Mr. Booth had friends here. He would be absorbed at once by them. Perhaps he would remember to ask us for an outing, but after the wig, I should not have been surprised had he put us all back in our proper places. And if the 'David Garrick' were not retaken — why, much of our happy comradeship was already over!

I was thinking of these things when a gentle voice said close to my ear: 'It is a good vision — is it not?' The voice was Mr. Booth's.

'You are glad to be back, are you not, Mr. Booth?'

'I am glad. I hoped I should be glad. Five weeks of it, too, and there are sights for us here!'

'But have you not thoroughly done San Francisco before?'

'I never *did* any town until my Chickens inveigled me. Let us hope I shall not become too lazy with one bill for two weeks. I may refuse to move from my chair!'

I longed to thank him for all the pleasures he had given us. As if reading what he deemed my fell purpose in my eyes, he turned the tide.

'You look as if you were working yourself up to say good-bye. Could you not — to that wig?'

'But I have not seen it yet, Mr. Booth! I may be

very glad to say it.' As I turned my head, there was the staff, also the ladies, being kept back by Mr. Chase. He was (as he said later) giving all the chances there were for me to *get my fine work in.*

Mr. Booth became silent. His gaze was upon San Francisco. All across the bay we rode so, close to the chain of the ferry. His eyes were shining. He seemed pleased with my unspoken sympathy. And then we bumped into the slip and Mr. Chase and Mr. Butler escorted the Star to his carriage and Popper placed us in ours and I was whirled all on a Sunday noon to creamed oysters served by the dozens on one slice of toast. I laughed to myself. The oysters were so out of proportion to all else that California grows, and then I laughed again as I remembered the soda fountains here, where champagne was drawn for ten cents a glass.

The day of the opening dawned bright and clear, as was to be expected of a climate that takes its rain in seasons. I came out of my night's sleep fresh as a breeze, but I was puzzled by the weight upon my heart until that Hamlet wig pounded itself upon my brain. Yes! This was the night! Ah, well, after all, Diplomacy was stimulating! On the preceding day I had absorbed the Sunday papers and searched the advance notices for a novel Edwin Booth superlative. It did seem as if the dictionary must have been raked for one. I also scanned the columns of the Opposition, so I might choose my Wednesday matinée and had thanked the gods for their propitiousness, for here was displayed —

that for our entire engagement would be appearing — Minnie Maddern — in *Caprice*.

I had also read with liveliest interest of the wind-up of the brilliantly successful engagement of the great Italian tragedian Tommaso Salvini, who had 'closed' Saturday night on the same stage upon which Edwin Booth would 'open' this Monday night. It was enthusiastically recorded that Salvini's 'impression' had been deep; that he was the *greatest living Othello* — yet filtering through all this Salvini fanfare was expectancy of Edwin Booth. Talent, even great talent, was not genius, and the Booth public knew it. I could not fail to catch the *vibrant* white heat of those advance notices. The writers' blood had tingled as they wrote, and it needed nothing — nothing — to make the reader's blood tingle. It was enough to print Booth! Booth! That one word drew in the audiences. And now, the night was come! The papers made headlines of it this Monday — *The great and only Booth opens tonight.*

Oh, those mornings when one cannot keep from dancing first on one foot and then the other! This was the beginning of such a day, and even Mr. Booth was to press down my little measure until it could not hold another grain.

I hurried to the Baldwin stage entrance. What a refreshing entrance it was — direct upon a clean street — after the usual thick mud approaches to a stage door! Five weeks in one town! It meant all my costumes were to be worn. I was eager to be settling my dressing-room. Smiles from the back-door man! Another one of these old dears remembering me! As I crossed the stage on my way downstairs, I passed Ido hard at work with her 'court ladies.' No one in the company was called to so many rehearsals as Ido and usually for an hour earlier than the regular call. I recognized several faces and wondered if their leader, Sophie, might yet be here. Yes, she was, and soon she hurried to me with her hearty 'Oh, I'm glad to see *you* back!' Welcomes from the house-people made all our theatres kin.

Now Mr. Doud appeared to assign my dressing-room. If I wanted to be alone there was a small room opposite the greenroom. And then Amo rushed by, calling out that Mr. Booth wanted Ido and me to come as soon as possible to the Palace — to see his rooms. They are 'all decorated' — it was 'wonderful.' She would not tell more.

When my golden locks were brilliantined and set up on the block, I went to Amo for her story. Mr. Booth had sent for them last evening to see his rooms, 'all decorated with flower-pillows — and lovely things — and he wants you and Ido to see them before the flowers wither.' Amo was even now in the throes of a stage fright, for this was her first appearance in San Francisco. She dared not go with me, and poor Ido was not yet free.

Mr. Chase escorted me to the Palace Hotel. He was so happy over the 'stupendous' business that his mood was sanguine, but he well knew I would not mention wig to Mr. Booth this morning. He reminded me he should be 'behind' for a last warning before the curtain rose, and so dismissed the diplomatic burden he had thrust upon me. But of the audience tonight he could not say enough. It was to be a 'wonderful audience, ladies all in ballroom attire, each carrying a bouquet!' He said that even the upper gallery had been reserved by society people. The local management said there never had been anything like the interest here that Edwin Booth had aroused.

Mr. Booth was busy with letters as we entered, but at once became the host. I limited myself to a mere snatch at a glimpse of the flower-laden rooms, for after all this was his opening day. From Mr. Booth's manner it might have been any day.

This is the story behind the flowers: A young actor in a far Eastern city had sickened and died in unusually pathetic circumstances. Mr. Booth had relieved and comforted. His stiff hotel suite was now homelike, cheerful, yet gala. There was a card on which was written, 'With a mother's gratitude.'

I did not get the characteristic story from Mr. Booth, but he did let me see how touched he was. He said, as if no one had ever shown him homage before: 'I am glad you came to see what is here done for me. I thought my Chickens would be happy for me — *with me* — in this tender welcome.'

CHAPTER XXII

MR. BOOTH WEARS A WIG IN HAMLET

I was in the Baldwin Theatre before the lights were on, made up and dressed by half-past seven — fully twenty minutes too soon, but I dared take no chance. Each necessary moment must be available for the deed. Again my heart was heavy. Mr. Chase appeared as he said he should, but only for a moment — 'just to make sure you were on the job.' He said amiably, but with suspicious emphasis, 'Mr. Booth must wear the wig tonight,' and I should peek at the audience. 'Never in all your life may you see another such house again. It's a ballroom and a flower garden — and of California flowers — rolled into one.' He was 'got up, regardless,' himself.

There was no opportunity 'to see the front' until Act First was ended. I snatched my peek-hole view then, and for its every vacant moment. All the company took turns in peeking, for the gas footlights made a flare that was difficult to penetrate when one was 'on.'

Only in California did such an audience assemble. There were so many flowers, their perfume reached those upon the stage. Mr. Chase put it well when he described the gowns as 'ballroom affairs.' Evening toilettes were in those days strikingly different from afternoon gowns. They were cut low and off the shoulder, and were sleeveless. That audience was a thing of beauty — right up to the roof. The picture of it is unforgettable.

I think I was sure, deep down in my heart, that Mr. Booth would wear the wig, for if he had resolved not to do so, he simply would not have discussed it. He could be impassably aloof, and then no one dreamed of not honoring the barrier. But when he was playing our game, he was *so* approachable, and this play-quality was in his manner when the wig was under discussion. Yet I was treading on very delicate ground, for if Mr. Booth's ideas were not yet fixed, a wrong word might prove fatal. I could now do no more than wait for his mood to guide me.

I had the greenroom to myself, for every one was dressing. Not one of the company was aware of my diplomatic mission. The partition did not run up all the way, and as far as hearing went, Mr. Booth might have been in the same room with me, but not a hint of what was to be floated over the wall. At last overture was called, and almost on the instant the dressing-room door was thrown ceremoniously back, and a voice said from within, 'I am coming out now.'

The bowing dresser was holding the door wide open. I tried not to appear concerned, but my heart was pounding, and then I heard a chuckle and Mr. Booth walked out into the greenroom — *with the wig on his head.*

Even on the stage I never saw such a tantalizing smile as he favored me with now.

'How do you like it? Shall I wear it?'

MR. BOOTH WEARS A WIG

I fancied I detected a threat in his question. If I gave the wig too much approval, off it would come. Once in a while there lurked a contrary little twist upon Mr. Booth's lips. It was there now.

I mustered my most casual tones. 'It is a good wig. Isn't it?'

He admitted it was.

'It is natural enough, but ——!' He experimented with it by running his fingers through the hair.

'You see! Each particular hair lies flat to my head — flat as my acting will be — with this wig on my head! I am hampered. I have much business with my hair. I like to run my fingers through my hair, in *Hamlet* ——'

'Yes,' I conceded — I wanted to be fair, even generous — 'I hate not to see you do that business.'

'Oh, I can invent something else,' rather impatiently, 'but I'll show you' — he clutched the thing he loathed, as if to pull it off.

'Oh, please, wait. Let me study you in it.'

I didn't think it diplomatic to harp on my admiration for the new youth of his Hamlet. I was not prepared for his younger face, with its eager spiritual beauty, accustomed as I was to this very face. I got in as quickly as I could: 'Is this the exact color of your own hair?'

'I suppose so. Really, I have forgotten'; and then he smiled rather mischievously, 'I see you approve!'

As carelessly as I could contrive it, I said: 'It *is* becoming. Could you not wear it once, just once? Do try it out! One night won't matter to you, will it?'

'W-e-l-l! It is on my head.' But, fiercely, 'Keep close

to me until I am on the stage, for in the very last second I may yank it off.'

Anything to divert those itching fingers, and then I believed myself inspired: 'Oh, Mr. Booth, perhaps you may have your longed-for stage fright if you wear the wig.'

He favored me with a look permitting varying interpretations, and none of them flattering to me, but he did keep the wig on, and I rattled on lamely, just to fill in time — for that call boy must appear any moment now — 'I like the line by your ear. Do you put on your own wigs?'

'I do.'

I felt the uncertainty of his resolve. He had not yet decided whether he would wear it or not. This was plain.

I hurried on. 'It doesn't weaken your expression, does it? You have combed it so naturally, it really looks as your own hair must have looked.' (Heavens! Won't they ever call Act First?)

'My head is too hot ——'

And then (and for this relief, much thanks) Act First!!!!!!!!! was shouted.

Mr. Booth's fingers savagely pulled his new dark locks. I kept still. What was there left to say? He was studying his own face in the large mirror before which he was standing and slightly frowning — and perhaps my heart-quaking eyes, whose reflection he saw in the mirror, appealed to his ever kindly nature: 'Oh, well, I will keep the d——d thing on!'

Call boy rushes in — 'Curtain up, Mr. Booth!' — rushes out!

MR. BOOTH WEARS A WIG

The dresser appears next. 'Ready, Mr. Booth?'

Mr. Booth turns and starts up the stairs. I follow closely.

'You need not come. I'll wear it.'

It was a very human Edwin Booth who was mounting the stairs for his stage to face that gorgeous audience. Even now he did not seem to be thinking of fresh triumphs knocking at his door, waiting impatiently for him, but rather to be understandingly reflecting upon how hard it may have been for me to 'persuade' him to wear the wig, for he gave a friendly chuckle even if he did look surprised that I kept close to his heels.

'I am coming up to hear your reception.' This was stark fact. Not for worlds would I miss hearing that San Francisco reception, even if I had no conception of its magnitude.

He twisted his mouth deprecatingly, but all rankling over the wig was gone, as if by magic.

'There will be nothing out of the way tonight. It is ten years — you know. They have forgotten me.' But he was smiling now, I thought more for his pleasure in being back in San Francisco than for the welcome he must have been sure of — forgotten after ten years as he might suppose himself to be. Had he not read his advance notices Sunday? It was quite possible he had not.

The curtain music was already playing. The stage manager had given the warning; he was standing in the centre of the stage to see if all the extras were 'just right.' He had timed the music to a second to enable

Mr. Booth to reach his 'property' chair. Now Mr. Doud was ready to give the curtain signal, after his own scamper from the stage. Mr. Booth dropped into his tragic pose and mien. But before he nodded his head to approve the curtain signal, he espied an old lady in the 'first entrance,' and without more ado he was out of that chair rushing across the stage and being enveloped by the old lady's clasping arms. Yes, he was being kissed, while the kisser pranced up and down as if she had lost her mind for joy. The music had to be repeated. Mr. Doud was at his wits' end. I do not believe he ever had had a curtain delayed from such a cause. It was enough to make him 'froth at the mouth,' and he almost did.

I knew the hysterical old lady well. She was Mrs. Saunders, a cousin of Joseph Jefferson, a great local favorite who was always added to the Barrett personnel when we played in San Francisco. She was a privileged being in the Baldwin Theatre, and was now on her own initiative intending to 'see' *Hamlet* from the first entrance. She could not have anticipated Mr. Booth's affectionate welcome, or else she would have come down into the greenroom, probably, and upset all the wig's possibilities. Horrible fears possessed me, that Mrs. Saunders might now spoil the wig; that Mr. Booth would snatch it off and be glad of this excuse even to himself. But no, the experienced actress might embrace an actor ready for the stage, but, even in her hysteria, never, never, disarrange him. She kept her hands from the wig, and I was only too grateful to her that she had waited, according to etiquette, in the first entrance. Not so Mr. Doud. I think he could cheerfully have wrung her neck, for the audience was already showing its impatience, and this was not to be borne with ease by a self-respecting stage manager. He could not do a thing to hurry Mr. Booth. That was not within his province. I never saw him so upset.

The music was played three times over before Mr. Booth returned to his Hamlet chair. He realized, of course, each complication that might arise from his keeping the curtain down, and he 'took in' Mr. Doud as he passed him briskly, all the boyish mischief in his nature alert. He ignored the worn-to-a-frazzle expression upon his stage manager's face, and slid into his Hamlet pose, turned his face to me, and *winked*. Nothing of the situation had escaped him, and he was inwardly convulsed over it all, probably telling himself he was *bad*. His spirits had not shed their fun when the curtain went up almost with a clang — for its rising reflected the stage manager's temper. As for that wink, it was still in the Star's eye when the curtain reached his shoulders; there was only time — not a split second to spare — to compose his face into Hamlet's gravity before it became exposed to that crowded house that from the stage resembled a wall of flowers.

CHAPTER XXIII

APPLAUSE IN SAN FRANCISCO

CONTRARY to the Booth Hamlet Prompt Book directions, edited by William Winter, Mr. Booth did not enter on the cue given therein by King Claudius — *And now our Cousin Hamlet and our son!* This business must have been used in the past, but the change was made before I became a member of the company. Hamlet was 'discovered' — one of the assembled court to receive the first utterance *from the throne* since the marriage of the King with Hamlet's mother. Hamlet's chair was placed as near the footlights as possible for the shifting scenes — about *left centre*. The throne upon which Gertrude and the King were seated was placed at extreme left. The Court was grouped about the stage. Laertes and Polonius stood near the throne.

This change from 'entrance' to 'being discovered' (even as late in his career as the first edition of the Booth Hamlet Prompt Book) is enlightening, for it proves Edwin Booth did not stop searching for ways to improve his art. He said he let his characters take possession of him in his wee, small hours when he could not sleep, but this 'being discovered' proved also that *the play's the thing* had more and more become an integral part of his interpretations. The 'centre of the stage' or 'an entrance' was discarded along with all that he had *imitated* when, in his early youth, he assumed his great rôles. His art had for long been a *development of the play*, even if at times, for lack of proper support, he apparently *did* the plays in monologue. He was never selfish as artist or man. His mind could not have conceived art to be selfish. If it seemed so, at times, it was that one did not grasp the lights and shades of the character Mr. Booth was impersonating. He did not discard 'traditions' if he found no improvement for them. Novelty without rhyme or reason did not appeal to him. By being 'discovered,' he deprived himself of that keyed-up 'entrance' that artificially stimulates an audience's expectancy. He might very well have assumed the effect of his 'appearance' would so be dimmed. It was not.

Quietly seated, the scene proceeding as if the Star were not on the stage — with the King speaking at once — Mr. Booth's 'reception' at each performance stopped the play. In vain he did his best to avoid this.

Sometimes one hears it said, or reads it, that the methods of Edwin Booth would be too out of date to sway a modern audience. No one who saw his art as he *listened* to the new King's first speech from the throne could endorse such a mistaken estimate of the art of Edwin Booth. In this scene he sat in unaffected quiet — not a muscle contracted or relaxed — yet his audience read each separate thought of his mind; he did not even shift his eyes, but their color changed from flame to smoke and back again.

> Though yet of Hamlet our dear brother's death
> The memory be green; . . .
> Therefore, our sometime sister, now our queen,

The imperial jointress of this warlike state,
Have we, as 'twere with a defeated joy, —
Taken to wife: nor have we herein barred
Your better wisdoms, which have freely gone
With this affair along; — for all, our thanks.

Modern methods? His eyes were a study in listening during the King's speech.

Motionless as a statue with ceremonious dignity (was he not at court?) at the words, 'Our sometime sister, now our queen,' and again at 'taken to wife,' his audience saw his pain as if the skin were suddenly torn from his quivering nerves. Irony, even while listening, mastered his mind, and his thoughts exposed the bruise upon his soul. When later, he spoke his line to the Ghost, 'Oh, my prophetic soul, my uncle!' it came not as surprise to his audience. They had already seen his prophetic soul. He shook himself out of his listening absorption when the King-Uncle directly addressed him. In Hamlet, as in all his great characters, he set up a limitation to develop his rôle within, and made this limitation felt by his audience, even with his first appearance. In Hamlet this limitation was so thin and penetrable it seemed as if the prison house would of itself set the soul free.

The audience must have been expecting the Star to walk on, for the curtain went up without a sound from the front. The King began his speech. Then the inky-cloaked figure was recognized, and they broke loose. I was in the first entrance, prompt side — where the clock was. I timed that San Francisco reception. It lasted more than five minutes. It waxed in volume until it seemed nothing could exceed that steady flow of tireless energy.

Mr. Booth held his sombre mood and posture as long as he could, then bowed gravely — not a trace of a smile upon his face. But they — out there — kept it up, until he was forced to step out of character and wanly smile upon them. More applause. He rose now, but in his dignity, and reseated himself. More applause. He rose again, and bowed a slightly more human smile this time, and sat down. The applause was gaining in volume and intensity. At last Mr. Booth recognized the feeling back of this ovation, and in spite of himself responded — with all of himself.

I had not seen this Edwin Booth before. Again he rose, bowed and waited, but as that 'reception' would not let up, he came down to the footlights and just stood there helplessly. As if he had forgotten he was on the stage, he looked out upon that wonderful and beautiful audience and his eyes filled with tears. Aggressive tears they were — no blinking them back. When his audience saw those tears, they began all over again. The miracle had happened, the leopard's spots paled, but I was too excited to think of this. I saw him utterly conquered by his audience and his audience utterly conquered by him before he had spoken one word. And how young he looked with the border lights shining upon his brown hair! Why, he's just a boy — San Francisco's boy — even the Fire Boy come again. How could he help it after that welcome!

The night threatened to become a demonstration to Edwin Booth, with Hamlet left out. The actor compelled quiet by slipping into character, but a Hamlet that made one feel as if Jove's lightning bolts had been turned loose and were striking all about one. I had not seen this Hamlet before — but then such is genius; it always astonishes. The first note of that voice of molten gold came from a heart that was throbbing beat by beat with the heart of his audience.

Once his hand went involuntarily to his hair and he turned his face to me. I felt the fun in his challenge, yet his face and mien were tragedy, but after this one resentment he evidently accepted the wig with all its imperfections on his head.

I wished for Mr. Chase to be with me to rejoice in that young Hamlet. I was overjoyed that his 'Opera audience and a California garden rolled into one' was seeing *the wig* on Mr. Booth's head. They interrupted him all through the act. This was usual, but even the applause did not sound usual this night.

The first great outburst came from 'These but the trappings and the suits of woe.'

'Frailty, thy name is woman!' brought down the house.

The third great point, 'I'll speak to it, though hell itself should gape And bid me hold my peace,' received a terrific burst, as did also, 'Foul deeds will rise, Though all the earth o'erwhelm them, to men's eyes.' They tried their best, when the scene shifted here, to turn his exit into a recall.

After the Ghost scene, as the curtain fell upon his line, 'O cursed spite, That ever I was born to set it right... Come, let us go in together' — there were eight calls. I counted them, and I was sorry, for how could any audience keep up such enthusiasm. They would be too worn out.

The lights always went up on the instant Mr. Booth's curtain fell. There was no wriggling of the curtain, nor a darkened house to suggest further calls.

Of course, those eight calls were wonderful, yet I feared the rest of the play would be an anti-climax. It was not!

Act Two had ten calls.

'The play's the thing' had sixteen calls and asked for more.

> Why, let the strucken deer go weep,
> .   .   .   .
> For some must watch, while some must sleep:
> So runs the world away.

sounded like another 'reception.' I thought they would never stop.

Act Third, 'I will speak daggers, but use none' went beyond ten.

The closet scene was constantly interrupted.

> ... look, how it steals away!
> My father, in his habit as he lived!
> Look, where he goes, even now, out at the portal!

was an ovation as if there had not been 'a hand' before for him, and when the curtain fell upon the closet scene, I lost all count of calls.

I missed the graveyard scene, but I was up for the last one. For the most pitiful cry I have ever heard,

'Oh, I die, Horatio —' sobs echoed him from the front. Mr. Booth was not philosopher, here. It was youth robbed of life before it had lived. His pathos was unbearable. He was so cheated by death. By now there was not a sound in front. The rest was indeed silence — even after the curtain slowly descended.

Lights go up at once. No one moves out there. The orchestra is playing its Hamlet dirge and then, after complete quiet, reaction sets in. Ladies climb upon their seats, scream out for Booth! Booth! It is refined Bedlam, and then more calls. I no longer pay attention to them. I am too used up. — And then — it is over. Edwin Booth has opened in *Hamlet*, and the curtain is down for the night.

Mr. Booth passes me, after taking his last call, with a suspicion of a flicker in his eyes, and I know then he knows my feelings. I make way for Mrs. Saunders, who rushes upon him. But it is another Edwin Booth from the playful actor of curtain-rising time. That audience tonight had done something to him. He welcomes her with a gentle smile, but gets away almost at once, and soon — very soon — he is out of the theatre.

When I returned to the Baldwin Hotel after the play, I went directly to my own room. I did not even think of supper, for I could not have swallowed. That hopeless picture of Hamlet lying in death clutched my throat. Always Mr. Booth's death scenes tore at my heart, but on this night it did seem as if I could not bear the grief of it. The next morning I did not even hurry to have the papers sent up. There could be only one verdict. Mr. Booth must have been touched when he read those eulogies. They reflected his audience.

Amo, too, had made her hit. This was not surprising after the way her mad scene had been received the night before. Miss Vaders had 'arrived' in San Francisco.

CHAPTER XXIV

A HOLIDAY AFLOAT

OF course, that opening night demonstration was never quite repeated, but successive audiences made it clear San Francisco had surrendered to Edwin Booth. The wig was in evidence for each performance, and became a detail of the Hamlet costume permanently. Much to my own ease, Mr. Booth did not by a look remind me of all that had gone into the wearing of that wig. I was even ashamed by this time of the diplomatic conspiracy and hoped there might never be another for me. These two weeks I watched Hamlet often and it was evident Mr. Booth had accustomed himself overnight to the wig. If he did not run his sensitive fingers through his hair, he seemed to be doing it. I could have sworn he did. Mr. Chase, too, wished to forget — conveniently.

Mr. Booth inspired such a delicate sense of loyalty, we avoided the appearance of discussing him. I shrank from quoting him, and Amo and Ido felt as I did. It is for this reason there are few Amo and Ido anecdotes connected with Mr. Booth for me to record. There must have been many of them. By unvoiced common consent we established our unwritten law — our finger upon our lips for whatever Mr. Booth might say to us individually.

One night in the greenroom, Mr. Booth took my

breath away by telling me he had accepted an invitation to go yachting on the Pacific conditionally.

'You must keep me in countenance by accepting, for I have given the impression my ladies are included in my invitations.'

Oh, what a darling little lie!

I remember well Mr. Booth's soft laugh here. 'Are you planning to accept?'

'I do not think I was ever happier in my life, Mr. Booth, than to realize you have not been bored by us in the "David Garrick."'

'I shall keep the "David Garrick" to the end of the season.'

There is a deeper overtone to yachting on the Pacific than yachting on the Atlantic. When I first came to California, I could not shake the feeling I had reached the jumping-off place. I never felt so far away. Mr. Barrett, who planned his route to close his season in California and was particular to arrive here after the rainy period, was again giving to his partner the benefit of his own luxurious taste. As usual, Mr. Booth had requested Mr. Chase to plan carefully each detail to secure our physical comfort. Carriages collected us. Our hosts received us not only with cordiality, but with marks of gratitude as if it were recognized we with themselves shared the responsibility of giving the guest of honor his good time this day. We were so at home with Mr. Booth and he with us that almost at once was recreated that out-of-his-shell atmosphere of the 'David Garrick.'

Mr. Booth was a delightful conversationalist when he

shed his diffidence. Our part was done when we bridged for him these first few moments, for it needed very little tact to withdraw into the background when Mr. Booth took the lead. If the habit of his shyness showed its head or cast its shadow before, his ladies had on the tip of their tongues some pertinent question to ask of him, and straightway in giving answer Mr. Booth was again revealing his humor and his charm. Conversation was easy today, for our hosts tossed the ball back and forth.

The boat was not a yacht, but belonged to a line of which our host was the owner. She had a broad deck and was steady, and for this trip was sacred to Mr. Booth's privacy. As she ploughed her way out upon those blue waves under a bluer sky, I tingled as if I were turning a living page of an animated volume of the 'Arabian Nights.' For how else was I here, soon to eat lunch with Edwin Booth on the glorious Pacific Ocean, if some genie had not snatched me up and dropped me to this white deck. There is the picture of Mr. Booth standing by the rail and looking out over the waters and up at the clouds and saying he was succumbing to an enchanted spell. He seemed utterly unconscious that to his companions he in himself was the magic of this lure.

Not at all too soon it was asked did not the salt water breezes make us hungry. It had been considered in the arrangements that the actor dined at three o'clock. The engine was stopped, that there might be no motion when the good things to eat were served. I dare say there would have been much that was good to drink but for Mr. Booth's total abstinence.

We coaxed from him some of the tales of his California

days. Out here on the Pacific the stories of his early hardships acquired an even more fascinating tang than when we were whirling over the rails. He drew an amusing picture of his boyish misadventures, but no one but his own flesh and blood could have coaxed from our Star a story of his triumphs around the world. He shut out his brilliant life from his conversation as definitely as if he had pulled down a shade of a window.

If today launched my social mingling with those (apart from the theatre) whom Mr. Booth admitted to his private hours, I nevertheless came to the boat with an almost defined impression of our hosts. Our Star's personality projected the quality his friends would be rich in. Our hosts for the day were perfect dears, without a drop of Leo Hunter blood in their veins. Reverently, yet tenderly, underneath a gay hospitality, they watched over the guest of honor; our comfort, too, was arranged for each moment.

No hostess ever had foisted upon her 'party' a less smartly gowned set of guests. At times I fancied that in Mr. Booth's eyes our very lack of smartness was the reason he desired to introduce us to his friends. Through us he conveyed a sort of pride in his profession from which at random — so to speak — might be culled this group of actresses. As a bouquet picked in the garden of the theatre, we were drab, and many a manager would not have been proud of our appearance in our street clothes. Had Mrs. Foster been met, leaving the vestibule of Grace Church, she could have been set down appropriately for no less a personage than the President of the Woman's Auxiliary. Stability and respectability were stamped upon her. She today, as for all 'occasions,' donned her widow's weeds. They were sprightly weeds as weeds go. Her dress-parade bonnets were enlivened by crisp crêpe flowers. She was the dowager perfect. Mama Baker was frankly the grandmother type, although she had no grandchildren. Her skin was white and pink. There was never more than a thin dusting of powder for her face. Not one of the Booth ladies used make-up out of the theatre, nor needed to. The 'Chickens' were a tailored lot; even Ido, who made her own dresses, affected the severe. Amo had her songs of praise for her Ophelia success, and she responded so modestly, yet with so much pleasure, that her Star smiled upon her in warm approval. All in all, it was a rare day.

When the boat docked, there were our carriages waiting for us. It had been 'perfect,' for Mr. Booth said so and hinted of a very near drive to the Cliff House. He played his great rôle that night as if he had brought away with him the tang of the sea.

CHAPTER XXV

MINNIE MADDERN

MR. JOHN T. SULLIVAN [1] was staying at the Baldwin Hotel. Once in a while we passed one another and paused to jest at our 'strange encounter,' for seldom were we under one roof. He, being outside the 'charmed circle,' was not so happy-minded over the situation as I was. Upon one meeting he said he had nothing to read, and I offered to lend my copy of Rider Haggard's 'She,' of which everybody was talking. Mr. Sullivan decided not to wait for me to leave the book at the desk, but to borrow it that very night after the play. Dressing-room visits were in fair repute, but unless one had a husband present, hotel room visiting was *not the thing*.

A bell-boy knocked upon my door, and blandly said: 'The gentleman in Number so-and-so wants you.'

Of course, he had made a mistake in the room.

'No, lady, he told me to go to this room and tell the lady I want her.'

I closed the door with full faith in the mistake.

Soon there was a second knock, and a note this time, signed John T. Sullivan, apologizing and explaining he was asking for 'She.' I delivered the best-seller of the day to the young grammarian. The next night, on my way to the elevator, Mr. Sullivan overtook me.

[1] Mr. Sullivan later became the husband of the superb Rose Coghlan.

189

'I have been trying to waylay you to apologize for my stupidity.'

We entered the elevator and descended, then the car stopped to take in another passenger, a little fashion plate, which at once exclaimed as if delighted to see him: 'Oh, how do you do, Mr. Sullivan?' And straightway that gentleman was absorbed in this young person of much importance — for such his deference indicated her to be. She was uttering words more quickly than I had ever heard them flow from human lips, and she had a promise of an infectious laugh in her voice that did not materialize, but kept one expecting it. Her eyes — I did not miss her eyes, but they were too restless to do more than give out a hint of what they were like. Who was she? By her very endeavor to render herself unnoticeable, one knew she was somebody — and then I caught a glimpse of her full face. Of course! She was Minnie Maddern.

Once down in the lobby, she was the first out of the elevator and vanished as hurriedly as she spoke.

Mr. Sullivan was preening himself.

'That was Miss Maddern. You may not know it, but I was her leading man for a while last season.'

'In *Caprice*?'

'In *Caprice*.'

'Oh, I am so glad to have seen her close by.'

I suppose being outside the royal circle made him sensitive, for he said loftily: 'Miss Maddern is charming always. Supporting her was a happy experience!'

She had greeted him cordially. There was no condescension in her manner to her former leading man.

MINNIE MADDERN
In the days of 'Caprice'

MINNIE MADDERN

Mr. Sullivan was right. She was charming. I was impressed by her clothes. They were the latest thing. She had such an air of success, and she was *so* young. On my way to the theatre I wondered how it felt to be a star while yet a girl.

I was to hear much said of this comedienne who had just emerged from soubrette ranks, for the head waiter seated me next to a young man who after a few days asked if he might introduce himself, as he had seen me on the stage several times. 'I am Arthur Miller, Miss Minnie Maddern's manager.'

During the next five weeks we became dining-room friends. I do not remember even catching a glimpse of him away from the table except when attending the Maddern performances. He was a listener made to order upon Edwin Booth. No rhapsody of mine could be too torrential for his eager ears. He craved tales of Edwin Booth, but he was a loyal manager and he had his own rhapsodies of *his* Star to pour into my also eager ears. Miss Maddern was rehearsing her first great rôle, Frou Frou, and from now on each dinner was seasoned with how the *Frou Frou* rehearsal had gone that day. Once he said with meaning: 'Her channel is not wide, but it is very deep.' As a prophecy of the art of Mrs. Fiske, Mr. Miller's words are interesting. They may have been the first to record 'the deeps of her channel.' But one wonders that the *breadth* of her channel escaped his intuition. Mr. Miller pledged a box for the first *Frou Frou* night. As it was to be on a Sunday, I was free to attend, and in the mean time there came a free Wednesday afternoon for *Caprice*.

BEHIND THE SCENES WITH BOOTH

One evening at the Baldwin, Amo impressed upon me: 'Do not let anything prevent your seeing Minnie Maddern in *Caprice*. She's different. And when she sings — croons rather — "In the Gloaming," you will choke up.'

My legitimate training had not developed respect for this type of play, nor usually for the actors of them, if I did like to see them. But as Amo said, Minnie Maddern was 'different,' even if she had not yet taken Lotta's place as she had been advertised to do when she first went starring. But then, Lotta was in a class by herself. That irresistible little clown left the theatre before I came into it. But Minnie Maddern was not a bit like Lotta, and almost overnight the 'successor of Lotta' went up in smoke and the real Minnie Maddern took her own rightful place.[1]

It was something of a shock, if pleasurable to the public, and not according to Hoyle for the producing managers, when young ladies went starring without properly climbing the ladder.

Managers were assuring every young girl that youth was not an advantage. To be young was against one. Youth was gawky, raw. Experience that enabled one to simulate youth and the skill to make up to look young — that was what was wanted. We heard this constantly. It was the accepted standard of the theatre. They 'got around' Minnie Maddern by saying she was *born on the stage*. They overlooked the fact that other

[1] A booster, who entered heart and soul into much of that advance puffing of Minnie Maddern, told me that he 'couldn't do enough for the red-headed little daughter of Tom Davey, for he was such a dear fellow.'

young actresses were also born on the stage, but for all
this did not go starring when they were fifteen. Then,
too, there was Mary Anderson, but — one hated to be
so unoriginal as to be always quoting her career in
reply.

For this *Caprice* performance I sat me down to study
the methods of a soubrette: for I had worked hard upon
soubrettes. I could not help but think it a pity that
Miss Maddern had not the advantages of supporting
Edwin Booth for one season, at least. Mr. Barrett,
too, would do so much for her. Perhaps they would get
her for their Perfect Theatre. Of course, Mr. Barrett
knew all about Minnie Maddern. Her father had been
his own agent-manager for years and her aunts also
supported him. And then the curtain rose.

There was presented a pleasing if stereotyped picture
of a rustic bridge. It was not quite so 'elaborated' as
was Minnie Palmer's in *My Sweetheart*, which was higher
up and had a real waterfall. Today's little thin play
moved on as such daintily labelled scenery or acting
usually does, until there came on a figure clutching a
bunch of fagots. She knew how to make her entrance,
but technique had nothing to do with the vitality she
at once revealed. Years after, when I saw my first
Romney portrait, I was reminded of the laughing eyes
of Minnie Maddern. While her costume was wholly of
the theatre — as unreal as it could possibly be — her
study in brownish reds deceived us into accepting it as
something drawn from life.

I did my best to catch her methods. That vital being

up there on the stage let her methods tumble over one another like bubbles in a cataract. She put as much meaning into her *listening* as into her *speaking*. Once in a while she was plastic even. Always, even in her hurry, there was repose. She could sit still; she could smile from deep within her as she listened. She was always thinking before she spoke. This would delight Mr. Barrett in her. 'Gesture to the thought' was his instruction. I do not know if Minnie Maddern gestured at all, but I do know she moved about and *did things to things*.

It was some time after she came upon the stage that I asked myself if she were beautiful, but when I once thought of it, I was very sure she was — at least some of the time. Managers demanded beauty. She was a cloud through which the sun was ever trying to shine. It was interesting to be expecting the sun. I do not think I thought of the sun when she was on the stage. Probably I did not think of genius at all. Great acting was gauged for me by Edwin Booth, but Minnie Maddern made me laugh and cry. And I liked her hair so very much, almost as much as I liked her eyes. It was oftener golden than red. At times it was deep auburn. That magician-y old gas-light flicker perhaps played tricks with her hair; perhaps, too, with her eyes. I wondered what *was* their color. Blue, one was sure of it — at first. Then, they were green, no, black — they even might be yellow. They were basilisk-y! Oh, no, they were little suns. But they were the right sort of eyes for an actress to have, and I let it go at that.

She was a finished soubrette and knew how to get her

laughs. In Act Second she did a bit of clowning and was 'funny,' but she soon shed this phase, crouched on a stool in a very red fire-glow, and, accompanied by the full orchestra, sang 'In the Gloaming.' She made people cry their eyes as red as the flare of the firelight. Perhaps we did not quite know why we cried, but if we thought about it afterwards — and I did — that slumping girl was hypnotizing herself as she sang. Her gentleman husband was ashamed of her, and she was saying this to herself in her mind, over and over: 'He is ashamed of me.' The words of the song were apt, but they were not important. Any other song — while she sang it — would have told the same story. We should have known the girl was saying: 'He is ashamed of me.'

At the end of the act she gave a cry that was as natural as any Modjeska had torn our hearts by. I had not before heard just such a cry in the theatre. Yet I knew it was right — for I heard a girl cry out like that once! But it was in real life!

In Act Third there sailed on a full-fledged society belle who coquetted with her own dazed and unsuspecting husband until the poetic justice of her victory made the audience gurgle. She seated herself nonchalantly at the piano and sang to him tantalizingly until he was helplessly in her web. Here she wore a pale blue satin ball dress with a train. Her bare arms and neck were as lovely as her back was dimpled. She was charged with the joy of 'getting even'; with mischief, happiness, and charm. When she had her husband eating again out of her hand, she revealed her identity and threw herself into his arms — to his bliss and that of the audience, and — it was over. I had seen Minnie Maddern.

I hurried to the hotel to eat before dressing for our own performance. I do not think I speculated upon the future of Minnie Maddern. She was an established Star, and of course would 'grow.' However, through some optical illusion my memory of her was not of an actress, but of a real girl whom I had seen wander into an unreal play and somehow live there her very real life. Unconsciously I was placing her by the side of Mary Anderson, Modjeska, Ellen Terry. Not comparing them, no, indeed! They were legitimate Stars, but then I should not have dreamed of comparing Minnie Maddern with any one.

CHAPTER XXVI

WE DINE AT THE CLIFF HOUSE

IT was a far cry from the gossamer threads of the dainty *Caprice* idyll floating airily and inconsequentially on gentle breezes to the storm-tossed rocky coast of the tragedy, *A New Way to Pay Old Debts*. Almost from one to the other I went. The chasm between them separated two worlds. Sir Giles Overreach was embodied evil. Mr. Booth revealed that, through his mind the horrid could express itself in completeness.

A New Way to Pay Old Debts had no part for me, so I was able to see from the audience Mr. Booth act a monster. He played Sir Giles but once this season. Mrs. Foster shone as Lady Allworth. I was impressed by the sweetness of her far-reaching voice and truly amazed by her appearance. At close range she was oldish and fat, but from the front as Lady Allworth she was in her prime and most attractive to look at. I liked her voice better than any on the stage except Mr. Booth's — always except Mr. Booth's — always!

He did not give the impression of making the least effort to speak loud, yet his lowest tones carried to the limits of the theatre. In his bursts of passion each syllable was distinct. Not anger nor emotion marred his perfect elocution. About me people were saying, as the curtain fell, that his speaking voice gave as much pleasure as a great singer's. One marvelled at its beauty and his diction.

BEHIND THE SCENES WITH BOOTH

Considered as a play, I thought *A New Way to Pay Old Debts* old-timey, but Mr. Booth's acting was ageless art. His Sir Giles Overreach tore my nerves apart. He stung me to the quick. My skin felt as if it were shrivelling under acid burns. I knew there was some one walking on my grave all through that performance, from my constant shivering. Every one about me, too, was shrinking and trembling. Mr. Booth made not one appeal for sympathy. Uncompromisingly he let himself be written down a monster without one redeeming trait. He stripped the villain's soul naked. People slunk out of the theatre looking upon one another as victims who had for three hours been saturated with evil, had it injected into their veins. The amazement of it was that Sir Giles was filtered through the *mind of Edwin Booth*, and yet had come out wholly obnoxious. If there were a Sir Giles in that audience, he must have felt as if he was gazing at the head of Medusa and had a bad night of it later on. My own was quite bad enough. That monster mocked me for a long time!

His audience that night, if comments in the lobby and in the aisles meant anything, felt privileged for this opportunity to estimate Edwin Booth's versatility, to have a completer range of his powers, and broaden a realization that for him it was as easy to plunge into hell as to join in anthems of angels' choirs; that he was native to the universe, and the deeps of his genius were soundless.

The third week of the engagement introduced the full repertoire. Mr. Booth owned San Francisco by this time, and each succeeding bill but paved the way for a demonstration for the next play.

We were riding the crest of one wave after another. The houses were jammed. Finding new superlatives for Edwin Booth seemed to have become a contest among the critics. As if they had dipped their pens in a living fluid, they wrote in ecstasy of King Lear, Bertuccio, Richard III, Macbeth, Shylock, Petruchio, Iago. One read daily, 'The king of them all!' 'The only Booth.' 'The incomparable genius.' 'The supreme actor of the age!' In every character *but one*. Here was the rub! Edwin Booth was not the greatest living Othello! This crown was worn by Tommaso Salvini!

In all this harping upon the Salvini-Othello superiority, there never was a suspicion of desiring to belittle Edwin Booth. On the contrary, it was proclaimed that his supreme position was San Francisco's glory, that he had gone out from San Francisco to conquer the world. But since he had made Iago his very own, it did seem a pity San Francisco should not have the combination of Salvini's Othello with Booth's Iago — made famous from the Metropolitan Opera House engagement last spring. Why had not a joint engagement of one week been arranged for the two actors; one outstanding as Othello and the other outstanding as Iago? With one artist's engagement immediately preceding the other — why had the opportunity been missed?

The almost daily repetition that Salvini had wrested the Othello crown seemed not a sting, but a thinly veiled managerial device to arouse in Mr. Booth an 'I'll show them' feeling. Mr. Chase's conviction that a bad notice would do his Star good seemed to underlie all that was being written on the Salvini Othello. Down in my heart I was sure as sure could be that Mr. Chase was working the press to do what he himself wanted to do most of all, prod Mr. Booth into playing Othello. If this were so, the management failed. Our Star ignored the challenge.

In the greenroom Mr. Booth demanded to know why no one was planning to take him for a drive. Were there not seal rocks here to be seen, even with seals barking upon them?

'Oh, yes, and the Cliff House for a lunch or three o'clock dinner,' answered Mr. Chase, 'but the ladies are rehearsing daily ——'

'Please arrange with Doud to let them off for one day.'

So again the carriages collected us and every one was happy. Mr. Booth repeatedly spoke of his daughter's regained health. Amo on this day was a sunbeam. How could she help being one? The critics were thanking Mr. Booth for bringing Miss Vaders to them. The engagement was continual honey for her; and then, as we sat on the veranda of the Cliff House listening to the barking seals and laughing at their clumsiness, Mr. Chase contrived, without raising his voice, to convey to my consciousness that he had another confidence for me, and would I saunter down the porch with him? I had become wise in his ways by this time, and knew another nefarious scheme was lifting its wily head. Perhaps I even suspected the plot.

As we came out of earshot of the others, Mr. Chase

said at once that he couldn't 'stand it' — about Salvini's Othello!

'Mr. Booth's Othello costumes are along! All he
needs is one rehearsal. Barron is up in Iago. I asked
him. Don't you think, Miss Kitty, that Mr. Booth can
act Othello better than any other actor in the world?'

Of course I did. 'But then, too, there are the laws of
the Medes and Persians and there were fixed stars, too,
in the firmament! One of these is as fixed as Julius
Cæsar ——'

'Yes, and what happened to him?'

'Is this another of your "persuasions," Mr. Chase?'

'Just think how easy that wig was for you!'

There is a courage born of despair. I soberly reasoned
with him that in the case of the wig I had merely been
up against Mr. Booth's hesitancy. 'Really he had
decided to wear it before I ever said one word to
him ——'

'I know all about that wig! Will you try for Othello?
Because you must get Mr. Booth to go on as Othello
here. It should be done for the last week — say on
Tuesday.'

'I don't think this a situation for *tact*, Mr. Chase; it
lies between Mr. Booth and you ——'

'It requires more tact than any situation that has
come up.'

I told him I couldn't and wouldn't. It was too soon.
Mr. Booth would resent it this time — and, anyway,
it wasn't professional etiquette. I hoped this might
floor him.

But he drawled: 'Being here today at the Cliff House

eating with Mr. Booth, and driving from here in carriages with him doesn't exactly come under the head of professional etiquette, either. Now, does it? Mr. Booth never before took members of his company yachting on the Pacific that I have heard of.'

'But ——!'

'Let us keep all business out of this; professional etiquette included. In your place, when you mention his playing Othello to Mr. Booth, I wouldn't refer to a thing the papers have been giving out. I'd steer clear of any — managerial complication' — he smiled provokingly. 'I'd just let him see how much you want to see him act Othello! You do — don't you? He's going to thank you when it's over.'

'I'd give a year of my life to see his Othello.'

So I weakly yielded to my desire. But I refused to violate hospitality. Not one word from me today. I would not be alone, even, with Mr. Booth, for the rest of this outing. But I was. Popper and Mr. Chase saw to it.

CHAPTER XXVII

I ASK FOR OTHELLO

THE reason Mr. Booth had given for his Othello obdurateness was 'too hard work.' Did he really mean this? Why should Othello tire him more than King Lear? Mr. Booth played each character as if he had been created for this very purpose. Not once did I see him come from the stage physically exhausted. On the contrary, he came off as fresh as a boy. I have seen him enter the theatre as if he were weary, but his acting soon exhilarated him. I would as soon have stood looking up at an eagle's flight and have feared for its weariness as to become apprehensive over Mr. Booth's fatigue from acting. Really, I believed and do now believe that acting rested him. That, as a ship is freed from barnacles by being scraped, the cares of the man were shed on the stage. Othello might tire him in anticipation, but I was sure the actual performance would prove a reviving tonic.

I do not remember the precise introduction of the Othello plea. I did not make mention of Salvini's name. Of this I am sure. Had it occurred to Mr. Booth that his manager was enticing him into answering a Salvini challenge, he would probably have declined to appear as Othello. Mr. Booth's position was one of resignation to the inevitable. There was a hue and cry for his Othello. He must comply.

Playing in masterpieces does fill one's mind with

poetic lines upon great themes. It was as simple to let sublime phrases trip from the tongue as slang. I should have felt at my ease could I have thrown myself at Mr. Booth's feet and weepingly implored him to act Othello and that, 'when kneeling at the throne where Kings themselves need pardon, the deed shall shine beside thee as an angel'; only I did not think it appropriate to suggest Mr. Booth might need pardon. No, prose was all that was left to me.

Perhaps I had been unconsciously pleading my cause for much of the season, for Mr. Booth was already convinced that his acting was my chief pleasure in life. He knew what his genius meant to me, and perhaps he trusted his instinct to give me this pleasure for the reason that I had not fallen in love with him. He may have deemed it poetic justice to reward a girl who was unsentimental over him! Anyway, that very evening in the greenroom after making it clear in several different ways, with his Iago jaw finality, that he would not act Othello — it was too hard work, he suddenly switched to consent. He supposed he should live through it for one night; but that 'I had better get Chase here, for my mood may shift.'

With this 'too hard work' ringing in my ears, I scooted up the stairs to have them send out for Mr. Chase, and gleefully shooed him down to the greenroom, where he was greeted by his Star: 'She has done it.'

Mr. Chase contrived to appear as cool as a cucumber. 'Would Tuesday of the final week be satisfactory, Mr. Booth?'

'It will do, only get it over with'; and exit Mr. Booth.

I ASK FOR OTHELLO

Mr. Chase added a confidence, when he was sure his words might not be overheard, that he should keep out of sight until it was too late for his Star to change his mind. Mr. Chase was not taking chances for Othello.

'I'll send Mr. Magonigle to accompany Mr. Booth to the Palace after the play. I'll go now and settle the papers. When you wake up tomorrow, you'll see Othello bills everywhere from your window. They have been ready for two days.'

'Supposing Mr. Booth had refused?'

'It's easier to pocket a loss than to be held up by the printing!' Never had I seen the kindly Mr. Chase so genial.

And the next morning, indeed, the town was flooded with Othello posters. 'Edwin Booth as Othello' was to be read from every space a poster was permitted to be pasted.

As if no phenomenon had shaken our very vitals by a 'new sensation,' Mr. Booth again became our host for a drive in Golden Gate Park and through San Francisco streets generally. Lolling back luxuriously in the carriage, I heard Mr. Chase ask what my reward was to be.

'Why, Othello is enough reward for any one. Besides, I didn't do anything — not when one came down to it. Mr. Booth himself decided it so quickly ——'

'He says I owe Othello to you. How about a box for that night?'

'For me? Really, with a sold-out house!'

'Well, you've earned a box for Othello if I pay for it out of my own pocket. Invite your friends!'

'Oh, I couldn't share Othello with an outsider! I couldn't talk that night!'

'Would I do as an escort? I should have to be in and out — but — I'll sit there all I can.'

'I'll wear evening dress.'

'Full dress, of course, and the biggest bunch of roses that will come into the auditorium that night. You'll think you live on Nabob Hill. I want you to be perfectly happy. Is there anything else you can think of?'

'Something to nibble on — between acts.'

'Five pounds of fruit glacé! That's your number, if I remember.'

'Mercy!!' But I didn't mind his laughing at me — not with a box for Othello.

The memory of that performance is as cameo-like as if it had been yesterday.

Before it came off, it was clear that Mr. Booth was taking Othello seriously. He astounded me when he spoke of it as 'your performance.' He said — always with that play undercurrent of fun, yet contriving to make me feel the honor of it as sincere on his part — that he should act to me that night. 'You *would* have Othello! I shall give *you* an Othello after your own heart. I shall act to you.'

It had been absurd to ask Mr. Booth if he were 'nervous.' Had he been succumbing to even an approach to a stage fright, he would have boasted of it. But he was putting spurs to his art. As Mr. Chase phrased it, he was intending to act Othello for all he was worth. But there was never in his manner a suggestion of picking up the hat from the ring. Mr. Booth was not accepting a challenge, but Mr. Chase was — and working his publicity along this line, but warily — most warily — for he did not risk the consequences of Mr. Booth's refusing to go on at the last moment should that challenge become too impertinent.

When the night came at last, after my early dinner I ran to the stage door. I tried merely to walk, but there was a pent-up energy within me that would be spent. I should not have visited the greenroom that night (for it was not the thing to do when out of the bill) had not Mr. Booth asked me to come behind and *look him over*.

In later years I realized he did not want to miss the complete happiness he was sure my face would be shining with, in that hour. He told me that very night one was not often privileged to look upon such a happy face.

The greenroom was empty. All of the cast were dressing. I inspected my own self in the large mirror and suppressed a sigh. If only I could have afforded a complete new toilette and swept imposingly into my box and carelessly let slip from bared shoulders a gorgeous evening wrap! However, the night was mild and there would be no wrap at all.

I soon forgot myself as if I were wiped from a slate, for the dresser, with a responsible look in his face, threw wide open the door and Mr. Booth came out. His mind was on Othello as his slight nod indicated. Not before or since did I see him so absorbed in a character he was about to go on for.

There was nothing of Othello's usual majestic stride

as he hurried to the mirror to inspect himself. He gazed critically upon the reflection of a young Othello. I wondered if he had ever looked younger when made up for the stage. The youth in his reflection reacted upon him, for, like a daring hero about to set out upon his quest, Mr. Booth turned to me and asked: 'Well?'

'You are the most beautiful creature I have ever seen.'

'That is a valuable opinion on an Othello make-up,' he said unsmilingly.

'You are the first Othello I have seen, Mr. Booth, whose skin does not make me shudder at the very thought of Desdemona's marriage.' I was having a lesson in make-up, for his bronze make-up had erased each 'line of care.' He did not look to be more than twenty-four. I did not say another word on his appearance. What was the need? He knew what a thing of masculine beauty he was as Othello.

'You are a young girl. Desdemona's psychology is not unlike your own. She is not abnormal. I contend Othello should be attractive enough for Desdemona to fall in love with him. Othello is not a tragedy of abnormal passions. This is your night. I have not forgotten my promise.'

'I'm a King Ludwig — only there'll be an audience too ——'

'He, nor any other crowned head, could have bribed me to act Othello for him tonight. Make the most of it. You shall not have this opportunity again.'

He did not care to talk. I felt this. He seemed to be marshalling the reserves of his art. He was commanding his body to be his tool. The overture was called.

'Oh, Mr. Booth, it has come!'

'I shall act to you!' — said in his most professional tones.

'I feel sorry for every one in the world but myself tonight' — and I slipped out. From the stairs I saw him quietly reënter his dressing-room. What a lesson in acting he was giving me! Complete self-possession with his mind on what he was intending to do on the stage.

Others were leaving their dressing-rooms. In spite of the great occasion, all were serene, for none of the stage business was altered. Mr. Booth gave Mr. Barron the same privileges for Iago he took for himself in the part. However, every one, including the scene-shifters, was awaiting a new triumph on the Baldwin stage this night. It was in the air. Behind the curtain there was no doubt the Salvini Othello crown would be resting upon the brow of Edwin Booth when the final curtain fell.

Thinking upon how wonderful it was to be support-ing the greatest actor in the world, I flew out of the theatre — around the corner — to the front of the house. The lobby was already thinning.

Mr. Chase stepped forward. He had determined to do his part tonight. He himself led the way to my box and, taking the roses from an usher, ceremoniously placed them in my hands. He pulled out my chair, indicated the box of fruit glacé (all opened ready to be nibbled), and hurried away.

BEHIND THE SCENES WITH BOOTH

The overture was nearing its crescendo. There was just time to glance over the audience. Such an assemblage as it was! Another *Hamlet* opening night. Flowers, lovely toilettes, tiaras, a Court or Grand Opera audience! Not an empty seat anywhere! The gallery was jammed! Eager faces waiting for something out of the ordinary! Genius is to fight its fight tonight! For the challenge was felt, and tensely, too, out here. It was not a Roman holiday atmosphere, nor one of letting the devil take the hindmost — no, far from either! — but — it was Salvini *versus* Booth, with the verdict already given to Salvini.

Mr. Chase slipped into his chair. 'They are come to make the best of his being in second place tonight and to prove to him it does not matter, that he is first in everything else. A bad notice will do him good — and look at the house!'

'But it isn't going to be bad! You just wait and see. Why, he looked like the sun god mounting his chariot. Mr. Chase, you never saw anything so beautiful as he is in his Othello make-up. There is going to be another opening night hysteria ——!'

CHAPTER XXVIII

THE house darkened! I heard the warning bell, the curtain bell — a hush — a pause, and the curtain rose.

Mr. Barron is at home in Iago but the rest of the company is keyed up. They, as well as we, are waiting for that one moment — of Othello's entrance. Then the moment is come!

There is an intake of breath at this apparition of poetry before the great burst of applause. Already his physical charm is telling, and already, as always, Mr. Booth has let his make-up define the limitations within which he will portray his character. He has given himself romantic scope for his Othello. The instant he is seen, he has won the sympathy of his audience. They each and every one — one feels it — fall in love with him, even as Desdemona.

As Othello he uncovered his heart throbs, his fevered pulses, his coursing blood, before he had spoken one word — even as he made them see his soul in Hamlet before he spoke. Every one settles down as if suppressing a sigh of bliss.

They can understand Desdemona's infatuation for this Othello. They share it. The play is to be a love-story to clutch the heart; a sort of married Romeo and Juliet — at least until the murder! But the plot is so reasonable, all at once! Desdemona's love unescapably natural.

Othello stood forth, a vision of a slightly bronzed son of the desert. His straight black hair framed his young face, framed those flashing eyes, and that sweet, strong mouth. He brought into this Venetian Court no hint of indolent gondolas. In his own person he invoked his native background of cream-white steeds — Arabia's pride — galloping over burning sands.

Then he spoke! I heard the music voice uttering those words: 'She loved me for the dangers I had passed through, and I did love her that she did pity me.' It was a knight of the Holy Grail pleading his love now with faith in his justification. He lifted that line from earth and earthiness. We saw the angel in Othello's heart.

Of course, Amo was glorified by playing these love-scenes with Mr. Booth, and, of course, he knew it. I could have sworn a thought of this reached me from him even as he rapturously listened to Desdemona's exultant plea, 'Little Miss Vaders, get all you can out of this performance, since stage love-making means much to you. Why begrudge so small a thing as a bit of acting? How easy this part is, after all! It plays itself' — and so on and so on. Mr. Booth may not have thought one of these thoughts, but they came over the footlights to me with his spoken words, and the wonderful part of it was the illusion was not destroyed for me. I received two opposing messages, each distinctly, and I was saying to myself, I am glad for Amo!

The effect of Mr. Booth's acting upon me that night was to obliterate the audience. Behind the scenes I could keep tabs on calls; take note of the volume of the applause; let the enthusiasm 'out there' twist and twirl me until I was a part of it, but tonight, until the final curtain, there was no audience for me. I was in a trance.

In Act Second, Mr. Booth wore a costume that proved the artist soul of its famous designer. It was scanty of material, but gave the actor freedom for every muscle. It was of white and Nile green silk, very soft in effect. Everything about it suggested the spring season of life. So did the wearer's bearing. His quickened countenance; his utter unconsciousness of himself; his seeing before him only the hallowed object of his reverent love — but also his unattempted hiding of the tiger within him — were springtime both of civilization and the jungle. I chided myself for thinking of a tiger. It was too cruel a beast to associate with the Othello who had so radiantly and exaltedly defended his love before the Senate. Why did I think of tigers now? It must be Othello's leap from the ship to the dock. This was a leap as nimble, as sure, as light of foot, as a tiger's — for that ship was seen; we, too, saw plainly a lithe figure poise and flash down to Desdemona's feet. That my subconscious mind and my objective mind were equally functioning here did not bewilder me at all. What if the scenery on the stage included no ship so that the actor could not have physically made a leap from what was not there! Mr. Booth placed the picture — both of the ship and a leap from it — in the minds of his audience. Actually he did give us the last motions of an impatient lover-husband jumping to the side of his too-long-absent bride. He created, too, that tiger for us — not a sleeping but a contented tiger.

I had a curious sensation as if beholding the Booth

Iago setting snares for the Booth Othello. It was not surprising, for I knew each tone of his Iago voice. By shutting my eyes and ears to Mr. Barron, it was easy enough to vision the master-actor in both characters — to see them together on the stage. And when I did not so see them, Iago at once dwindled into a despicable hypocrite, for I did not feel one thrill of the exultant relish in Iago's villainy which our Star without fail stirred up.

And what a lesson *in method* his Othello acting was — for in this performance Edwin Booth utilized so very, very much of his art. Passion swept from him seemingly uncontrollable as wild fire, yet to the student observer right here was his art most calculated. He not only made us feel that chaos was come again, but he left us in no doubt what chaos is. In the big scene with Iago, I could only think of the crescendo of a great orchestra. His agonized fury mounted higher and higher until it did seem as if the gates of heaven alone could halt him, and if they did — what difference would it make? Did we not see him carry hell up with him? I was sure I saw tiger jaws shake Iago, for Othello was all tiger now. Then he flung Iago from him! Oh, his contempt for Iago! It was fearful. He played upon us in this scene. This word is misleading of his strength and sense of doom. He conducted his audience crash upon crash, until it could bear no more. Mercifully the curtain fell. The audience sat shrinking, gasping. It stayed quiet — until it remembered it was an audience — and then it gave way.

Calls for 'Booth! Booth!! Booth!!!' Flowers were

flying through the air to the stage. 'Bravo! Bravo!! Bravo!!!' No one thought at all of Salvini — not if those shouts and flower hurlings told their story true. Here was no longer a contest for the crown of Othello. Here was sheer adoration of genius.

The death scene is a blank in my memory. I do not know what Mr. Booth did in this act. I only know what I felt. He had reduced me to an unthinking state. I was nothing but feeling.

It had to end. There is a confused recollection of what took place after the final curtain. The audience seemed crazy and to be glad it was. They could not bear to let him go. Mr. Chase was as undone as I. We both realized I must get out before the crush if I was to catch Mr. Booth in his make-up. He himself had asked me to be prompt. I snatched up my flowers and my neglected candy and somehow reached the green-room.

Mr. Booth very soon came from the stage. He was not elated. It would have amazed me had he been. He was no longer Othello. He cast that character from him, and contrary to his custom all that season, contrary to everything, he did not rush into the dressing-room to prepare for the street, but sat down in a chair that had evidently been provided for just this purpose and settled himself to *talk it over*. I could not believe my ears.

It was not an altogether pleasant talk. He began it by glaring at me! I was the culprit who had made him work so hard this night. 'Too hard work,' he said, and resaid: 'Too hard work!'

He dared me too far! I broke through his line! I forgot professional etiquette — any sort of etiquette — and I told him what I thought of his acting. I couldn't help it! It swept through me and from me like a torrent. Mr. Booth gave me up, and let me rave. He did not smile, nor look pleased, nor laugh, nor poke fun, nor wax sarcastic. His hands were resting upon his knees as he waited for me to run down. He made no effort to deceive me that he did not fully understand that his acting was responsible for it all, and he wound up the situation by advising me with a hint of a threat in his voice: 'Make the most of it. You will never have another chance to see my Othello. It is too hard work. But I am not surprised you feel as you do, for I acted to you.'

'Oh, Mr. Booth, didn't you forget I was on earth?'

'I do not think you were on earth' — a tiny smile. 'I aimed my Othello at your imagination. But I would not go through with this night again! So remember you have had your Othello.' As if I could forget his Othello!

Mr. Chase came to take Mr. Booth to the Palace Hotel, and was too surprised to say so when he found that the Star had not yet begun to change for the street. Mr. Booth continued to harp on his *too hard work*, but there was no impression made upon us that he was tired. Indeed, he was so untired that he resumed his game of blaming me for it all — and for the manager to take note that there would be no more Othellos for the rest of the season. And he laid so significant an emphasis upon Othello that poor Mr. Chase blushed and felt very guilty, and I credulously hoped my hoodoo had been lifted — that there would be no more diplomatic missions for me.

And the next morning's papers! Not a writer did here perceive a divided duty; divided allegiance; divided acceptance; divided opinion. Edwin Booth was crowned the greatest living Othello.

The criticisms had come as an anti-climax for me had I not, in reading them, for the first time really grasped the notion that Mr. Booth and Mr. Chase *did* hold me responsible for that performance. Then I danced a jig about my room, and nearly missed my breakfast. But I could not come down to earth all at once — not even to eat.

CHAPTER XXIX

PEACOCK FEATHERS

Amo, Ido, and I went shopping in Chinatown, where I fell a speedy victim to the allure of a stuffed peacock which had been fashioned into a fire screen. But how to pack that spread and wavy tail? The shrewd Chinese merchant offered to ship the body, and to lap and pin the tail feathers so they could lie smoothly in my theatre trunk. When once that wavy tail reposed safely on the bottom of my least-used theatre tray, I confided my relief to Mr. Booth. By the expression of his face I wished I had not done so, nor ever seen the bird.

'Where is that peacock now?' he asked, as if his fate depended upon it.

'Why — here in the theatre — in my trunk ——'

'Already! Then something will happen to the baggage. Is it in your trunk now?'

'But I will take it out at once, Mr. Booth; I'll express it home. I did not suspect that you ——'

'It is too late. It will do no good now. The peacock feathers have come *into the theatre*.'

Oh, why had I forgotten New York and the broken mirror? Nothing had since reminded me that Mr. Booth dreaded these bad omens. He was so wise always, so just, and now I had brought peacock feathers to worry him! In San Francisco, Mr. Booth was more willing to enlarge upon his theme than in New York.

He trusted me by this time. He was convinced of my regret, so he explained why his faith in bad omens had become fixed.

He was not scolding, he said. I knew he was trying to shield me as well as himself. I was such a reckless lance-breaker with omens of ill — and I should get the worst of it, he was sure, because of his own experience.

'Peacock feathers are bad luck! The worst of luck! So are ivy vines. I let them plant ivy around my house — I knew better — and I lost my home!'

In his voice were tones that told me what this losing his home meant to him. Mr. Booth placed an emphasis on the word 'home' that I did not forget; but this was insignificant and shadowy compared to the emphasis he placed upon the loss of his theatre — Booth's Theatre!!

'I have a horror of peacock feathers. I do not know, even now, why — I let that bird come into my theatre. I should have refused point-blank to let the thing be set up. They sent it as a present to me — "something to adorn my office — something unique!" I suppose my own reluctance to admit, even to myself, that I was foolish enough to believe in omens influenced me. I was uneasy always, when I met that bird's eye. It was baleful. It glared down upon me — *and I lost my theatre.*'

I realized I was hearing what I should not hear — the pain in Mr. Booth's voice that told his story of the loss of Booth's Theatre. I wished I had not heard it! Perhaps he did not realize he had drawn his veil — that I was seeing within the tomb where was buried alive the heart of his art; where he had thrust his hopes for that which made his career important to the American Theatre as an institution. '*I lost my theatre.*'

Why had I not understood it all before? Booth's Theatre was his workshop! Without it his acting art would forever be incomplete. His acting upon changing stages where he was not his own producer was a fraction of his art as he conceived it in his own mind. He had built so wisely for the future of the American stage. It was to be a beacon light, this theatre of his! He had thrown his own fortune into it. He had earned every penny of that fortune — and lost it.

'I lost my theatre!'

Mr. Chase so often said: 'Would I had been there! I could have arranged everything so easily. Had Mr. Barrett been experienced enough, then! Any business man knows, who has looked into the history of Booth's Theatre, it could so easily have been saved.'

'I lost my theatre' became my Greek tragedy, while the poor peacock feathers magnified themselves into ill auguries of the gods.

With the whole country going mad over the Irving productions, it would have been human nature for Mr. Booth to remind the public, in print, of Booth's Theatre. It did not seem to occur to him. He always spoke of Mr. Irving's productions in glowing words and welcomed whatever development the American theatre might receive from the Irving-Terry tours.

A curious coincidence braced Mr. Booth's faith in the bad luck of those peacock feathers. The Interstate

Commerce Law went into effect about this time and the cost of our baggage dizzily soared. But I detected a note of triumph in his voice when he said: 'I told you something would happen to the baggage.'

CHAPTER XXX

'FOR NOT BEING SHY WITH ME'

In the first week of the season, when Mr. Chase distributed his little red leather-bound notebooks, in which, pasted on the inside cover, was the route for the entire tour, he had attracted my attention to the 'open week' following San Francisco, designated in the route 'Yosemite.'

Even when we reached San Francisco, it was understood that Mr. Booth, 'with a party of friends,' was to make the Yosemite trip. Mr. Barrett had painstakingly arranged for a week's absence from any reminder for Mr. Booth of duties and annoyances. His partner-friend had laid emphasis to me upon Mr. Booth's not even seeing the faces of the company for a week, and Mr. Chase had not gainsaid him.

But the best-laid plans of mice and men — as many a time before — did what Bobby Burns said they did, and upon one startling greenroom night Mr. Booth, in finest fettle, announced: 'We will take the "David Garrick" and pass the week in the car along the Pacific Coast. We will sleep in hotels when they are to be had. We will travel by stage when we feel like it. For one week *I shall do as I please*.' His eyes twinkled with his joy of defying whom it might concern. 'I seldom know what a real vacation means. There is usually a left-over responsibility. For one week there shall be freedom from — everything.'

'A cipher without a rim, Mr. Booth?'

FOR NOT BEING SHY WITH ME

'Let us hope it. The Chickens must stand by me. You know I cannot play by myself. The Yosemite will keep for soberer periods. It is my tonic that our profession breeds girls without jealousy. You make me happier than I expected to be again in the theatre. Three of a kind, and I have them in my company. Be kittens and puppies for a week. You are younger than one of you realizes, and this amuses me most of all. You do not have airs for one another ——

'I have told Chase, this week open is mine! We shall set out as vagabonds — back to my youth in California and — back to what I had no time for in those days — nor since, for that matter. I never did know how to thank any one! I wish I knew how to thank you ——!'

'Thank us, Mr. Booth!! Mercy, for what?'

'For not being shy with me.'

Mr. Chase referred to the coming week as one of lovely idleness on full salaries and all expenses borne by Mr. Booth.

The week was listed 'Yosemite' on the route. We went in the opposite direction.

To me there is no record of him that more illuminates the real Edwin Booth than this pleasure jaunt for which he paid all the bills and not an inkling of it got into the papers. In the middle of a record-breaking season, Edwin Booth laid off and took his ladies on an outing at his own expense! Such things were news.

Mr. Chase grasped the value of the publicity that was escaping him, but he had become used to Mr. Booth's unswerving dignity by this time, and 'confided' that to give us this pleasure trip Mr. Booth had abandoned the Yosemite plan.

The San Francisco papers wound up their reviews of the Booth engagement as the most brilliant, dramatic triumph of the decade — in fact, for the exact period of Mr. Booth's absence from the city. All of Mr. Booth's impersonations were again dissected, with Othello wearing the crown.

After a crowded closing week — of houses and doings — on the last Saturday night, as soon as we had jumped into street clothes, we jumped into carriages — and were off!

In the station as we waited for the train, there appeared a motley crowd in most incongruous costumes and of woe-begone countenances. It reminded one of Petruchio's wedding garments. Mr. Chase hurried to his Star, after a whispered instruction to us to 'keep Mr. Booth's attention from those people — or our trip is ruined.' There had been a fire that totally destroyed the Monterey Hotel — the very hotel we were now starting for. We took our cue, and contrived to place Mr. Booth with his back to the moving throng. His native shrinking from being observed saved the hour. He did not suspect that passing behind him was a crowd of fire victims. As soon as possible we boarded the 'David Garrick'; drew lots; ate supper; and every one said, including our host, how pleasant it was to be 'home' again. The Monterey fire was kept from him for this night. Mr. Chase had the latest information. No lives had been lost, and there was heavy insurance. The guests' possessions had been burned. This explained the ragtail attire. 'But,' Mr. Chase added, 'they are even now at the Palace! Don't let it bother you! They will enjoy shopping to-morrow. Rich and idle, it will give them something to do.'

On awakening the next morning, there came the wonder as to what might be that ecstatic thing awaiting me outside of those blue and golden curtains. Then Monterey seeped into my sleepy brain. We were here on the shores of the Pacific Ocean for one long week — with Edwin Booth! It was enough to make any girl wide awake. The car was at a standstill. I looked from my window to see the fire ruins. They were not visible, but the ocean was, and enticing green lawns.

When Mr. Booth came from his drawing-room for breakfast, there was content in his face, yet he was expectant. There were deeds to do, or rather there was the opposite of deeds to do — but we must *be at it*. We decided on a slogan. *Abandon care all ye who enter here.* We determined, without actually putting it in matter-of-fact words, to gird ourselves with sweetness of temper suggested by Mr. Chase, and, with something akin to bliss, suggested by me. We were so very happy that we really did not need to say so, but for politeness' sake, we did.

'Are you ready to set out upon our quest?'

'Quest for — what, Mr. Booth?'

'For Nothing! Nothing is what we search for this week.'

Yes, we were ready to set out upon our quest — for Nothing.

BEHIND THE SCENES WITH BOOTH

During breakfast, from the car window, there was not a human being to be seen on lawn or beach.

'I believe they did it on purpose, Mr. Booth, in your honor!'

I suppose there was not amongst us one sufficiently fiendish to have 'wished' this fire on the hotel, but since it had to be — why, it was fortunate Fate arranged the time of it — to the minute — so no curious tourist might follow Mr. Booth about. He owned everything in sight this week. He loitered where his fancy led him.

The solitary figure of Edwin Booth on that deserted beach — the Pacific Ocean rolling to his feet — was congruous. It satisfied one's sense of what should be. The lightest prodding of imagination — and the whole world was his. When I tried to put this in words for him, his eyes deepened, and he asked to be helped to see it as we saw it.

'Let us sit here upon the sand. See it for me, Chickens.'

We played up to this, even as the scene of which we were a part was playing up to us.

'We have stopped the sun, the moon, and all the stars for you, Mr. Booth! We have crystallized Time for you. We have drawn the circle around you, and no one will dare to set foot within that holy bound — not while we are in Monterey!'

He did not say anything. He may have been wondering how we got that way; but he gazed out upon the sea as if he were one with it, and then we spoiled it for him. One, not content to let very good alone, suggested he was another Count of Monte Cristo, who could exclaim: 'The world is mine!'

Mr. Booth declared he scorned the world. He refused it as a gift. He was modest in all his desires — all he asked for was the earth! with perhaps the sea thrown in!

Now we knew all was well. It was always so when he indulged in nonsense, and even Popper could not beat him at it!

CHAPTER XXXI

MR. BOOTH SINGS A COON SONG

WE began the outing proper by inspecting the fire ruins. The watchmen in charge were longing to pour out woeful tales. There had been no real tragedies, and Mr. Chase insisted there was no need to be sad. Souvenir vendors sprang up as if by magic. As there was not another human being to buy, Mr. Booth fell an easy victim to their pleadings. One of these lovely polished shells is on my writing-table. By the rarest of fortunes the fire had not destroyed the stables. The glad news that a rich tourist and party in a private car had dropped from the skies spread like another fire, and a wild one. Mr. Booth, incarnating the sole pickings, was implored to engage horses and all sorts of conveyances — anything he could use was offered at the smallest prices! Mr. Chase was told to 'pay the usual rates. Poor fellows!' As there was no food to be bought anywhere, and the 'David Garrick' was stocked, it was arranged to meet the car *en route*, or return to it as might develop.

But Mr. Booth wanted to loiter on the beach, so we hied ourselves back to it. Today's guest of honor was Mama Baker. Mr. Booth fairly assigned himself to her. The 'heavy ladies' and the Star and the manager formed a group to watch us as we scooped up sand with our shells, built caves, and threw sand at one another. In

vain we coaxed Mr. Chase to throw sand at us. He did
not know how to play so well as Mr. Booth did, and, unlike his supposedly melancholy Star, did not want to,
but he was not shocked — if our hair did blow about
like smoke in the wind.

Mama Baker's voice checked our antics when we
heard her say: 'You may have, in the beginning, imitated your father, Mr. Booth — since you say so — but
whom did you imitate when you went on for end man?'

Mr. Booth blushed.

From the Chickens, 'An end man! — Not in the min-
strels?'

Mrs. Baker added, in severe pride and slight rebuke
for our ignorance: 'Mr. Booth could have made his
reputation in black-face.'

'Oh, they cast me for an end man, because I could
play the banjo.'

We were at once in a small uproar! Edwin Booth a
minstrel performer — an end man! 'Did you *black*
your face — really?'

'Of course I " blacked " my face.'

Oh, couldn't he — now — for us? One tiny coon
song — or anything in dialect?

He couldn't and wouldn't — but he did! We swept
him into our gales of laughter. The breezes from the
Pacific, too, may have blown away his habit of reserve.
He softened his voice to Negro tones. We could not
induce him to sing a spiritual. He said he did not feel
sentimental enough.

When I told him of my relief in being able to laugh,
out loud, and not in honor bound have to hold in, Mr.

Booth changed from amusement to seeming distress, as if he feared I were 'telling on him' to the conventional members of his company. He tried to keep this up, but failed; the ludicrous side of it was too much for him — and for me, too. But he continued to appeal to me, as if for protection, from 'being found out.' Never was there a more delightful mental monkey-shines expert.

This was Mama Baker's day and she repaid her host. If she filled the position of Old Woman, the vigorous actress was never the old lady. None but herself in the company spoke of the Elder Booth from personal experience. At these times, there was a halo about her head, I believe, in her Star's eyes. She was 'Mama Baker' to the entire dramatic profession, even as Mrs. Eldridge was its 'Aunt Louisa.' She had known 'all of them' she said.

We loved to watch Mr. Booth's eyes when listening to a grand old lady of the stage talking to him of his father. The Palmy Days came into their own again on that deserted beach. Our host said it would do the Chickens good to hear these authentic yarns. He did not regard himself as a Palmy Day actor. Mama Baker, as usual, was dramatic. 'Grand Old Ladies of the Stage' are exceptional women! They have to be both old and grand. Mrs. Baker drew out for us the fact that the god of Mr. Booth's idolatry was his father's genius. Mrs. Foster, too, to the impertinent Chickens, seemed to go back almost to the origin of the species, but, she explained, her experience was confined to John McCullough. Hers was another generation, she said, from Mama Baker's.

230

MR. BOOTH SINGS A COON SONG

If Mrs. Foster lacked the background of the past for Mr. Booth, she was a punctilious guest upon matters of the present. Each day she asked him after his daughter's health and led him to speak of his wee grandchildren and other domestic topics of fond interest.

I used to think that Mr. Booth feared to bore people with his private joys or griefs, yet that he was grateful when drawn out. If so, Mrs. Foster was a boon to him, for I fear the tragedian would have derided the notion that the Chickens had an honest interest in himself as father or grandfather. But we had, and we were sympathetic, too, over worries from illness in one's family. Had we not homes of our own?

When Mrs. Baker was saying: 'They knew what acting was in your father's day,' we were humbled into silence. But Amo could not restrain her feelings. 'So do we today,' she interjected; but Mrs. Baker ignored her.

'Oh, I know they like to say that great actors of that school ranted. But they did not rant, did they, Mr. Booth?'

'Our *great* actors have not ranted — ever, in any school; but, Mrs. Baker, you and I *have* heard actors rant — occasionally.'

'I would rather hear an actor rant than not hear a word he speaks,' came from the Palmy Day actress defiantly. 'In my young days, no one could have secured an engagement without a voice.' O Regan, thou art rankling yet!

'Just what is the difference between your father's

acting and your own?' asked Mr. Chase, to change the subject, I suppose.

'The fundamental difference, I would rather not touch on, but the superficial difference lies — perhaps — in my voice. I make less noise.' He chuckled and we laughed. Mr. Booth, as if fearing we might attribute his merriment to the 'school' of his great father, added almost sternly that he had developed his own methods gradually and according to his own physique. 'It is rather safe to assume that actors establish their school upon their physique — for one must cover up what one cannot physically do.'

Mrs. Baker agreed, but continued: 'You are so considerate of your company, Mr. Booth. You are not like Mr. Forrest. What would he have said to a supporting actor who did not give him his cue in the proper pitch for one of his big speeches — did not build up for him, to make his points?'

Mr. Booth seemed to be swept by some irresistibly droll memory — perhaps of supports who failed to measure up to Mama Baker's estimate. His eyes were dancing; he made an impulsive and, oh, such a promising gesture — but, alas, thought better of it. After all, he was probably telling himself, these be supports themselves.

I watched the suspicious behavior of his shoulders hopefully, but Mr. Booth was himself again and turned the key upon all that treasure of atrocious acting, stage mishaps, and misfits generally. But he did not trust himself to meet our eyes. He gazed out to sea until the socially wise Mrs. Foster asked if one could gauge Edwin Forrest's fire by Mr. McCullough's methods.

'No, McCullough was less volcanic than his early model — so am I. I do not mean Forrest — but my father. He was my early model.'

CHAPTER XXXII

CEDARS OF LEBANON SEEDS

When Mr. Booth said he was hungry, his manager asked if after lunch a drive would be the thing, or would he rest.

'Let us drive a long distance that we may return in the sunset. When I am acting, I am shut up in a dark room while the sun is setting.'

I do not remember how the order of our going fell on these days. We were in and out of stages. We drove to the Seal Rocks; we drove through the Forest of the Cedars of Lebanon. The solitude everywhere, Mr. Booth said, made him feel as if he were dreaming of some exquisite, slowly fading beauty — too delicately intangible to remember it when he woke up — at theatre time.

Our driver (when we made use of the stage) kept on tap a supply of information. There had been a young lady whom he had driven, only the week before the fire, over this very route, and, although she had insisted upon the front seat, she had not raised her eyes from the pages of a novel the entire way. Mr. Booth's interest did much to comfort the poor man.

The driver also told us what might have been a legend — but he said it was true — that the cedars had in some mysterious way drifted over the Pacific Ocean and taken root on this far side of the earth. Fact or fancy, a flame kindled in Mr. Booth's eyes. He was fascinated with the

234

idea, that, long before Columbus, these trees had found the New World.

'Think of it! Vitality safe within those drifting seeds!'

'Tiny arks!'

He inclined his head. He was grave. 'Little arks, indeed!'

The observant Mr. Chase must have felt that the vicinity of our chatty driver with his modern stage-coach was an anachronism. Almost imperceptibly he guided his charges deeper into the forest. He shared his Star's mood of awe. An hour, even longer, slipped by as Mr. Booth lingered upon the wonderful thing Life was and the poetry of that long, perhaps dark, wandering upon waters to find a rooting spot on the shores of a New World.

'Right under our feet' — from Amo. In that solemn stillness, the Chickens, too, were reverent, and Mr. Booth understood when I said that for the first time, Genesis was real life to me. He placed his hand upon a gnarled trunk and, standing so, looked up into the over-hanging, widespread boughs. It was the gesture of affection. I believe, in spirit, Edwin Booth was caressing all that forest. At last, with the slightest of shrugs, as if apologizing for saying the obvious, he gave us Ruskin's line: It was a grand thought of God's when He thought the tree.

We were little more than chameleons, we Chickens, these holidays. We took on the coloring of the varying moods of our environment, even its hush. Mr. Booth asked me, as he came out of his own reverie, of what I

235

was thinking — and I confessed, of nothing. He smiled, and then I remembered our quest, the search for — Nothing. He said we had found it. 'I hoped it would be like this.' Nevertheless, the air we were breathing had a tonic in it, and nimble young bodies *had* to dart about, run races and climb trees. So overcharged with joy were we, our healths demanded safety-valves of laughter — yet with never a guilty feeling. Back in San Francisco, did not Mr. Booth fairly implore us to be young as puppies and kittens on this outing and not to forget that he could not play alone? So we did not forget. How could we with those sportive sunbeams and frolicking shadows to urge us on? Our games, however, were played more *before* our Star than *with* him.[1]

Mr. Chase contrived to keep Mr. Booth and 'the party' out-of-doors during the day. The first evening when we gathered in the 'David Garrick,' Mr. Booth teased us, saying he had never seen such sleepy faces — but that he himself could not keep his eyes open. 'Breathing fresh air all day should make us sleepy. I know I shall sleep soundly after a little reading.' He bade us good-night and retired to his drawing-room.

Stupidly I did not reflect upon our host's astonishing sleepiness until I awoke from my own long night's oblivion. Then doubts assailed me furiously. Of course! Why had I not suspected it was my own sand-heavy eyes and not our Star's that had sent him to bed so early —

[1] 'My father was not reserved or grave with those to whom he gave his friendship. With them he was playful. With his mother, he often acted a little boy, for this rôle delighted her. He was very sweet with his mother and tender, but nearly always sunny and playful. I am glad that my father was not reserved with you and that you remember him as he really was.' — Extract from letter to author from Edwina Booth Crossman.

'after a little reading'? Such unselfishness was truly Boothian.

In the *Julius Cæsar* tent scene, when Mr. Booth played 'Brutus' and spoke the line to his sleepy slave after asking him to sing to him, 'I would not urge thy duty past its might,' the actor was playing his own character. So would Edwin Booth have spoken to his slaves! So did Edwin Booth speak to those he employed.

Laurence Hutton, in his tender little book, writes: 'Only those who have known Edwin Booth in trouble and in sorrow, have known Edwin Booth at all.' These were not my trouble or sorrow days, but I was a member of his company and he was the man who paid my salary. But does not a salary-paying man reveal a very true side of his nature to the one who receives his money — sometimes a side no one else suspects?

With 'vulture hours' fresh in my memory, I conspired again, but this time without Mr. Chase, that Amo and Ido join with me to wonder in Mr. Booth's presence why we did not go to sleep sooner; that we did not seem to be able to break off our former habit of late hours — and many other silly little subterfuges — and they were effective, for that very evening, Mr. Booth, after saying good-night, returned and found three 'wide-awake' damsels who were 'so surprised' to see him.

He came almost too soon for Ido's tranquillity. Since New Orleans, those brass curtain rods had tempted her acrobatic instincts. 'I long to hang by my knees from them.' She was in full swing when she saw Mr. Booth. He gave a warning to the confounded one not to squeal.

237

He placed his finger on his lips and shook his head at the blue and golden curtains in mock terror of what might be behind them. And although he *almost* joined in our giggles — not quite — he moved us to a place of safety — that is, as far from the sleepers as it was possible to get — even right next to the kitchen. In this seclusion we sat down — four fell conspirators. I do not remember what was said, but I have not forgotten that Mr. Booth brought his pipe out again.

Our topic was probably that Nothing we had come in quest of. It was a merry enough Nothing, and it was not very late, after all, when Mr. Booth confessed he was truly sleepy this time, and said good-night again, after thanking us for driving away — his vultures.

One night, Mr. Chase was initiated into the conspiracy, and then there was chaffing of the Chickens. I had brought from the cedar grove a sprig with pods of seeds, and was finely working myself up over an enticing prospect of Cedars of Lebanon flourishing on my mother's lawn. Mr. Booth's interest in these seeds was to come later. On this stolen night, he eyed my prize dubiously as he listened to his manager's banter and smiled over our preposterous retaliations, for Mr. Chase was darkly hinting that these might be salt-water trees — 'but if so why not try crying on them, to make them grow? Of course, the young ladies will feel like crying, when the season is over!'

Not a Chicken so base as to ignore this challenge. 'What was "just crying"' from us? There'd be floods of tears in relays. They would all come and help. Those seeds would think they had been planted by the Pacific Ocean! Niobe would have nothing on us!

For this one hour, and only this one hour, taboo on spoken gratitude was whiffed through the open window on the smoke from our Star's pipe. He was too highly entertained by our powers of exaggeration to be mindful he was being thanked, and he even helped to swell the burst of laughter which greeted Ido, when, in sudden and palpably honest dismay, she exclaimed: 'Oh, how different all the future is going to be!'

After Mr. Booth's death I read a copy of one of his letters in which he had written that 'tears were being shed — as the season winds up' (or an expression of the same meaning) 'all because of a few rides.' In the Theatre, twilight was come and not yet gone when I read that letter; still came the moan from everywhere: 'His last cue has been given, he has answered his last call.' I wondered, and it hurt me to wonder, had we failed? Did we not, after all, convince Mr. Booth that it was he and not rides — nor anything but himself — that lifted us from earth, that season? Then the letter cleared. Thoughts creeping backwards became lighter and brighter until they fairly danced about in those buoyant hours of Monterey, and the days before, and the days that came after, up to the last night of the season, which, through the Star's own contriving, was to be the merriest prank of all. This letter belonged to the writer's playtime and what fun he must have had indicting his Chickens! — writing of their nonsense-tears, as if he had taken them seriously! It was, for us, a painless little jest, since we were not to know of it. It has delighted me that Mr. Booth all by himself carried the game on.

After one 'David Garrick' supper, our host said: 'No human being on his vacation has the right to ask for more than I have now. It takes so little, after all, to rest — only to stop thinking!'

'And plenty of money,' put in Mr. Chase. 'You are having an expensive outing, Mr. Booth. Closed theatres! Private cars!'

'Money is well spent that buys a week away from myself.'

This outrageous statement was challenged. 'You are having a week with yourself, Mr. Booth.' He hoped there was nothing 'left out,' that we wanted — that is, which might be procured.

'No, there was nothing — unless the week could be stretched like rubber'; and Mr. Chase teased us by vowing we were dying right then to be back in the theatre — to go on with Mr. Booth. Naturally we were not impregnable to assaults upon our contentment when Mr. Booth's acting was the weapon of attack, but — well, we thought better of it.

Even an enchanted week of crystallized Time has only seven days! Toward the last of these, make-believes were sent scooting, for reality was poetic enough. A few sneaky little glooms would bore in. Suppose Mr. Booth were disappointed in this outing. If only I knew — and then, upon the last day, I heard him say: 'There is Denver! I have a plan ——' He turned to his manager, as if to ask a question which Mr. Chase answered before his Star spoke.

'I have sent my wire to the General Passenger Agent, Mr. Booth. We shall know soon.'

'So will these Chickens if we do not take care! And Denver is my surprise!'

Oh, wouldn't he tell ——?

'Not one word!'

With something entrancing ahead of us, for Denver, we said good-bye to Monterey.

My mother's garden knew not those pods. During the supplementary season, Mr. Booth suddenly asked: 'Have you those Cedars of Lebanon seeds?'

'I have.'

'Would it break your heart — to give them to me?'

'No, Mr. Booth, it will mend any crack in my heart. Oh, do you really want them? How glad I am!!'

'I shall forward them to my gardener at Boothden — that is, Newport. If any one can make them grow, he can. It was so stupid of me not to think at the right moment! This is like me! I never do, or I should have brought away my own pods and not be begging for yours.'

To me, these cedars — yet in their pods — were that poor little Christmas tree way back in Syracuse come true for him at last.

CHAPTER XXXIII

A BRASS BAND MEETS US IN CHEYENNE

SOMEWHERE Mr. Magonigle united the sections of the supporting company. On the opening night in Salt Lake City, the bill being *Richelieu*, the 'heavy ladies' were out of the cast, which suited the pampered Chickens. Without critical eyes upon them in their dressing-rooms, they could give way to rapturous hugs. They conversed in squeaks, for the most part. In another moment, the curtain would be up, and Mr. Booth *on!* The elation of seeing him act again! This was the best of all.

Mr. Booth accepted an invitation for a concert in his honor within the new Mormon Temple. Our host could not have been more than fifty, yet, he told Mr. Chase, he was the father of forty children. The singer of the day was one of these. He was very proud of this accomplished daughter — she was his spoiled darling — but he did his best to conceal his heart's weakness, and begged Mr. Booth to believe the concert had been arranged that the guest of honor might gauge the acoustic properties of the Temple.

Mr. Booth was interested in acoustics. He told his host that no other physical quality of the theatre was so important. He asked many direct questions about the famous acoustics of the Temple, and when the time came for the demonstration of hearing the pin drop, he said he had been told of this pin often, and sighed that theatre architects in general evidently had not.

The young and attractive prima donna's voice had been trained in New York, and, even as Mr. Booth led the applause, his eyes roamed from this 'one of forty children' to her doting father and back again, deeply impressed. He said to me, when out in the open again: 'I did not dare whisper in there with those marvellous acoustics, but think of it! — a father educating forty children — like that!'

Mr. Chase added, 'Think of paying for such an education for forty children.' And our manager did look so aghast at this might-be expense account that I congratulated him upon being a bachelor, and advised him to remain one. Whereupon Popper told him he had brought it on himself, and I, ungrateful minx, accused my defender of having nearly burst from not airing Booth's Theatre acoustics. Many a time had I heard him boast these were perfect. Regretfully he explained that Mr. Booth wouldn't have liked it.

On the Southern and Far Western tour the engagement of Edwin Booth was celebrated by local managements with fancy programmes. Occasionally they were printed on satin. Whenever these souvenir programmes were distributed, Mr. Chase took his toll of them 'for the ladies' and a few of the company.

On one of these satin programme nights, I stood near our Guildenstern, who, after securing his coveted prize, directed it to Miss Mattie Royle, Salt Lake City, and said he could scarcely wait to get home. I congratulated him on having a whole week in Salt Lake, and Mr. Royle was polite enough to hope I might meet his mother, in fact the family. This was my first human touch with Edwin Milton Royle. His acting had intrigued me all the season — not as Guildenstern, for no actor ever yet shone as 'knife and fork,' as Rosencrantz and Guildenstern are nicknamed — but once in a blue moon one shines as Tubal, and Mr. Royle's moon was always blue on *Merchant* nights. With the opening of the Royle front door, one breathed the atmosphere of home. And the mother! Never yet was born a man or woman who in his drab hours did not yearn for just such a mother. During the afternoon, a Mexican saddle was proudly brought in and displayed as it lay on the floor. The whole family rejoiced in this saddle, for it was brand-new and out of the ordinary class of saddles, and the ranchman-brother to our actor was as proud of it as if it had been a curtain call.

This elder brother had 'come in' from the ranch to be 'home' to greet the actor of the family, who in his turn asked the right questions to draw the ranchman out. We listened enthralled to red-blooded tales of blue-blooded heroes, which the dramatic instinct of the actor-brother pounced upon. We were told that younger sons of English aristocracy were frequently 'ranching it' in our United States West — and even married squaws. These were called squaw-men, and back of these locally frowned-upon mixed marriages lay stories of self-sacrifice.

I remembered the afternoon in the Royle home when in later years I sat by my husband's side for the premier of the *Squaw Man*. Mr. Charles Frohman had chosen Mr. Goodale to be the dramatic critic to pronounce first judgment on Edwin Milton Royle's new play in which Mr. William Faversham starred so long and brilliantly.

On the train to Cheyenne, Mr. Chase fixed me with a baleful glare, and I knew a confidence was hovering over my head, and heavy, heavy, it was hanging. Confidences were thick as blackberries now, but usually they were agreeable ones, for next season was already more in the management's mind than this one. The Cheyenne confidence had nothing to do with futures, however pleasant. He said he had no heart for it at all!

Here was his tale, and of woe it was! Mr. Booth was going to be met in Cheyenne by a delegation of prominent citizens — even at the 'depot.' This was enough to upset his manager, but would I listen to this? 'They will have open carriages for Mr. Booth and the ladies — in fact for the entire company, and there is to be a parade from the depot to the hotel!' This was bad enough, but would I listen to this? There was to be a brass band to head the procession, and this was not all, either. That brass band would be playing full blast when the train pulled into Cheyenne, and what did I suppose the tune was to be? 'Lo, the Conquering Hero Comes!' What was to be done about it?

Laugh! I never felt less like laughing; it was ghastly. What was to be done, indeed? Hadn't Mr. Chase thought of anything?

'Never was so stumped in all my life!'

'Of course, it can't be done.'

'Of course, it must be done!'

'Oh, Mr. Chase!' — but I remembered his rank in time.

'Miss Kitty, I tried to impress you that these are prominent citizens. They mean this parade as a great honor — a sort of testimonial to Mr. Booth. We can't insult a whole town — not in the Far West ——'

I was too dazed to realize how stupid it was of me when I asked if he couldn't telegraph ahead that 'owing to the lateness of your delightful invitation ——'

'It's been letters for weeks! — but I've been hoping something would turn up.' He tried to smile. 'That somebody would die there, or something — perhaps the theatre would burn down. But we are out of luck — and we'll be there' — he looked at his watch — 'before you know it.'

'Mr. Booth will understand how hard it is for you.'

'Tell him anything you can think up! Anything! I'm desperate.'

I began to remonstrate, but he was already in his Star's drawing-room, and, before my breathing was normal again, he was out and, leaning over, whispered: 'Tell him the worst.' Then the manager ignominiously retreated to the company's special Pullman.

This was the wild-goosiest task that had been laid upon me yet. It spelled failure. Mr. Booth riding at the head of a procession after a brass band through a town! It was too ridiculous! Mr. Chase could not be serious! He could not be expecting Edwin Booth to parade with a brass band and in an open carriage. He could not! As I started for the drawing-room, it came over me Mr. Booth might become angry — and at me; and if Mr. Barrett heard of Mr. Booth's anger — how he would resent my blunder! Amo looked pleased that I was 'going in,' and so did Ido, but I thought on that brass band and wished it were the 'heavies' who had to face this music. I couldn't wish anything so horrible upon my fellow Chickens.

Mr. Booth was sitting in the warming sunshine by his window, carefully choosing his pipe. He proceeded to stuff his selection and asked, apropos of nothing, if I indulged in alcohol rubs.

'No, Mr. Booth, I do not.'

'I am glad to hear it. I do not approve of them. I have given them up long ago. My doctor advised them; in Booth's Theatre I was always rubbed down after the performance, but they made my voice husky.'

Had he taken cold more easily after these alcohol rubs?

'I took a slight cold. After I gave them up, there was no more huskiness.'

I thought I knew why Mr. Booth was introducing the first topic he could think of, for it was not the custom for the ladies to enter his drawing-room unless the suggestion came from him. And this invitation was seldom given. He wanted me to feel at my ease without a special welcome from him.

I was stricken dumb. Mr. Booth looked his surprise, and then again assisted me over what he must have believed was something hard to say, by asking me if I had been in Cheyenne before.

'No.' It was Amo's first visit, too, and she was all worked up over seeing the corral here, because she played in *Ranch Ten*, and the second act was laid in the Cheyenne corral.

Mr. Booth chuckled. It was plain to see he thought it an odorous location for an act. As if dubious of what might be underfoot he asked: 'Did the actors walk on stilts in the corral scene?'

'I saw *Ranch Ten*. That corral in the play was probably like the Saenger Saal in *Tannhäuser* on the Berlin stage.'

Mr. Booth did not know the story.

'There was a Berliner who went to the Wartburg to see the Saenger Saal because he was such a devotee of *Tannhäuser*. They took him to the Saenger Saal, but instead of being impressed by the frescoed, vaulted chamber, the man from Berlin said it wasn't correct. They couldn't fool him. He knew how the Saenger Saal ought to look, for he had seen *Tannhäuser* on the Berlin stage often enough. The original Wartburg Saal was all wrong.'

Mr. Booth said after a few moments — but in those moments he favored me with one of his unreadable gazes — 'The Saenger Saal of the Wartburg and the corral in Cheyenne — well ——?'

He was so perfectly delightful this moment that my heart became leaden when I reflected that in the very next minute he might be angry. If only I might influence him to see that this brass band in Cheyenne was prompted by the same appreciation of his genius as Germany's tribute — his laurel wreath in leaves of gold;

that it was the same homage the Berlin stage manager had been carried away by when he knelt to 'Herr Meister' — so I tried to carry a pint of coals to the Barons of Anthracite. It did not enter my head that Mr. Booth would ride in the parade, but before I could mention the matter I had been sent in to break to him, he interrupted me by saying dryly: 'I will try to remember your comparison when I take my curtain calls in Cheyenne. Now be happy again' — and the train was slowing down! Could it be so soon? Poor Mr. Chase!

'I think we are here,' observed Mr. Booth genially.

Yes, we were here. I heard the band playing. It was blaring to my ears!! The tragedian listened, and smiled approvingly. Evidently he relished a good brass band!

Then the train stopped. My unsuspecting Star chatted on, but he was listening to the music. I couldn't think of one thing more to say to him. Travellers were hurrying past his window. He leaned back not to be visible to those on the platform. He did not move — he was taking his leisure — was there not all day before him?

Then I blurted it out. I mixed everything up. 'That band is for you, Mr. Booth. They are going to parade you through the streets.' He jumped up and pulled the shade down. I think Mr. Booth was under the impression that he was assisting me to rise — and he was. When I was on the other side of the door, it was banged and bolted. The very click was ominous. That traitor of a manager was waiting. He did not even ask what had happened; he knew. Mr. Chase knocked politely.

249

But there was no reply, and the door stayed shut. I thought Mr. Chase looked *grateful*. Neither did he give any indication of being disappointed. This surprised me until I became suspicious that he had put me in that drawing-room to bear the brunt of it. I hardened my heart, but Mr. Chase quickly melted it again, for he confessed that he had not expected anything of me. 'Miracles do happen, perhaps — but I knew you must fail this time.' This was small consolation.

He had, after all, been thinking to some purpose. He had drafted Charles Hanford to impersonate Mr. Booth: I suppose because Mr. Hanford was so good-looking. The ladies were instructed to hover about Mr. Hanford and 'cover him up' from the gaze of the reception committee as much as possible. 'Treat him as if he were Mr. Booth. Surround him, hang upon him.' And so we proceeded to the carriages, casting, I fear, smirking, fatuous glances at the impressed impostor, and passing through the station in a fashion the extreme opposite to our decorous Star's manner of slipping through.

When the carriages were reached, Mr. Hanford hung back and waited for some one to get in first. He was very embarrassed, and Popper pushed him in with such force that it reminded me of my own recent exit. The mock Edwin Booth at once took the wrong seat with his back to the horses, and jumped up confusedly when Popper hissed in his ears, 'Not that seat.'

Mr. Chase had been shaking hands with the committee and trying to explain that the 'greatest tragedian' was *shy*, and with flourishes and overemphasis, introduced Mr. Booth's *brother-in-law!* And the band was playing, 'Lo, the Conquering Hero Comes,' as we drove through the streets. Mr. Hanford kept his hat on when the crowd cheered, and we had to tell him to take it off and bow. In surprise, he said, 'Oh, is that for me?' He bowed after this, but never did a hero look so sheepish. Amo almost had her laid-aside hysterics again.

ˉhe substitute was worried. What was he to do? He wasn't intending to stop at that expensive hotel, but he was escorted by some one to the bridal suite, and then, fortunately, Mr. Chase appeared and instructed him to 'hang around a while and later sneak out the back way.'

When we registered, I was confronted with a raise of rates. The clerk explained: 'They're running excursion trains in for the Booth play tonight. You are lucky to get in this hotel at all. We're turning them away.' Our Star was almost too popular![1]

When Mr. Chase had a breathing space, he hurried to the 'David Garrick.' He said he 'crept back.' He found all shades drawn down tight and the doors locked, but the cook let him in by way of the kitchen. The tragedian remained barricaded. The manager returned to the hotel to secure Popper, who rushed down to instruct the cook what to serve for dinner. They were both on hand to escort Mr. Booth to the theatre; neither was desirous of being alone with the outraged Star, who commanded them to drive through back streets. Mr. Chase said with that sold-out house he didn't mind so very much.

[1] Edwin Booth attracted out-of-town people in such numbers on his Far Western tour that frequently hotel rates were raised.

I tried to keep out of Mr. Booth's sight during the performance, but when, against my will, I encountered him, he was as sunny as if nothing had happened — ever — to annoy him, and his acting was wonderful. Mr. Chase said people were saying in the lobby, 'That wasn't Edwin Booth who rode in the parade this morning.' 'Of course not,' he heard some one air; 'they keep a dummy to take his place for parades.' Whatever local resentment there may have been was wiped out by Mr. Booth's acting. His genius swept them off their feet, and perhaps, when they came face to face with him, they realized the eternal fitness of things for themselves. Anyway, the Cheyenne engagement was another triumph.

Mr. Booth asked me on the next day's train if I had recovered from my fright. *My* fright was a new aspect on his barricade. He hoped there had been no tears shed. Mr. Chase avoided the Cheyenne incident as if it were something contagious which he might come down with.

CHAPTER XXXIV

THE PLANS FOR THE PLAYERS

MR. BOOTH lingered over his supper the night we crossed the Rockies. Why hurry? The next town did not occur until tomorrow. The air outside was nippy. And then — the moon rose! Nature composed an impromptu to challenge the Golden Gate. We said the beauty outside the car windows made our blood run cold, it was so unearthly. But chills gave way to thrills, for here I was on top of the Rocky Mountains; snug in a private car; eating a luscious supper, *and* across the table sat Edwin Booth! On such a night he could not fail to think aloud — nor did he, for he told us the story of the club he was founding to honor his own profession. The beginning was frothy enough. He asked us to trace the lady in the moon. He scorned the poor old man up there. Even as he jested, I could not but again notice the entire absence of all flirtatiousness in Mr. Booth's manner and threw myself some invisible bouquets that my own manner was ditto. The car was whisking along a trestle that bridged exquisite, shimmering water, and we wondered that so high in the mountains there should be so large a lake. It reached as far as we could see from the windows on either side. I thought the scene perfect, but there is a contrary streak in me, so I bewailed the coldness of that clear-cut circle of light.

'Just a thread of a cloud, Mr. Booth — don't you think it would soften the outline?'

He did not. 'We should then miss the contrast of what the moon shines upon. See the softness in that radiant loveliness beneath the moon.'

Some one said it was like diamond feathers, but Mr. Booth changed this to 'vapors of diamonds,' and then excitedly exclaimed: 'It is not a lake! It is a cloud! *We are above the clouds!* We are living the proverb. Those vapors of diamonds are our silver lining.' He was fascinated with supposings of what might be hidden to our eyes — of what was lying beneath. 'Might it not be a black night of storm? Not a ray of this moon's glory can pierce that thick cloud. I have lived to see the silver lining of my black clouds.' He looked up at the moon as if it had become to him the symbol of his life.

When the tables were cleared, he spoke of *his club* and as if it were an accomplished fact. His voice held the same certain tones he might have used if speaking of a theatre about to open — and we, knowing the conservative way Mr. Booth ever regarded unfinished ventures, accepted 'The Players' tonight as something born into this world.

Whether or not Mr. Booth made use of the name 'The Players' I have forgotten. It is easily possible later association with this name has intertwined itself with my memory of the night when we crossed the Rocky Mountains. We crossed them in the spring of 1887 — some months before the summer of that year which is the time given by Laurence Hutton and other writers for the club's inception — the place being the yacht Oneida on whose deck the founder's close friends were gathered. I shall not try to reconcile anything. There is an Edwin Booth-iness about the later yacht Oneida 'inception.' It would have been so like him to be silent and let his best friends believe that to them he owed his inspiration of that which had been his long-time dream. To the majority of the race, a man's dream is the most precious part of himself — to himself. Some have died defending dreams and some have copyrighted them. Those who listened to Mr. Booth on the yacht Oneida were his chosen friends, yet even with all barriers down, it does seem he could no more dissect his spiritual heart than he could pluck out his physical heart for inspection.

On another day Mr. Booth instructed Mr. Magonigle to bring several actors from their Pullman into the smoking-room of the 'David Garrick' that he might lay 'the club' before them. I begged to be permitted to sit in the smoking-room and hear 'all about it, too. Might I?'

I might come! So we went into the smoking-room, and again I see Mr. Booth riding with his back to the engine, and the actors — only a few, including Mr. Malone — taking their places. I, an acknowledged intruder who had no business there whatever, was seated on the floor close by the open door. My sex was taboo. This wonderful club was not for my gender. This was brought out by the actors through their questions and Mr. Booth's answers. It was an earnest discussion, right to the point, and took place months before the summer of 1887. The Founder said 'the benefit of the club should extend beyond those of our profession.' He said much of outsiders respecting the actor's viewpoint. But Mr. Booth seemed most of all to yearn that the character of the actor — his human side — should be better known. He saw actors with actor eyes — exactly as they were, normal human beings — as unlike to one another as are any specimens of the human race. Mr. Booth assumed that we knew he had all sorts of opinions upon actors, just as he had all sorts of opinions upon the rest of the people on this earth.

'We do not mingle enough with minds that influence the world. We should measure ourselves through personal contact with outsiders. I do not want my club to be a gathering-place of freaks who come to look upon another sort of freak. I want real men there who will be able to realize what real men actors are! I want my club to be a place where actors are away from the glamour of the theatre.'

The actors present responded heartily. Even dues were mentioned, as this was a practical exposition of the club's purpose, and the listeners wanted to know if they would be able to afford to join. Some one asked if actresses were included (it was not I — I did not open my lips). A troubled expression akin to a small terror leapt into Mr. Booth's eyes. Actresses meant women members outside of the profession, and, well I knew, there could be no sanctuary in the club-house for Mr. Booth should 'ladies' be eligible. Afterwards, he smiled grimly over the 'absurd picture of myself trying to hide in the club from women members.'

THE PLANS FOR THE PLAYERS

Mr. Chase, accustomed to pouring oil on troubled waters, suggested this club idea might be taken up by some of our lady stars for their 'sisters,' and Mr. Booth warmly hoped it might be.

CHAPTER XXXV

HOSPITALITY IN COLORADO

WHEN Mr. Chase said he had another confidence for me, I threatened to jump off the train, but the manager assured me it was something that I should be sorry not to hear and that it was Mr. Booth's own contriving for *Denver*. Soon there was a conference held out in the open car that 'the ladies might participate.' For the surprise he had been storing up for us since Monterey was a drive through the Garden of the Gods. No one could conceive how the trip might be made. The excursion required more than a part of a day's absence from Denver, and ——!

Popper said the usual two carriages appealed to him.

'Plus a railroad train,' added Mr. Chase.

Some one asked had tracks been laid in the Garden of the Gods. Then the host advised that Mr. Chase lay his information before us.

'It is carriages through the Garden of the Gods, Mr. Booth, but a train to get us there and back — as you know.'

'Then we shall run the "David Garrick" up there ——?'

'I fear not. The road is narrow-gauge. It cannot carry the "David Garrick." Any night you prefer, Mr. Booth, the road officials will have a special train waiting for you after the performance. We shall eat supper and pass the night in a sleeper and wake up in Manitou Springs; drive through the Garden of the Gods to Colorado Springs and find our own train there, to bring us back to Denver.'

The Chickens bubbled in anticipation. This sort of gratitude Mr. Booth did not check. There was something so romantic in running away — out of town — between bills. There was the risk that we might not get back were there an accident; a sort of playing-truant disposition that we all relished. I think Mr. Booth did, too. The risk was our spice.

Mr. Chase said of this outing: 'I took the General Passenger Agent's breath away when I told him Mr. Booth wanted to make this excursion between theatre nights. He is doing everything for us. It comes high, but our business warrants any indulgence Mr. Booth may give himself; and I do not think the opportunity may come again for him. Next season he and Mr. Barrett will be more conservative ——' He checked himself. His unruly member was under control in spite of all he said of it to the contrary.

From the hour we breathed New Orleans' balmy air, spring had travelled with us. Here in Denver nothing marred anything, weather nor business! I used to wonder how it would feel to go on to a poor house. As sure as the curtain rose, it went up on — not one empty seat. After New Orleans, choice Edwin Booth tickets were — for the most part — five dollars apiece — an extraordinary price.

At last the great night came for which Popper had

instructed us to bring our needies to the Tabor Opera House — for we should drive direct from the theatre to the station.

Almost as soon as the house was emptied, we were on our way. My Denver friends said they could not believe their ears when I gleefully told them we were to drive through the Garden of the Gods tomorrow and be back in town in time to go on at night.

On the train, the General Passenger Agent became master of ceremonies. Mr. Booth was expecting Mr. Cooper, yet when the latter waited for *royalty* to lead the conversation, we — knowing that it was this very respect for royalty that often sent Mr. Booth into his shell — at once flooded the General Passenger Agent with questions, sedate or giggly according to our ages, and before he had replied to even a part of them, Mr. Booth was asking his own questions. Mr. Cooper admitted that though he was with us to secure the right of way and take general charge he had 'snatched at an opportunity to thrust myself into this delightful company.'

Mr. Booth expressed his appreciation of the bountiful supper the road had provided. Mr. Cooper apologized that there was not wine. 'It would improve the supper, but Mr. Chase impressed upon me that you do not care to have it served. If you would change your mind, there is time enough to get anything — before we start. I can fix any schedule, you know, for this short run ——'

Mr. Booth was in high fettle tonight. He thanked Mr. Cooper, and declined the wine. He smiled: 'You have already been too heedless of our digestions ——'

There were rumors that **Mr. Booth** needed to be careful what he ate! It may be — very likely!

Mr. Cooper had brought gifts of bound books for the ladies — 'railroad literature' he called it.

The next morning, when we awoke bright and early, the car was standing in Manitou Springs. Our train after ejecting us was sent by Mr. Cooper to Colorado Springs, to await us. The General Passenger Agent bade us good-bye after breakfast.

We walked 'just across the way' to a wooden hotel. Never, never, shall I forget that breakfast table. Dickens would have adored describing it. Ido whispered, 'Breakfast! Why, it's all the meals put together!' We must have gazed in awe, we three, for the elder ones and the men laughed at us, Mr. Cooper especially. He said: 'The road values your estimate of the food we serve.'

Mr. Chase told us to do justice to everything because there would be no midday meal! The dining-room had been reserved for this occasion, and when we could eat no more — try as we might — we drove to various springs to taste their waters.

During the drive, when some of the formations were startlingly magnificent, Mr. Booth ordered a stop for a saunter and he skilfully apportioned his companionship. When my turn came, he asked, 'What manner of gods be these who walk in this garden?' He was not looking at me. He was asking his question of himself.

I, as every one, saw the old cathedrals and castles in the great rocks, and I ventured that perhaps this was a mirage of Europe — a frozen mirage. Mr. Booth was unsympathetic to this notion. He said, 'These were here first.' He gazed out upon those glorious rocks and said again: 'They were here first. And before them — what an upheaval! I feel as if I had been caught in arrested motion. I feel as insignificant as a horned toad.'

'Oh, Mr. Booth! When you give, as you do, *what a piece of work is man!*'

'I will let Hamlet have it his own way, but when the poet comes, he will tell us what these rocks are saying to us!'

After a while, he said: 'I am thinking of the Cedars. When you call this a frozen mirage — of Europe — you put the cart before the horse. This was here first. Suppose we accept the mirage idea — but keep it *our* mirage — not Europe's.'

'You mean, Mr. Booth, that architects in Europe may have had visions of the Garden of the Gods and been inspired for their cathedrals ——'

'I fear I do not mean anything. But poets see mirages — I suppose there are always mirages of something hovering near poets. It fascinates me — that, in the guise of inspiration, pictures of this — visions — floated over to Europe. *How* they got there I have not thought out — unless' — he chuckled over it — 'they drifted like our cedar seeds, on a "sea of thoughts."'

'Whose thoughts, Mr. Booth?'

'There you have me! Supposing Nature does think — say in mirages and other phenomena. But let us be prosaic again! Why Europe, when we have our Indians to talk of? A redskin is the proper make-up for this scenery. I am too pale — too pale!'

HOSPITALITY IN COLORADO

Mr. Booth put so much meaning in 'too pale' that I was puzzled. I did not think he expected me to understand him nor did he try to help me. He was seeing vistas of ages backwards and forwards.

Carefully had the day been planned. At Colorado Springs we were driven immediately to the hotel. There was only time for dinner, and then began the short journey back by train. The curtain went up to the minute that night, but we sped from train to theatre. Mr. Booth said he did not miss his dull afternoon lying down, and added, raising one eyebrow: 'Had I been so foolish as not to accept your invitation to your first supper — my season would have been like all of them. Even at this moment I should be a prisoner in my hotel rooms.' He must have thought of that brass band, for he almost laughed...

The sands of our lives ran through hour-glasses as regulated as were our 'curtains' and our trains. Every hour of the day was scheduled. We had no more than left our carriages, which Mr. Chase had sent to bring us to the Denver Club, and entered the ladies' reception room, than Mr. Booth came in from the men's side of the club. He was in his freest of moods today. He was accompanied by a distinguished-mannered man, who impressed one as positive and unsentimental, and yet, how his voice caressed the guest of honor! His eyes softened in homage to him. Was there ever anything like the way he wins them, I thought. Sex has nothing to do with it, nor age, nor cast. A charmingly cordial hostess approached, and Mr. Booth presented us name by name. He made a little ceremony of this, as if he enjoyed it. He amazed me, he was so un-shy with his hosts. I had not seen him so animated as he was at the table, and it was he who kept the conversation general. As usual, we received warm thanks for sharing the responsibility to the guest of honor. The satisfied hostess said, when it was all so successfully over, 'Mr. Booth tells me he has become dependent on you.' I had often wondered what Mr. Booth did say when he coaxed those invitations for us. Our Denver hostess was so simply gowned, in such contrast to her lavishly decorated table, that I suspected she had taken a hint from Mr. Booth — for, alas, he must have known our wardrobes by heart. Lucky for us, Mr. Booth liked his actresses mousy, whom no stranger would suspect of being *on the stage*. They did not even need to be young. I believe that no woman, apart from his family, truly appealed to him until she was old enough to wear caps.[1] Today it was Mama Baker whom Mr. Booth thrust into the centre of the stage. It was he who answered a question of his host's to Mama — 'Oh, yes, Mrs. Baker knew my father.'

'How interesting! The Elder Booth! Really!!'

'I supported Mr. Junius Brutus Booth.'

'It's unbelievable. Oh, tell us of him.'

'Mr. Booth was a great actor and a grand man,' Mrs. Baker said with finality.

After a little, the Younger Booth changed the subject

---

[1] 'My father adored old ladies, real old ladies, and made me promise him that when I became an old lady, I would wear caps.' — Extract from letter to author from Edwina Booth Crossman.

JUNIUS BRUTUS BOOTH AS RICHARD III

with his remark that Mrs. Baker was — 'as we say in our profession, born in the theatre.'

Again I felt his pride in her, as if he were saying, 'Look at her. Can any *grande dame* improve on her?'

'Are you all born in the theatre?' asked our hostess.

Mrs. Foster said: 'Only Mr. Booth and Mrs. Baker.'

But this left out dear Amo, who never did speak up for herself, so I added, 'And Miss Vaders. The rest of us were just stage-struck.'

Mr. Booth must have enjoyed this party — as Ido called it — for he did not hurry away, and his lingering brought exultant smiles to the faces of the charming pair who had been at so much pains to do him honor. This formal lunch was the last of the cannily contrived invitations Mr. Booth secured for us, but for all this our happiest days with him were yet to come — at least for the Chickens.

Life in the theatre is not all flowings of honey with violets tossed upon cream. Ido said she supposed she had had it coming to her ever since Regan. In Denver, she was late on a scene. 'Stage-wait' were too ponderous an appellation for her tardiness, since she had no lines to speak, but the Queen did have to cover up some business. And when poor Ido, through inexperience of stage etiquette, did not apologize the moment the curtain fell, the Heavy Lead was incensed by what she felt to be spoiled-child heedlessness if not impudent disregard of rank. She appealed to the stage manager, demanding what, of course, was her due, an apology from Ido before all those who had been on at the time. Because he liked the weeping one, Mr. Doud contrived to arrange this ceremony when Mr. Booth was near by.

The surprised, even perplexed Star paused, but punctiliously listened to penitent mumblings, and he waited for the acceptance as if for something pleasantly customary; he asked some casual question of Mrs. Foster and, drawing Ido into the conversation, slowly walked off with the lady in the right on one side and on the other, the lady in the wrong. Nobody dared meet anybody's eyes. Faces had to be kept straight.

But Ido was crushed, and warned me that my turn would come next. It did, almost at once, even on the next jump to Omaha, although it was not I who had gone on for Regan in Cincinnati.

After the last Denver matinée, Mr. Chase took me for a short walk. He began by asking if life were still an unbroken dream of bliss for me? Had I no forebodings. 'Don't you feel hoodooed?'

'Not at all.'

'Well,' he drawled — and nobody could drawl as Mr. Chase when he wanted to tease — 'to put it plainly, you have been complained of to me. That makes it official, but to clinch it, your accusers have appealed to Cæsar.'

'To Mr. Booth!' I began to feel queer. That the manager would take this revered name lightly on his lips even to emphasize his jest was inconceivable. What was this ominous thing that was bolting from a clear sky, just for my benefit? And what a shame to trouble Mr. Booth!

266

'Of course, I shall not tell you what *Mr. Booth* is saying or doing about it. I shouldn't have troubled him except that I wanted to get this to him first. I think I am the best one to handle it for every one concerned.'

'If I had the slightest suspicion of what you are talking about!'

'You are called a fearful name.'

'Mercy!'

Mr. Chase was really laughing now. 'It's the worst the ladies could think of. It's "Beggars on Horseback"!'

The porter had 'informed' the early-rising elder ladies that because I lay in my berth so late mornings, he could not sweep, dust, and air the car, in time for Mr. Booth's breakfast. 'It seems you upset his routine.' I demanded to know why I had not been called. My tormentor guessed it was because he himself was asleep in his own berth about this time; then, too, *somebody's* curtains had to be the last to come down, and, so far as he could see, Mr. Booth had had his breakfast when he wanted it and in a well-aired car, too; the porter couldn't call a guest of Mr. Booth's without instructions, and as for any one else who was up early enough — some people thought I should be punished as well as reformed.

'Mr. Booth has appointed tomorrow on the train for the hearing. A sort of Star Chamber trial in more senses than one. You see, you are to be absent.' Mr. Chase grew more sober as he asked if I couldn't 'just leave it to Mr. Booth.'

But that was it! I was guilty. Mr. Booth couldn't be kind to me now without being unkind to Mrs. Foster and Mrs. Baker, and he would never humiliate them. Besides, they outranked me, But the very worst of it was that, if Mr. Booth's decision were partial to me tomorrow, he would topple from his high pedestal and no longer be *Edwin Booth*, and the day I had dreaded from the first of the season would be come for me at last. There it was! Everything was perfectly hopeless and here was Mr. Chase treating it all with levity, passing it off as 'one generation against another.' I didn't think the ladies were fair. They might have warned me! But I suppose they didn't think Regan was fair either, and had smarted under the good times we had out of Regan. But 'Beggars on Horseback' was too much! And why I? If there was one 'Beggar on Horseback,' there were three. 'But,' said Mr. Chase, 'you are the one who broke the camel's — tongue loose.'

I felt myself ill-used, but not enough to forego *Othello*. On this last Denver night all the play meant to me was Iago and Desdemona. Amo would be sympathetic as was Desdemona with Cassio and she would be equally helpless. It was Iago, the cruel one, who would be my judge tomorrow, and never did I so forget our gentle, patient Star in his pet villain! He flung deviltries from him and they were so contagious that he transformed his audience into Iagos. While he was on, nothing was so fascinatingly desirable as to dupe the one who trusted you!

At supper afterwards in the 'David Garrick,' there was much laughter. I suppose I, too, laughed, but I was

268

wondering what had become of Iago. Somewhere in Mr. Booth's mind his Iago was shut in! Well, why not? Wasn't his Hamlet shut in there too, and his Brutus and that delicious player of antics, his Petruchio? When I slipped behind those blue and golden curtains that had disgraced themselves by being the last to come down mornings, I gave them a vicious tug — and felt better.

How time did drag next day! But at last Mr. Magonigle threw open the drawing-room door. Most of those in the car were ostentatiously preoccupied. I was, myself. My eyes were not raised, but out of the corners I saw the procession sweep past me and be ushered within and the door close upon them. Not a head had turned our way, but there was solace in Popper's shoulders. They were too perky for a foreordained defeat of the Chickens.

Ido rushed to me. 'What's up?' As 'I knew nothing,' Amo was asked if she did. Yes, the cat had been let out of the bag in their dressing-rooms. 'They are telling Mr. Booth, we are "Beggars on Horseback."'

'Good Heavens!' from Ido.

Things were not so bad, now that I could air a few epithets. Almost at once, Popper threw the door open again. He blocked the way long enough for us to scatter, if he did look over our heads. They came out as if they were yet listening to Mr. Booth, who was following and seemed to be giving out information. The Star's manner was interested, but did not suggest anything unusual. He must have been saying that he was a poor sleeper, for he was now condemning himself for this failing, yet was hopeless of changing.

'I seldom sleep before three or four. I depend upon the hours between dawn and breakfast for my sleep. The lightest sound awakens me. Making berths! carpet sweepers! opening windows ——!' He was quite sad. He became appealing. He looked directly into my eyes and said, almost sternly, that he disliked to be fault-finding, but there *was* his acting! He knew young creatures were restless in the morning — but would I mind *not* getting up so early?

A pause! I suppose there was humor in this situation, but it was not for me to react to it — had I felt like it, which I did not. I was thankful to be able to say from the bottom of my heart: 'I would not disturb you, Mr. Booth, for worlds.'

Our blessed Popper took charge. 'But, Mr. Booth, you do not quite understand. This young lady is —— she is the last one to get up mornings!'

Mr. Booth turned to his manager for confirmation and got it; he addressed those who had been in conference, as if he were sure of their relief for my guiltlessness. 'You see, it is not she who has disturbed me by getting up too early.' The incident was closed, and Mr. Booth, as if he considered this good news had restored every one's spirits, brought out his pipe and seated himself amidst us, and by his own cheerfulness signified that, as far as he was concerned, 'Beggars on Horseback' might ride to their widely advertised destination.

It was some days after that Mr. Booth asked me

dryly if I noticed that at times he suffered from —
denseness? It might trouble his physician. His eyes
held no smile.

No, I had not noticed *that*, but, if he would forgive
me, now that we were on the subject of his health, at
times I feared he was absent-minded, a little, for he
gave the impression of being on the side of the guilty —
and of course this was not possible.

He remembered an occasion when he might have
given such an impression, but absent-mindedness was
not a symptom of his. The tragedian was looking out
of the car window as he said: 'I should diagnose it as
presence of mind!'

This was the last allusion from any one to the poor
little 'Beggars on Horseback.' The brief thunderstorm,
however, cleared the atmosphere of little hurts and mis-
understandings, and I was so ashamed that every one
helped me to reform. Even the porter let me be the
last to be called 'mornings.'

CHAPTER XXXVI

THE BOOTH-BARRETT COMPANY

As there was everything in an actor's world to confide these last weeks, I had many short afternoon saunters with Mr. Chase, for he said he did not like to talk in the 'David Garrick.' It was 'too sociable.'

I could not help wondering at his need of a confidante at this late day, but he said that the end of the season was more trying to him than all the rest put together. 'For every one is begging for a hint if he is to be reëngaged. This is the time for me to be wary.' So our manager confided that, although Mr. Barrett had reached his decisions, Mr. Booth had not relinquished his privilege of settling matters with his own O.K. 'Things were hanging fire until the conference!' Yes, there was to be a conference — and on a Sunday, in a town that lay midway between the cities in which the two Stars respectively opened on the following Monday night.

'We can make it, and be back in time for our openings. I am to take Mr. Booth over to meet Mr. Barrett next Sunday, and everything will then be settled.'

The conference came and went. In my memory was locked the completed personnel of the Booth-Barrett Company for the season of 1887–88. Not one of the Booth ladies was to be reëngaged. There was to be a private car, but only the two Stars were to travel in it. It was further confided that Mr. Barrett had urged his theatre project, but to these pleadings his partner had replied in tones that had a ring of finality; that Mr. Barrett, undaunted, was again filling his letters with eager arguments for his heart's desire, yet his partner's sole response was, 'Get thee behind me, Satan.'

I was sure Mr. Barrett could materialize his dream. Was the money not all pledged? He would persuade Mr. Booth, when they were constantly together. But something more obstructive than Mr. Booth's reluctance was pressing onward as an avalanche to crush this great 'dream.' To carry it out and then carry on — Mr. Barrett's health was needed, and, alas, his health was already undermined. He did not know it. In Lawrence Barrett's death, when he was only fifty-three, the *Perfect Theatre* was lost to the American Stage.

The regular season ended in Kansas City, but at once began the supplementary season of six weeks. So we wended our way East, stopping overnight in New York that Mr. Booth might contribute an act of *Hamlet* for the matineé benefit for Mr. Couldock at Wallack's Theatre.

One by one Mr. Booth killed off his heroes for the last time this season, until the repertoire dwindled to *Hamlet* and *Richelieu*. My eyes were often red when I returned to the car for supper, for I did not miss one death scene in the few precious nights that were left to me. I gave my feelings full play and thought myself unstrung, yet the instant Mr. Booth appeared, cheerful, expectant — as if he had never heard of tragic heroes — I was ready for the merry game. The present was unsurpassable — pooh for any future! Mr. Booth and Mr. Barrett and the repertoire of poems would so soon be mine again. Was not Mr. Barrett assuring me only three years of society plays would be asked of me, and did I not hear Mr. Chase saying in the most every-dayish tones — beyond contradiction — 'Why, you'll be running into us all the time, and any off night you get hold of, there'll always be seats up my sleeve for you.' The night I went in front to see Mr. Booth take his Iago curtain calls for the last time, Mr. Chase warned: 'If you lose your head over Mr. Booth's acting tonight and applaud, and he catches you at it — how will you feel after all he has said about being dragged out to be approved of — by — what was it?'

'Unripe judgment! I'll try not to applaud.'

I did try, but I forgot.

Again I watched the Olympian make his stately bow, and again wondered at the contrast of this grave being to — his own Iago, for instance. It did not seem possible they could be the same man. When the house darkened and the warning bell sounded, my heart was pounding as upon a first night. After forty weeks of daily seeing Mr. Booth on and off the stage, I blushed in the dark at my own silly words to Mr. Barrett that I didn't want Mr. Booth to become *a man* to me, and here he was — at the very tag-end of the season poised atop that pedestal without a thought or a care for his dizzy heights.

There were long jumps on our way East and short runs, but our daytime travel hours were as ciphers

274

without rims, for we beguiled **Mr.** Booth into reminiscing. These were the days of stories of Booth's Theatre and of the Lyceum Theatre that Henry Irving had made the leading playhouse in the English-speaking world.

Before Henry Irving had 'arrived,' even in the provinces, Mr. Booth was offered control of the Lyceum by his brother-in-law, John Sleeper Clark, who had an option on the lease. There was an ingenious plan for interchange of casts from Booth's Theatre. And foreign artists were to come to Booth's while Mr. Booth played in London.

'I should have had longer runs by this arrangement, more profits without much more cost. Once the Lyceum were running, the extra labor for myself would not have been beyond a bearing point. There were already some bids for the Star system end of the project.'

We were too familiar with Mr. Booth's tender affection, from boyhood up, for his brother-in-law, not to realize the sentimental value to him of this partnership. He said that the scheme could not help be enticing to an American tragedian. His taste, his art, his judgment would have practically guided the English-speaking stage; that the risk — as theatre risks go — was nothing to speak of; that every one expected him to accept; that he believed, even today, with longer runs — 'for of course I should have taken only tried successes to London' — that the risk would not have been 'more than I usually face, but ——!!'

We were all worked up over it! It was startling!

fascinating! Oh, why had he not taken over the Lyceum?

Mr. Booth said that he did not know! 'It was opportunity! With good management ——! There it is in a nutshell! I am an actor, not a manager. I wanted the Lyceum — but I could not decide — and in the mean time, some one else did.'

Mama Baker said: 'Yes, I know, Mr. Bateman, and he engaged an unknown provincial actor for his daughter Bella's company — whose name was *Henry Irving*.

Mrs. Foster then said, with oracular intonations: 'Had you taken the Lyceum Theatre, Mr. Booth, there would not have been a Henry Irving.'

What would Mr. Booth say to this? Some one was always throwing bombs. Up to now these — in the Star's presence at least — were friendly ones filled with rosy blossoms to decorate our reflections, but *this* bomb! 'Had you taken the Lyceum, there would not have been a Henry Irving,' came too close to a left-open trapdoor on a dark stage directly in Mr. Booth's path. There were critics and followers who saw in the great English actor Edwin Booth's only rival. Mr. Booth knew that we knew this — and here was Mrs. Foster with a smile on her lips implying, nay asserting, that the American tragedian had once held the career of Henry Irving in the hollow of his hand. My imagination soared. I forgot this past was deader than a doornail. It was such an intriguing might-have-been that it charged the moment with situation.

Then Mr. Booth made me feel as 'mean as pussly'; he shot the 'situation' to pieces. There was nothing to trust us with; he made it quite plain no thought of his upon Henry Irving needed to be guarded.

'I dare say Irving would have had a harder — a longer — climb of it. He himself spoke of this to me upon several occasions, and I reminded him there is always more than one road to Rome. Irving might perhaps have taken a thornier path, but it would have led him where he is today, of course. When I am criticised by friends' — he lifted that expressive eyebrow — 'for vacillation, and losing the Lyceum in consequence, I congratulate myself upon possessing this trait, since through my hesitancy our theatre gained a great artist — sooner. A pleasant feeling steals over me when I reflect that by keeping our super-productions at Booth's Theatre, and not transplanting them to the Lyceum stage, Irving's opportunity came — almost at once.

Having beguiled Mr. Booth into the Lyceum, we were not willing he should leave it. We coaxed for Lyceum stories. He said he was glad to gratify us, as the engagement had been rich in pleasure for him.

The importance of dress rehearsals came home to him when for this final rehearsal Mr. Irving, failing to make up as Othello, gauged his make-up incorrectly on the opening night. That Mr. Booth considered dress rehearsals to be important surprised me, for there had not been a call for one the entire season. He explained that at Booth's Theatre dress rehearsals were his custom; that he designed or supervised scenery, lighting, costumes, properties; that in his own theatre he passed upon all 'effects.'

'Irving was the only one in the cast who did not make

up for the dress rehearsal, and on the opening night his face was too black. Irving afterwards said to me he had learned his lesson not to trust the lights in his dressing-room, for there his face was the shade he intended it to be; the borders darkened it.'

When we asked why Mr. Irving had not made up at the dress rehearsal, Mr. Booth replied: 'Irving did not take the time. His mind was on the production as a whole.'

While he was on the subject of make-up, Mr. Booth revealed that he did look his company over even if his support failed to realize this, but it was not necessary to inspect older actors who had previously gone on with him, and most of them had, at some time. I must have made his heart sink if he took my Bloody Apparition make-up as a sample of what was to come! No wonder he sent for me on the first night of Jessica!

By this time there was little new for us to hear of *Miss Terry* from Mr. Booth's lips. Often he had spoken of her acting as 'bewitching, exquisite, delicate in method, of subtle humor and even subtler pathos.' He said that her Desdemona was the girl he himself saw when burning his midnight oil over Othello; that she made the tragedy sublime. Miss Ellen Terry, in her 'Life,' writes of the Booth guest engagement at the Lyceum Theatre. She prefers the Irving Iago to the Edwin Booth Iago. She delightfully gives her reasons. Her book is not at hand, but Miss Terry conveys the idea that Sir Henry was Satanic, while Mr. Booth did not equally suggest this diabolical ingredient in his appearance and manner.

278

THE BOOTH-BARRETT COMPANY

Miss Terry is high authority — but so is Edwin Booth.

Any one who saw Sir Henry as Mephisto will credit easily that the Irving Iago was more Mephistophelian in appearance than Edwin Booth's Iago. But is Iago supposed to look devilish? No one in the play suspects him until the plot winds up. Not until his fiendish work is done is he called a villain.

During this season I had tastes, but not opinions. My unformed mind was blotting-paper to absorb Mr. Booth's impressions. Yet even I perceived a justness in Frank Mayo's criticism that Edwin Booth's Iago was inartistic — standard though it was! Mr. Mayo backed up his position with reasons which I hoped would entertain Mr. Booth. They did.

'He says your Iago is inartistic!'

'Did Mayo say why?'

'Because you are too good-looking as Iago, Mr. Booth. No new husband who is not a born fool would select such a guardian to escort and protect his young bride — on a long sea voyage with sunsets and Italian moonlights, and he himself far away. Then, besides, Mr. Mayo emphasized that every one in the play calls Iago honest.'

'Do I look unhonest?'

'Mr. Mayo says no good-looking, graceful man is ever spoken of as honest. Any other adjective almost, but not honest. When there is no adjective people can think of to apply to a man except honest — they mean he is close to being a fool. I suppose he meant not shrewd enough to be dishonest. That's why every one trusts Iago and calls him honest. Mr. Mayo says Iago should be fat; a blond; almost lazy; even perspiring! No romantic girl would, of course, fall in love with *that* type, and a smart, unscrupulous man could easily be of this type.'

I thought Amo, at the very notion of a perspiring Iago, would have a fit.

Mr. Booth, without even lifting his eyebrow, said: 'Some prefer a Hamlet fat and scant of breath. Do you?'

'But, Mr. Booth, Hamlet is not chosen to be Ophelia's guardian! She is warned against Hamlet.'

'"Look to it." You are right!'

'But nobody warns Desdemona or Othello against Iago! Doesn't every one think him incapable of mischief? The plain truth is, Mr. Booth, your Iago does not have the chaperon look.'

Mr. Booth smoked a puff or two, then said: 'I think Mayo named his son for me.' His manner implied this act in itself was proof of mental derangement and would account for his fat Iago. 'Edwin F. Mayo. Edwin for me; F — Frank — for himself.'

'No, Mr. Booth, you said this before, and I asked Mr. Mayo. He named his son for Edwin Forrest.'

'Ah!' — the tone conceding there was hope then of the Mayo's recovery, after all.

When Mr. Booth decided I had been teased long enough, he gave us some charming Mayo anecdotes and reminded us that this fine artist had been engaged for Booth's Theatre.

THE BOOTH-BARRETT COMPANY

While yet stories of the Lyceum Theatre held us enthralled, Mr. Booth recalled 'one of the desperately trying moments of my life' — 'When only Irving's fine breeding saved me from crushing embarrassment.'

'When playing at the Lyceum, I received a letter from Mrs. Irving asking for three seats for herself and her two sons. The letter was peculiarly worded. I puzzled over it. It permitted a double meaning. The writer phrased it: 'I wish to bring my sons to see you so they may see *what great acting is*.' I read a mere bit of gracious compliment to myself into Mrs. Irving's note; naturally, I knew what she meant, but on the surface the note seemed to say that the writer considered that up to now her sons had not seen great acting.'

Mr. Booth said he could not resist a chuckle over that unconscious *double entendre*. He laid the note on his dressing-table to later note its address; he was puzzled, too. Why should he be asked for a box by Mrs. Irving in her husband's theatre? While he was making up, the dresser announced Mr. Irving, who walked at once to the dressing-table to put a question of immediate importance to his guest co-star, and his eyes lighted on the letter.

'Ah, Mrs. Irving!' — pleasantly. Mr. Booth would not have his most considerate associate read that seeming slur on his acting — and yet — there was nothing between the husband's mortification and his own discomfiture but his host's breeding. Mr. Booth trusted to this breeding.

'I picked up the letter and gave it to Irving. It was an uncomfortable moment for me — but it passed harmlessly, for Irving refused to read his wife's letter.

'"Oh, no," he said lightly as if he were already forgetting its existence — "oh, no!"'

Mr. Booth laid the letter down, acting the rôle of a man thinking of other things, and one who realized that Mr. Irving's mind was also on other things, but the mind of one of them was not — and the letter was destroyed at the first opportunity.

The two first gentlemen of the English-speaking stage came rather well out of this bit of intimate drama.

CHAPTER XXXVII

THE CHICKENS IN 'RICHELIEU'

BACK in Kansas City, Mr. Chase had confided he was booking his Star for some one-night stands on the last two weeks of the supplementary season. He read from a letter in which one manager offered one hundred per cent 'to secure Booth.' 'All I want out of it is to be able to say Booth played my theatre.' Mr. Chase explained: 'None of them are getting real profits. They are glad of the publicity. Ninety per cent and up, right along. Ninety-eight and ninety-nine.' If ever a manager was satisfied with his business outlook, it was Mr. Chase.

One hundred per cent staggered me so I forgot etiquette and asked, before I knew it, what we were to do on the one-night stands. Would he please forgive my indiscretion? I really had not asked one question on the 'business' before. He laughed and admitted this was true. 'But why should you? Don't I tell you everything as we go along? We do *Hamlet* the last two weeks.'

'I should want *Hamlet* if I were a theatre manager.'

'They all want *Hamlet*.'

Then, one day, when the Star was admitting how much diversion and relaxation he was getting out of the present season, I said, without a hope of its coming true — 'Wouldn't it be wonderful, Mr. Booth, if you did *Richelieu* for the one-night stands?'

No 'heavy ladies' went on in *Richelieu*, so this bill held possibilities for the Chickens that *Hamlet* did not offer — and Mr. Booth saw these opportunities at once, but he made no reply and smoked on. I was relieved he did not answer. Silence was part of his form with us. Never had he scolded and hardly ever praised. Whatever his opinion of us might be, it was shaped by now, and not likely to change in the few weeks left to us. I felt so confident he would pass by my idle speech that I was startled when he said, after a pause, 'I will think it over.' It had been on my part no more than a half sigh for the moon — and who expects the moon to tumble into one's arms because of a foolish hankering after it for a moment or so? We came into Mr. Booth's presence sure of his indulgence. One could fling hopes and wishes and wonderings about; toss them in a blanket. He knew our reckless phrases were mere breeze wisps, even if they began — 'Wouldn't it be wonderful ——' We could say anything before Mr. Booth if we did not touch on himself or ourselves.

Shadows fell upon the hitherto unruffled spirit of our manager, for his Star suddenly decided to substitute *Richelieu* for the last two weeks. He said, if Mr. Booth really preferred *Richelieu*, he was satisfied, of course — but he couldn't understand it, because *Hamlet* had been the Star's own suggestion. 'You have no idea what I am up against. They all want *Hamlet*.'

Mr. Chase wished he knew who had interfered at the last moment — with the printing all sent out — and then memories of his own machinations intruded. He gave me a searching look under which I failed to stand up. 'So you are at the bottom of this?'

I tried to persuade him his was a case of guilty conscience; that he had made use of me so often to contrive against his Star that now he was suspicious Mr. Booth might be retaliating in kind, but the manager had seen his light. 'Who knows it?'

He was assured that none but Mr. Booth even imagined this audacious secret.

'It's all right if it's just Mr. Booth. He's like a boy putting this over on me ——'

'He's getting even with you, Mr. Chase.'

In due time was posted the announcement that *Hamlet* was dropped and *Richelieu* substituted. On the surface, it did not mean much to the company, but underneath was the edict that Mr. Barron, Mrs. Foster, and Mrs. Baker were to be left behind in New York. Mr. Barron, they said, was thankful to join his family two weeks earlier on full pay. How would the ladies take it? This was the rub. Would they feel nothing worse could happen to them? To our surprise and my own relief, Mrs. Baker and Mrs. Foster said they had dreaded those one-night stands in hot weather — for the season was getting late — and now they would be resting in comfort and the ghost would be walking just the same. We were speechless when they thanked Mr. Booth for this latest expression of his kindness. I did my best for my own sake to believe them, but each day I felt more guilty, for no argument could convince me any sane woman on earth would cheerfully forgo two weeks of Edwin Booth in his private car.

BEHIND THE SCENES WITH BOOTH

There was the night in New York after the Couldock Benefit! I went behind at Niblo's where Mr. Barrett was playing. He congratulated me at once for being in the *Richelieu* cast. His manner was casual enough, but his smile was crammed with meaning as he said: 'I hear the change of bill was made suddenly. I am not surprised. The bill for these last two weeks was bound to be *Richelieu*.' He meant me to know he knew. Discipline went by default, however. Was not the season so nearly over? Had he not tucked me out of harm's way for months to come? Since he could afford to be merciful, Mr. Barrett gave way to a hearty laugh. He told me to stand by, for Mr. Booth was coming behind. When Mr. Booth left his box, Miss Gale was presented. She was looking most lovely, but was awed speechless and could do nothing but gaze upon the genius, who slipped quickly into his shell, like the Mr. Booth of the first of the season.

We left New York the next day at noon. Mrs. Baker and Mrs. Foster came to the train to say their farewells in the 'David Garrick.' Mr. Booth had arranged for a visit in the car for the Misses Magonigle, his two nieces, Popper's daughters. When they said 'Uncle,' I almost gasped. It was like hearing Shakespeare or Goethe, or even Jove, called 'Uncle.' They were so gentle and appealing that one thought of sweet peas. I wondered if the girl wife of Mr. Booth's youth had this same expression. He was sombre and seemed to be studying these flower-like faces. The Chickens tried to efface themselves and go out on the platform, but Mr. Booth would not permit it. He chatted for his nieces and asked questions of them, but seemed to be shy even with them. Mr. Booth gave a little book to Mama Baker. 'It was my father's.' I was told when she opened it a check lay between its leaves. Then Popper announced it was good-bye time, and they were all — gone.

Mr. Magonigle seemed to be drooping. It was evident he needed to be tormented into a gayer mood, so we asked what we should do now for chaperons, and he brightened at once and fixed us with eyes that he meant to be baleful, but which were only twinkly, and said that *he* was here and would be on the job — and he was, to his own amusement and to his brother-in-law's and ours.

The gayety of these last two weeks was intangible but not elusive. It was always there to elate the Chickens with their rare good fortune. When we awoke in the morning, we had no fear Mr. Booth's mood might have changed overnight. He came to the breakfast table ready for merry quips — his own chiefly; but he made us believe we answered them in humorous kind. There was never an overflow of youthful spirits — even if we re-accumulated ardor while we slept, to throw into each new day; even though our reverent awe of Mr. Booth had become honeycombed with his own enjoyment of an almost imagined game — for we did not forget, not for an instant, that monkey-shines delighted him not — no, nor cheerful idiotics either.

Mr. Booth declared he had misnamed the Chickens. We were *owlets*. Who could have wanted to pack off to bed these wonderful nights with Mr. Booth saying he had forgotten what fatigue was like and that he never felt less like sleeping. It was one 'final' smoke after another. Even Mr. Chase and Popper sat up for them. Mr. Booth made no sign that two of the group insisted — to every one but himself — they were in love with the Star. I suppose he had accustomed himself to such things for years and may have felt that young ladies, who in his presence remained natural and sweet, and were entertaining in spite of their *tender passion*, deserved his respect.[1]

There were times when Mr. Booth needed the 'David Garrick,' and then we sought out the Coney Island localities of the town, had our tin-types taken and the rest of it. At night we rode in Mr. Booth's carriage either to the hotel or to the car. It did seem that there were carriages for every occasion. On one drive Mr. Booth reproached himself that he had not arranged a visit in Newport.

'We may have another month of this. It is like me not to think of things in time, if you would come to Newport ——?'

We knew it would not do, but there was one Chicken who had ecstatic spasms. Did not Mr. Booth make himself believe he wanted us for another whole month? It was such a delightful O.K. to my timid suggestion of the first supper invitation way back in Bay City, during our second week of the season. Many of his little speeches were broken to say, 'If I had thought in time — I should have my Chickens for another month.'

[1] For these last One-Night Stands, on very short runs, the entire company travelled in the 'David Garrick.'

CHAPTER XXXVIII

MR. BOOTH BURLESQUES A PART

ON the closing night, Mr. Booth sprang a surprise. He named his impromptu a little wind-up for the Chickens. For once the usually guilty ones were innocent if one discounts their proper appreciation of this unlooked-for good fortune. It was the *house* that was to blame.

Mr. Booth said he played that night to the coldest audience of his career. I said they sat out there like bumps on a log. Mr. Chase said it was all because they wanted *Hamlet*. He was rather special about the change of bill being responsible (for my ear alone); so I sniffed that this was not reasonable, for the other towns had hankered after *Hamlet*, too, but in spite of their disappointment had accepted *Richelieu* enthusiastically. Far from me to resent that audience for what it did or did not. I blessed those arctic ones out there. Did not Edwin Booth because of them release his genius for comet-flights in strange skies — the very strangest his versatile talents were ever permitted to illuminate?

When Amo came down from her scene with *Richelieu*, Ido asked why she was 'laughing.'

'Oh, Kitto — Ido — his faces! He turned his back to the audience and — made faces at me! I thought I should die.' She could tell no more; she had to change.

As I mounted the stairs, my hopes ran high. I, too, might have Mr. Booth making faces at me. Then came a damper — suppose that audience had warmed up by now. It would be like Mr. Booth to be sorry for them. But, oh joy! the stage manager savagely whispered: 'They are asleep out there. I never saw or heard anything like it.' Soon after I was on, Mr. Booth (entirely changing the business) rose with dignity, waved me upstage, grandly swept past me down to the footlights, turned his back to the audience, stood there, and then — I knew it was coming, but that did not help. The reputedly melancholy tragedian began a series of diabolical grimaces that sculptors of gargoyles would have given their souls to model. One followed another — no two alike. He interrupted the gargoyles for serious acting — when he had to — now and then, for the play's sake. These reprieves were springes to catch woodcock — just to give himself time to observe whether I were holding out or if he must turn off the current to save my life. Oh, how grateful I was to Mr. Barrett for training me to stand by my scenes as if they were guns in battle. Several times over the Star manœuvred me into position where I was exposed and he protected, until I longed for François to come on.

With François's entrance Mr. Booth gave the audience another chance. His acting became spirited, and he sent his line which audiences always seemed to be waiting for, 'In the lexicon of youth, which Fate reserves for a bright manhood, there is no such word as fail!' — like a rocket in the dark — and it dropped back to earth like — Why say it? There was not a hand. It made me think of going on for farces in tombs, playing to coffins. When the curtain fell, there was a feeble effort made to get it to go up again, but the Star did not wait. He detained me to warn me with a snap of his jaws akin to Iago: 'If they do not rise to the Curse of Rome — I shall burlesque the rest of the play. Be up for it.'

The Curse of Rome came. There may have been a 'polite response,' but compared with what we were accustomed to it was — to make use of the Star's pet expression — 'a cipher without a rim.' We three whom he had let into his very open secret held our breath. Would Edwin Booth actually turn his great Cardinal into a monkey on a stick? It was too much to hope for, yet he had made his threat with something very like unholy joy.

When Mr. Booth poked fun at himself, in his looking-backward version of the San Francisco Fire Boy, it was skirmish to battle beside his satire of Richelieu. To-night he was burlesquing one of his greatest rôles on an actual stage before an audience that was taking him seriously — the very foundation he needed — and was supported by his own company also taking him seriously. Amo and Ido, being on the stage with him, at attention, suffered more than I, but my handkerchief was stuffed in my mouth, for the stage manager was patrolling the wings.

Mr. Booth's gargoyles had but awakened the snake. The serpent's darting sting came — as he had warned — right after the Curse of Rome. He then tossed his tragic art in the flames and I saw it come through the fire, pure gold. It was Edwin Booth, not a lesser, who caricatured his Richelieu. That ruthless satire is yet vivid, and the impression clings that it was not intended for mere clowning in a great rôle, but rather that there was now seeping to the surface the sum total of this artist's sufferings from poor supports in his whole career; that the long-tortured actor was not only remembering the *dogans*[1] stingy managements had foisted upon him, but was now boiling all this down to its last essence, and was, for once, *letting off*. Mr. Booth was too gloriously pleased with himself not to have been evening things up.

Is the record of Edwin Booth's acting complete that does not include an analytical tribute to his talent for satire, caricature, and burlesque? I glory that mine was the privilege to see this extraordinary display of his many-sided art, but only a *critic* should attempt the description. I pass it by.

When the final curtain was rung down and Mr. Chase, Mr. Magonigle, and myself were waiting for those who were dressing, our manager said he had not realized that the tragedian could be so full of the Old Nick. Popper was not surprised, not he! Mr. Booth bade us pile into his carriage and admitted everything. Upon his acting, for once he let us rave and even laughed (if it was the most unvocalized laugh I ever heard) when he was called a gargoyle.

Mr. Chase arranged for a drive this last Sunday, but left himself and Popper out. 'We are too busy. Mr. Booth and the three of you may have the last outing to yourselves.'

About the middle of the afternoon the 'David Garrick' was to carry us to Worcester, and from there

[1] Mr. Booth to his intimates named incompetent actors *dogans*.

Mr. Booth would travel alone to Boston. The company under the care of Mr. Chase was to return to New York. Happily for us — or it may have been by design — Mr. Booth's train left first, so we were there to see him off.

The intervening hours were winged. It was a gentle, whimsical host who on this last drive insisted upon condemning himself again for not having arranged for our Boothden visit. He clung to his regret that we were not to be with him for another month, when it might so easily have been accomplished if he had given us time.

Richelieu as a topic was not avoided, but it was not encouraged. Mr. Booth's eyes twinkled as if it were difficult not to laugh, but that he had resolved, after sleeping on it, that silence was golden. When it was said to him, 'It was high to high fortune for us, Mr. Booth, for you may never play *Richelieu* — like that — again. Do you think you will — ever?' He thought it more than likely he never should — ever! And then we ventured too near the holy of holies! We trespassed — even to the steps of the throne.

'If the bill had been *Hamlet* — you would not have ——?'

He gave us no time to finish. He sat up and rigidly straight. He was for a few seconds almost fierce.

Part of the time of that last drive, Mr. Booth devoted to appealing to us not to desecrate the Shakespeare plays. He implored us to realize what our heritage was — not to forget what a noble thing these great poems made of our profession.

I think taking it all in all this was — almost — our most cheerful, our merriest drive.

CHAPTER XXXIX

HOW WE SAID GOOD-BYE

FOR days past Mr. Chase had been worried. He said something superfine hung heavy over his head. Had it merely been *fine*, he could have handled it without a care, but when the *superfine* was involved, one needed to watch one's step. At length he asked did I think Amo and Ido were yet in love with Mr. Booth.

What did *he* think?

'Oh, I don't know what to think. I know they *say* they are — both of them.'

'Do they say this to you?'

'I think they say it to anybody who will listen.'

'Not to Mr. Booth, though.'

He admitted they had not lisped it to the Star. 'Mr. Booth says, if it had not been poured into his ears by others, he himself should not even have suspected it, and I don't believe he takes stock in it any more.'

'Who told him, in the first place?'

'I did, and I am sorry. I did not understand the situation the first few weeks. I was trying to shield Mr. Booth — in case they lost their heads — but they have not done so. But they are bound to make scenes, they both declare, when it's good-bye time. Something has got to be done about it.'

'Oh, Mr. Chase, they are just teasing you. Don't let them!'

HOW WE SAID GOOD-BYE

He hoped it was teasing. 'Haven't they said anything to you?'

'Of course. They both swear they'll disgrace themselves, but they won't.'

'I have an idea. Couldn't you fix up a little speech or two for them? If they have something learned by heart to say, they will come to the good-bye as if they were acting a scene. I think everything will be all right — in that case.'

I tried to convince him they could do it better alone, but as I did believe it would be a help to them to have their good-byes by heart, I promised to talk it over with them.

'I'm depending on you. You are so cool-headed!'

'Heavens! If things go wrong, please do not blame me!'

'But I shall! Now, for Mr. Booth's sake do something about it, for you know it may be your last chance ever again to do anything for him.'

The Chickens — the three of them — took this good-bye situation seriously. The two who bewailed their anticipated disgrace loved to talk it over. They would give anything to do and say the right thing to Mr. Booth.

Ido said that she had been living in another world. She didn't know how she should 'stand it' to go back again. It wasn't the luxury of it, no, nor how good Mr. Booth had been — she knew that couldn't go on; but it was just Mr. Booth himself, and she wasn't in love with him — hadn't been for a long time, but she didn't know how she could put up with ordinary people any more — and she should never see him again!

'You and Amo are going back to your lovely homes, but it's different with me. I don't want to trouble Mr. Booth when I say good-bye, but I know I shall do something crazy.'

We changed cars at Worcester. Here the 'David Garrick' was switched into storage. Our departing Star was now standing by the steps of his Boston Pullman with the ladies near him and the actors withdrawn farther down the platform.

Mr. Booth walked to them, alone, and chatted with them a few moments. Whatever he said to them made them happy, for all were smiling, even jesting.

When Mr. Booth returned to the Pullman steps, Mr. Chase and Popper stood on either side of him. He slipped an envelope into his brother-in-law's hand. 'A little commission if you will attend to it?' Of course this was another gift of a check. And then — Mr. Booth spoke to us! The moment had come when my sex was on trial.

It was an unsmiling Edwin Booth who put out his hand to Amo. When his expression was both unsmiling and sweet, then it was most dangerous. Poor Amo! He could not have made it harder for her.

She came to Mr. Booth, took his outstretched hand, met his serious eyes with her own earnest ones. She was poised; she was charming, and she spoke with sincerity and with feeling.

'I fear, Mr. Booth, I have not let you see how much I appreciate your patience with me as an actress, your inspiration on the stage, and your hospitality in the

"David Garrick." All my life I shall look back to this season. I have had the honor to support you and I hope I may be fortunate enough to be professionally associated with you again; but, if not, I shall always have your kindness for my brightest memory. Good-bye.' She let go his hand, smiled a lovely, genuine smile, and stepped back — a dignified young lady. Mr. Booth's eyes shone with his pride in her — and then he extended his hand to Ido.

Ido stepped up to him impulsively.

'Oh, Mr. Booth, it's been too wonderful for anything! I can't thank you, but you do know, don't you? Good-bye.' She blushed the tiniest bit, and her voice had a catch in it, but she smiled brightly. Never had she been more girlish nor darling, with her blush and her smile and the catch in her voice. It was just right.

Mr. Booth smiled back quite as brightly, and I know he was hoping Mr. Chase was ashamed of himself for having accused two perfectly innocent young ladies of the folly of falling in love with him. He exonerated them completely.

Up to this very second I had not once thought of my own good-bye. I had not the faintest notion of what I might say. Every one was sure it didn't matter about me. I was so cool-headed.

Mr. Booth held out his hand to me. I took it. And then — mercy — I was sobbing and couldn't stop — and didn't care who saw me!!

'All aboard!'

Mr. Booth mounted the steps. He stood on the platform, his hat off. The actors cheered him lustily as long

as he could hear and see them. We waved our handker-
chiefs! Mr. Chase and Popper stood bareheaded, as if in
salute. No one laughed at me, or teased me. I did not
try to hide that I was crying. It would have been use-
less. The train was no longer in sight. Mr. Chase said
there were tears in Mr. Booth's eyes. I did not see them.

It was Popper who, squaring his shoulders, held forth;
'If you, child, hadn't put your pride in your pocket and
let Mr. Booth realize that you were fond of him — after
all he has done for you — for the three of you — I'd
never have got over it!'

On the way back to New York, Mr. Chase teased me
for the last time. 'Still waters!'

I told him to rub it in. I could already see how ridiculous those tears were after all those 'cool heads' they
had heaped on me.

Mr. Chase became thoughtful. 'You used to tell me
you were afraid every morning that this was the day
Mr. Booth would do something you would be sorry for,
and at night you'd say, one more day has gone and he
has not made me sorry.'

'I think that is why I cried. I shall not see another
perfect human being very soon.'

'You believe Mr. Booth is perfect?'

'I don't suppose he was born perfect. He is fifty-four.
He always speaks as if his life had been a fight with
himself — but those fights were over before this season.'

'Yes.' After a while he laughed a little. 'There's one
town he won't ever play again!'

CHAPTER XL

WHEN A. M. Palmer produced *Partners* at his Madison Square Theatre I was of the cast, and when *Captain Swift* followed in which Maurice Barrymore shone, Mr. Palmer had left over enough talent on his salary list to present *Partners* in various theatres. Once in a while there was an idle week, and to my own great good fortune one of these coincided with the New York engagement of the Booth-Barrett combination.

The dear and generous-minded Mrs. Le Moyne had given me a 'friendly tip' which she said was imperative for an actress to observe.

'Choose your pose — then stick to it.'

I had chosen the *sophisticated*, but had not yet succeeded in screwing it to the sticking place.

Arrayed in my pet finery of black velvet and furs of Russian lynx — and sage-green kid gloves, a telling touch — I sallied forth to meet my 'best friends.' I fondly believed I looked the part, but I was far too happy to be *going home* not to have quakings over keeping up my pose before the very two whom I was most eager to impress. Unsensing, like a fluttering butterfly among the last roses of summer, that gardens sink deep under winter snows, I felt no nip of frost tonight. Mr. Barrett was not yet stricken; Mr. Booth was not 'patiently waiting' in that room of hallowed memory, which remains undisturbed in The Players.

BEHIND THE SCENES WITH BOOTH

A beaming Garry took me in charge, and I was so glad to be back that my sophisticated pose was endangered, but it was on full blast when I entered Mr. Barrett's dressing-room. Even his delight in it did not phase me — not all at once.

'Look at her, Garry. She has come to dazzle us with her *grande dame*-ness! Tell Mr. Booth there is a strange lady here to see him. Be sure you say a *very* strange lady. You may sit down, for Mr. Booth does not take to strangers, so there is time for a visit with me.'

Garry returned bearing the tidings that Mr. Booth was awaiting me in his dressing-room. The grinning one was again despatched to announce that there had been a mistake, that Mr. Booth did not know this lady. An even more grinning messenger came back to say Mr. Booth asked for the honor of an introduction — and he would be waiting in his dressing-room when he came off. The game between the tragedians was on, and all to make happy one whom they knew to be so homesick for them both.

When Mr. Barrett was called to the stage, he said I was not to leave the room while he was gone, but the look he gave me showed he was not expecting to be obeyed. As soon as Mr. Barrett was on the stage, I rushed to Mr. Booth. He stood laughing his silent laugh just as if I had been going on with him yesterday. To my sophisticated toilet, as well as the appeal of my pose, he remained impervious. I was yet one of his Chickens. No welcome was given me. Why was one needed? I belonged. And how happy I was that he was the same Mr. Booth who always saw through me at once. When he led me to Mr. Barrett, I had so forgotten my pose that I was startled to hear the latter playfully protest: 'We have to put her in her place, Mr. Booth. Flaunting a woman of the world before us — with the marks of the nursery on her yet!'

Mr. Booth turned his glowing eyes indulgently upon me. To Mr. Barrett's amusement, my pose had evaporated. It was the old story. No one could be artificial in Edwin Booth's presence. It was good to see these friends standing side by side. I knew I should not forget this picture. I left the theatre in the gladdest of moods, but with Mr. Chase's old question tossing about in my thoughts. Which is the greater friend — the one who inspires or the one who serves?

Far away on the Great Lakes I read in the 'Detroit Free Press' of the engagement of Booth and Modjeska at the Detroit Opera House for the last three nights of this very week. I travelled home by rail without loss of an unnecessary hour.

I arrived the next morning at the Russell House on actor time — eleven o'clock — and sent up my card. As if the mere attempt to come into Mr. Booth's presence were magic enough to bring the past to life, a single step over the threshold of a prosaic Detroit hotel took me back to the romance of Golden Gate drives, of *Hamlet* openings, departures for Monterey in the 'David Garrick,' of a special performance of *Othello* — all my very own; of adventures piled up mountain high — impossible and true — for here in the Russell House Ladies' Parlor was Sophie of the Baldwin Theatre!

She rushed upon me and cried out how glad she was to see me!

Yes, she was dressing Madame Modjeska and adored her.

'They showed us your picture in a photo gallery yesterday, and I told Madame you were an old friend and that Detroit was your home and perhaps you would be here — and Madame is so sorry for you.'

'But why?'

'Because I told her all about how Mr. Booth used to drive in San Francisco. I told her of the Hamlet wig, and that the ladies went for a week to Monterey with him. She could hardly believe it. He never does anything like that now. Madame is so interested, but she hopes you won't feel hurt.'

'Hurt ——?'

'If Mr. Booth doesn't see you.'

'Not see me? Oh, Sophie!'

'It won't be personal! Mr. Booth doesn't see Madame to visit with her sometimes for weeks. He has changed!'

Mr. Booth changed! I did not quite know what this meant! Mr. Chase had not said Mr. Booth was changed. But then he would not in any case. That I should call upon the Star was too much a forgone conclusion to need mentioning. I listened to Sophie, who was doing her best to keep me from being hurt — and by Mr. Booth. The thought of his hurting any one's feelings made me want to laugh. I had taken such a hard journey to see him. That didn't matter. But, he, actually in Detroit — and I not to speak with him, if only for a moment! It just couldn't be! I asked after Madame Modjeska's health, with my thoughts on the bell-boy and my eyes on the door through which he should come!

And then he brought his message — ·Mr. Booth will see you!'

'There! I knew it! Oh, I am so glad!' and Sophie sped off with her news!

Mr. Booth's suite was one flight up near the elevator. The boy indicated a wide-open door and went his way. I knocked. There was no one in the sunny parlor, nor did any one appear when I knocked again. It must be the wrong room. I'd ask the elevator boy — and then, from the hall outside of the door, a hand gently touched my arm — and there in the corridor — stood Mr. Booth! Changed? No, he was the same Mr. Booth.

He plunged into an explanation with the old, half-amused-at-himself, half-seriously-defending-himself manner that I knew so well!

'Oh, Kitty! I am so relieved! After I sent the boy away to bring you up, it came over me — suppose it is not she! It might have been, you know, another Miss Molony. My child, next time write a message I can't mistake. Put "David Garrick" on your card. I hid in an empty room down the hall where I could watch the elevator — to see if it were really you. And it *is you*.' For the first time he smiled.

'Come in, and I will make myself comfortable.' It did me good to see him whimsically raise one eyebrow. Changed! No, indeed!

'Is it rare discernment to suspect that making your-self comfortable means you will smoke, Mr. Booth?'

'So, you are seeing churches by daylight yet. Will you share my three o'clock dinner?'

It was not much more than eleven. By three he might be tired! Oh, if there had been no harping upon he was changed! I avoided answering him by asking if there would be lots to draw. He gave a pleased chuckle and the 'David Garrick' was come again!

If I would smoke, he would order *cubebs*. 'Come, let me see if you have kept faith with me. How is your little finger? It was a shame to stop the lessons — just because ——!' It was an almost audible laugh by now.

'I would rather watch you smoke, Mr. Booth. You are too much the stickler for finesse! Is Skill your god?'

'Oh, nonsense! One of my minor gods, perhaps! I have not thought of it before, but if there were worship-pers of Skill they would find a beneficent god. It pays in our profession to acquire skill, whatever name we give it!'

There were allusions to trifles I had not dreamed he noticed. So delicately were they touched upon one needed to be quick to catch them.

When Mr. Booth leaned back contentedly, I hoped for his mood of moods, the one I loved best of all, for then he had his being in a remoter past than the 'David Garrick.'

'Will you tell me of your father?'

'What do you wish to hear first?' This was asked as if it were important to him.

There was little for me to do now but listen. Mr.

304

THE SAME MR. BOOTH

Booth had crossed the barrier of his own fear of boring people by talking of himself. The old unrestraint of thinking aloud was with him again. He broke off at times to be silent — then took up his thread.

Cautiously I slipped in: 'Your mother? California? Booth's Theatre? Australia? Germany?'

I do not believe I was remembering that in all my chats with Mr. Booth he had not once told me his story. I took it for granted that he willingly led one he trusted within the Temple of Isis, but that the veil would stay his hand. Only once and for a moment had he lifted the curtain for me to see the ever-alive pain hidden deep in his heart over his loss of Booth's Theatre.

'I declare I have not talked so much of myself nor kept it up so long for years. Not since the last time my Chickens were with me. Shall you be in New York soon?'

'Oh, I hope so!'

'Come to The Players. I will take you all over the club. Is it a promise?'

I needed no urging. Mr. Booth's pride in The Players was a revelation to me. There had not been such a light in his eyes nor joy in his voice that night when he crossed the Rockies and unfolded his dream. He let me see he was not disappointed, that his club was more to him than his hope for it, and that he was rejoicingly grateful.

'You shall go into every nook and cranny at the club with me. It is against the rules, but *you* will not mind that. *I* may show you The Players.'

'Your own rooms, are they your real home now?'

'I hope to die in that room of mine. You will come and see its treasures.' He was gayly pleading. He spoke of the night we crossed the Rockies and of his inspiration from the silver lining. 'On a wakeful night I sit by my window in the club, and it is not hard to imagine I see the mirage of our diamond feathers hanging above Gramercy Park.'

I asked after Popper, but I called him Mr. Magonigle.

With the heartiest satisfaction Mr. Booth told me: 'Oh, he has been fixed up with a life berth in The Players. I am happy over it. I miss him on the road, but he is there to go back to.' Again that winsome smile. 'He will do his share to welcome one of my Chickens.'

'It will never do now to call him Popper, will it?'

'He will be hurt if he thinks you have forgotten his nickname.'

Mr. Booth spoke affectionately of Amo and Ido.

He told me of his nephews, Sydney and Junie, Agnes's boys, and that Junie (whom I knew well) was to be married and had called upon him to tell of the 'wonderful girl.' I noticed his old reserve, as he spoke of his daughter, but the adoration I remembered so well was again in his voice and eyes. When I asked of the *babies*, then came his human touch. He wanted me to see his little 'pets' as he saw them and even let my 'I suppose they have the Booth beauty' go unchallenged, although he switched the subject to his absent partner. I repeated some happy words of Mr. Barrett's upon their walks together the season before.

'Yes, we took our walks in each town. No, there was

no sight-seeing! What sights did the Chickens leave for me to see?'

He became serious when he told me of cutting his hand badly in the dagger scene in *Macbeth* in Boston last season, and how he *covered up*, and how he worried that he might stain Miss Gale's dress with his blood. 'My own blood' — he was smiling again — 'not the property blood you used to hide your poor abused face behind — until I stopped it!'

How he did remember! He recalled trifles here and there and even bits of frolic from his whole life!

'You do love to laugh, Mr. Booth, and so few people believe it!'

'Few see me laugh. I am laughing more this morning than I have — all this season.'

The characteristic quality of Mr. Booth's laughter was soundlessness.

He gave a vivid description of his father's acting; its terrifying effect upon those who went on with him.

'I have seen them forget that a frenzied scene was not actually happening to them personally.' Mr. Booth so stressed this effect of his great father's art upon his supporting actors, as if this ability to overcome them were merit extraordinary, that I could not bear it, and boldly reminded him of the story in circulation in the theatre of the poor ghost who was supporting *him* and who in terror ran off the stage into the alley when he looked into Hamlet's eyes.

'The horror in your own eyes, Mr. Booth, is something fearful to endure!'

He listened with more amusement than interest —

307

and with the tiniest of impatience thrust his acting out of the conversation.

I studied Mr. Booth sitting in the warming April sunshine, and from his manner I could not perceive that he was not just the same as on that day in Worcester when he had bidden us good-bye. By now I had lost all sense of time, and I think Mr. Booth had, too, for he seemed to be startled when his waiter brought the menu card. It was three o'clock!

'Will you not dine with me, after all? We have two hours — all the afternoon! I am not tired! I rest too much for my own good.'

I longed to stay. If Mr. Booth had not always been so considerate, so delicately thoughtful of others, I should have taken him at his word. It was only for one day, as he said, but it was like him to be willing to be tired out rather than hurt my feelings, and Hamlet was ahead of him — a big part, no matter how often he had gone on for it. He might be relying upon *my* own delicacy to decline. He knew I knew that he always did rest before his acting, and then, too, they had frightened me — in spite of all his vitality and cheerfulness — by saying he was changed.

I refused as beamingly as I could, and I heard him say with a mere ghost of a hint of peevishness: 'Tomorrow is the matinée. Why did you not come yesterday!' — and added pleadingly: 'Come to New York. When the season closes, we will have another visit, and do not put it off. You think you have years ahead of you. Try to look at time from *my* standpoint!'

THE SAME MR. BOOTH

'I do not wonder you think of me as a child, Mr. Booth. I fear I acted like one, many times, in the "David Garrick."'

He poohpoohed this. 'Were you in front last night?'

'Wild horses could not have kept me away.'

'There was a Richelieu once' — and the playfulness of his nature came to the surface again. 'Have I spoiled Richelieu for you? I hope not.'

All the morning I had been hoping Mr. Booth might feel the occasion worthy of an unreadable look. And now with the allusion to his burlesque of the Cardinal, his eyes tantalizingly lingered in their inscrutability upon mine. When the look had sunk in, he added: 'If I had known you were out there, I should have forced you to remember. Why did you not let me know?'

'I was too afraid of Mr. Chase!'

'Chase would, no doubt, have thrown a damper on it, but then he knows I am conservative this season. There is Madame Modjeska's art to respect — but the hateful truth is I do not feel like *cutting up!*'

'Nor I!'

'Oh, you never did — not much; you took it out in getting me to misbehave!'

So, Detroit was my home — he had forgotten! 'How little we of our profession know of the true lives of another actor. I *do* think of you as a child, but I dare say some man thinks you are old enough to be a wife!'

'Gracious, Mr. Booth, I *am* old enough!'

Mr. Booth said he had, for some time, wished to warn me — for he thought he understood my character better than I did myself: 'I shall speak to you as if you were my own daughter. You will marry some day, I hope — but do not marry a careless man.'

'Careless?'

'You think you are an inveterate genius-worshipper. You dazzle yourself deliberately with brilliant doings. You turn up your nose at goodness — I mean in the poor wretch who is trying to fascinate you. Now, do you not?'

'Usually, Mr. Booth.'

'The things that make you happy are all made up of goodness in others. Will you think of what I am saying — of what I am warning you against? Try to please me in this. Do it for me.' And then he smiled brightly. 'As if you would be thinking of me in that great moment! But I mean it!'

The waiter brought in the dinner and set his table.

'It is not too late, now, to dine with me!'

'No, Mr. Booth. I am going before you *feel* tired.'

'But you are coming behind tonight? And do not forget you are to call upon me at The Players.'

I went in front for the first act of *Hamlet*, and in the lobby Mr. Chase said he had a confidence for me. 'You should have dined with Mr. Booth. He was disappointed. Why did you refuse?'

I told him why, and begged him to repeat to Mr. Booth that I longed with all my heart to remain.

'After this, don't let any one tell you anything about Mr. Booth being changed. He does not change to his friends! He knows what he wants, and what he enjoys does not tire him — as you and I know!'

After the first act I went behind, and Sophie took me

to Madame Modjeska's dressing-room. I was furious
with myself that I was not telling her one half, nor half
of that half, of my long admiration for her. It seemed
so superfluous to say it when one was in her presence!
— She was interested in a young friend of Mr. Booth's.
Did Mr. Booth know I was here?

My visit with Mr. Booth was brief. I was always shy
in his dressing-room. My consciousness of his being
here the great actor overpowered me, while in the wings
he was so sociable one was at ease with him.

There were many reunions for me this night. The
handsome and dashing *Otis Skinner* came behind. My
good friend Charles Hanford presented the very young
Mr. Duval who went on for François. Mr. Booth had
said to me this morning that his François was a bit of a
genius. When I repeated his great Star's praise to this
young actor, 'he nearly dropped dead,' as he expressed
it, and flushed through his make-up.

On my way to the stage door Mr. Hanford followed
me. 'Ah, Jessica, at your old tricks.'

I indignantly advised him to ask if Mr. Booth had
not said it.

'Ask Mr. Booth? I would not dare! You must take
me for one of the Chickens!'

We laughed together and I left the theatre as happy
as in the 'David Garrick' days.

CHAPTER XLI

THE LAST TIME OF ALL

THE bill for the closing night was *The Merchant of Venice*, and I stayed behind until Mr. Booth's acting was over. Madame Modjeska again sent Sophie for me, and once more asked, 'Does Mr. Booth know you are here?'

Having been enjoined to keep out of Shylock's way in the old days, no rôle was less familiar to me than Shylock, except his scenes with Jessica. Tonight Shylock absorbed me. It was Shylock's reaction to the 'Quality of Mercy Speech' and not Modjeska's beautiful rendering of the lines that I was watching. It was Mr. Booth's acting-art of listening that compelled all my attention. As so often before, tonight I again lost all consciousness of myself in the hypnotic spell of his acting. I lived with Shylock. I followed that trial as if I had never seen it before! — as if the verdict were unknown to me. When it was decreed by the Court that Shylock must be baptized a Christian, I saw his soul twist with the shame of it. It was agonizing to see. With other Shylocks my sympathy had been with Antonio. Tonight I forgot Antonio and his cause — I saw only Shylock and his cause!

Mr. Booth for his final exit did not stagger off; he dragged off. His knees were feebly bending, his shoulders were pitifully drooping. His Shylock was dying before the curtain fell. One felt he was going out to slow death of body and horrible rebellion of mind.

UNVEILING OF THE STATUE OF BOOTH IN GRAMERCY PARK, NEW YORK

NOVEMBER 13, 1918

THE LAST TIME OF ALL

From a clairvoyance born of overstrained nerves, I knew that, when Shylock passed through that scenery door and it closed again, it would shut from me — for all time — the acting of Edwin Booth! I went to pieces. A newspaper woman, Johanna Staats, a stranger to me, took me in her arms, whispering: 'Why, you are just a bundle of nerves.'

I made my way to Mr. Booth's dressing-room for my good-bye. Remembering Worcester, I was on guard this time. A very much-alive actor spoke through the curtained door and gave me a shock, he was so cheerful. One would think he and tragedy had nothing in common. Would I meet him over at the Russell House by the stairs on the parlor floor? He was leaving tonight, but there would be time for a short visit. He said, in his teasingest tones, 'I would prefer not to say this good-bye in my Shylock make-up — I remember it had the effect of making you lose your head.'

Regardless of my prophetic heart, I determined that this good-bye should pass off as if it were the most pleasing thing in the world, and if I had not come to it fresh from Mr. Booth's genius I should not have been fearful for my poise. But I had not recovered from his acting! To safeguard my behavior I conscripted Johanna Staats! Would she come up with me — stay far enough away not to trouble Mr. Booth, but close enough to restrain me? Would she? She would, and gladly. Just to see him without his make-up was enough. I could depend on her.

We did not wait long. Mr. Booth came with Mr. Chase, ready for the train, and said at once: 'It is like me to have taken you from the last act and Madame Modjeska's acting. I never think in time. You look, child, as if a happy ending would do you good. Throw Shylock overboard.' He smiled, and far from sadly.

'I was priding myself, Mr. Booth, I was behaving this time! I really believed I was looking happy. But I always did contrive the wrong thing for *The Merchant!* Didn't I?'

He nodded.

'Why — what?' asked Mr. Chase. 'I never heard of this.'

'Do not ask her, Mr. Chase, or she will slip out of promising to come to The Players. There is only time for a threat — to punish her — if she does not.'

'Miss Kitty, you do not need threats to call upon Mr. Booth, I am sure!'

'I was born with a caul! Do you remember?'

'Yes, Mr. Booth.'

'Something tells me you will not come.'

'But I want to come — so very much!'

'Good-bye!'

I leaned over the railing as he went down the stairs with Mr. Chase. Twice Mr. Booth stopped to look up, and each time there was a little twinkle in his eyes. At the foot he stood and looked up again. He lifted his hat! My eyes may have become too sober, for when the contagion of his own smile forced one from me, he nodded in playful approval. For an instant I saw again the boy he had coaxed from his soul leap into his glowing eyes! He

314

THE LAST TIME OF ALL

was our Mr. Booth! He was the host of the 'David Garrick'! He held his hat a little higher — but he did not wave it! He was yet looking up — the tiniest teasing in his eyes — as Mr. Chase guided him away — to pass from my sight — forever!

CHAPTER XLII

CONCLUSION

THE years rolled by. In moments when the spirit of my girlhood seized me, I loved to give imagination reign and pretend I was rushing to The Players to be greeted by Mr. Booth and pour out my great news that I had heeded his hope for me — and that I had married a man after his own heart. It has been easy to conjure up that alive face with its glowing eyes and watch it become whimsical in its amusement. For he was sure to say: 'So, you did not forget my warning — you did remember me in your great moment — and by now you know how right I was to insist upon *the good man*.'

No, nothing concerning Mr. Booth was forgotten. The memories of the 'David Garrick' chats and the outings were a source of delight to the man I married, who had known and loved the great genius of the theatre before I was born. My husband's Pipery became a shrine for Booth mementoes. Mr. Goodale it was who first urged me to fix on paper my memories of these wonderful days — 'for our increasing pleasure as shadows lengthen.'

Then he, too, withdrew from human vision, and of his friend G. P. G., Mr. George Broadhurst wrote in that hour:

> 'His voice was gentle, his smile was sweet,
> His heart was strong.
> If all those he helped should chance to meet,
> God! What a throng!'

CONCLUSION

When I had been married almost as many years as I was old the night I leaned over the stairs to watch Mr. Booth go down them, Mr. Goodale asked me of what I was thinking.

I told him I was wondering — if I were to die and be greeted by one with authority and he should say: 'You have enough good to your credit to make it possible for me to grant one wish. You may ask for one perfect thing. What earth-experience re-lived will give you the most pleasure and happiness? This one thing is yours now — on the instant! After it, comes another story.'

Mr. Goodale, no more than Mr. Booth, poked fun at one's spoken-aloud fleeting thoughts.

'I understand. Would you know? What would you ask for?'

'I should say: "Let me see Edwin Booth — in *Hamlet*."'

My listener was leaning back in his easy-chair smoking, finding such comfort in his pipe that he recalled that other smoker and his pipe, and his comfort in it. My husband reflected, and then said, with conviction: 'I believe I should ask that too.'

THE END

INDEX

INDEX

25; effect on audience, 25; make-up as Macbeth, 26; criticism and correction of Miss Molony's make-up for 'Bloody Apparition,' 28, 29; 'horror' in his eyes a greenroom topic, 29; actor into man, 33; supper with members of company, 35, 36; study of Hamlet, 36; recipient of 'love,' 37-39; 'kissing' episode and its effect, 40, 41; aversion to strangers, 41; judgment on Jessica costumes, 42, 43; his make-up for villains, 44; excursion to Minnehaha Falls, 44-47; as Iago, 48; Joseph Jefferson 'opposition' in Chicago, 49, 50; critics compare them, 50; his marriage, *note*, 51, 52; attitude toward newly engaged actors, 52, 53; instructions to Jessica in relation to Shylock, 53, 54; visits Shaw's Gardens in St. Louis, 56; first acting of *Richard III* in St. Louis, 57; appearance and reception as Richard, 57, 58; manner of taking curtain calls, 59; colloquy on curtain calls, 59-61; experience in Boston in *Richard III*, 61, 62; wail over far-fetched psychology, 62, 63; reflections on endowed theatre, 65, 66; acting detached from company, 66; headed for New York, 67, 68; opening night, 69; manner toward audiences, 69, 70; told of Miss Molony's broken mirror, 70; premonition of harm comes true, illness closes theatre, 71; pays salaries in full while ill, 72; recovers, theatre reopens, 72; Miss Molony dissipates memory of broken mirror, 73; never burlesqued as was Henry Irving, 74; Nat Goodwin's explanation therefor, 75; opening night in Boston as a shrine, 76; his début there recalled, 76; when they put the orchestra on the stage, 77; incident repeated, 78; plays full repertoire in Boston, 80; effect of Tubal scene, 82; warns Miss Molony away from first entrance, 83; 'lost' Tubal scene, 84; Philadelphia *via* one-night stands, 86; *en tour*, 87, 88; describes interesting room in Philadelphia, 88, 89; life in his company compared with Barrett's, 92; refuses to play Washington, plays Baltimore, 94; pales at mention of floral tributes, they are forbidden, 94; golden wreaths and laurel leaves, 94, 95; miracle of box-office tribute, 95; naming brothers and sisters, avoids mention of John Wilkes Booth, 95, 96; outwitted Fate in London with Stars and Stripes, 96; his child born under flag, 96, 97; towns that claimed him, 97, 98; 'would not go to Washington, and Washington came to him,' 98; opposition from Frank Mayo in Pittsburgh, 99; permits Miss Rock to play Regan for one performance, 100-03; hires private car

'David Garrick,' 104; invites members of company as guests, 104, 105; psychology of acting death and insanity, 106, 107; phenomena of cauls and their significance in his life, 107, 108; story of attempt to shoot him, 108, 109; locked jaw of Iago, 110; loathing of long hair, 111; effect of his Fool, 112; aboard 'David Garrick,' 113 *et seq.*; origin of his given names, 115; a Richelieu memory, 116; sighs in vain for Napoleon play, 117, 118; letter from Mrs. T. B. Aldrich, 119, 120; the Aldriches in Egypt, 120, 121; 'a cipher without a rim,' 121; kiss earns forfeit from Miss Molony, 122, 123; story of Magonigle's Solon Shingle, 124; a judge of acting, 125; socks darned, 126-28; kissing psychology, 127, 128; accused in London of using dummy in *Fool's Revenge*, 128, 129; never had stage fright, 129, 130; Germans insisted on his Othello, did not want his Iago, 131, 132; their eloquent tribute, 133; worried about daughter's health, 134, 135; inveigled into playing $3000 matinée, 137-39; studied insanity for his mad scenes, 141, 142; skill in fencing and blowing smoke rings, 142; teaches Miss Molony to blow smoke rings, 143; played leading rôle in *The San Francisco Fire Boy*, 146; big scene, 146-48; insomnia's grip, 149, 150; memories of his mother and daughter, 151, 152; advised to wear wig in *Hamlet*, 158; approaching San Francisco, 162, 163; harping on the wig, 164; gaze on San Francisco, 165; 'opens tonight,' 166; his room at Palace Hotel, 167; story of its flower decoration, 168; eve of the wig, 169; wig on, 170; feels hampered by it, 171; wears it throughout play, 172 *et seq.*; changes directions of his Prompt Book, 176; development of his rôles, 177, 178; reception forces tears, continues through play, 178-82; death scenes, 182; eulogies, 183; wig still in evidence, 184; yachting on the Pacific, 185-88; subject of tales, 191; advantages of his association, 193, 194; his playing of Sir Giles Overreach, 197, 198; Salvini's Othello a challenge, 199, 200; at Cliff House, 200; plan to lure him to play Othello, 201, 202; acting a tonic, 203; consents to play Othello, 204; host to party in drive through city and Golden Gate Park, 205; preparing for Othello, 206, 207; make-up, 207, 208; to play to Miss Molony, 209; house packed, 210; thrill of his appearance, 211, 212; reactions to his playing, 213, 214; audience frenzied, 215; complains of the hard work, 216; crowned greatest living Othello, 217; omen of the

INDEX

INDEX

Chase, Arthur Branscomb, manager for Booth, 13, 18, 20; asks Miss Molony to be his confidante, 33, 34; at supper with Booth, 35, 36; concerned over 'love' for Booth, 37–39; makes up party to visit Minnehaha Falls, 45–47; remorse over photograph with hat on, 47; smiles at 'opposition,' 49; suggests riding in engine cab, 55; importance of bad notice, 63; in Cleveland, 64; prospects of New York, 67; optimism on New York business, 69, 70; worried over Booth's illness, 71, 72; not referred to again, 73; gave him fright, 76; hears story of orchestra on stage for Booth's *Hamlet*, 77; sees incident repeated, 79; sceptical of old tales, 85; at Syracuse, 87; takes Miss Molony to New York to see Barrett, 91, 92; inspirer vs. servitor, 93; fails to induce Booth to play Washington, 94; puzzled over box-office miracle, 95; in poetical mood, 98; Miss Rock for Regan at one performance,

INDEX

INDEX

324

INDEX

Philadelphia from Booth, 88, 89; sticking door causes stage-wait, 90; sent for by Barrett, 91, 92; compares life in Booth's company with Barrett's, 92; questions Booth on brothers and sisters, 95; given new readings and change of interpretation by Frank Mayo, 99, 100; invited to be Booth's guest in 'David Garrick,' 104; mother danced with Barrett, 105; sight-seeing drive in New Orleans, 105, 106; study of death and insanity in acting, 106, 107; phenomena of cauls, 107, 108; Booth tells story of attempt to shoot him, 108, 109; watches Booth's locked jaw of Iago, 110; effect of his Hamlet, 111; aboard 'David Garrick,' 113 *et seq.*; dubbed 'cipher without rim,' 121; a dream, a kiss, a pair of gloves, 122, 123; better judge of acting than Booth, 125; darns his socks, 126–28; inveigles Booth to play $3000 matinée, 137–39; taught by him to blow smoke rings, 143; *The San Francisco Fire Boy* and Booth's part in it, 146–49; his tender memories unfolded, 151, 152; good title for a mystery play — maybe, 153; more diplomacy to be engaged in with Booth, 154, 155; expected to persuade him to wear wig in *Hamlet*, 155 *et seq.*; warned of her imminent mission, 162; shadow of the wig, 163, 167; beholds it on, 170; apprehensive of its remaining on till end of play, 171 *et seq.*; effect of Booth's death scenes, 182; yachting on the Pacific, 185–88; sees Minnie Maddern in *Caprice*, 193–96; outing at Cliff House, 200; urged to persuade Booth to play Othello, agrees, 201, 202; obtains his consent, 204; box and fruit glacé for reward, 205, 206; asked by Booth to look him over, 207; passes judgment on his make-up as Othello, 208; effect of his acting, 212 *et seq.*; buys peacock feathers, they become an omen, 218 *et seq.*; off for holiday week in 'David Garrick,' 222 *et seq.*; on the beach at Monterey, 228 *et seq.*; search for Nothing, 236; seeds of Cedars of Lebanon, 238; to go to Boothden, 241; at Royle family home, 244; hovering Chase confidence, 245; epic of the brass band, 245 *et seq.*; crossing Rocky Mountains, above the clouds, 253, 254; hears of Booth's 'club,' 254; 'The Players' outlined, 255, 256; women members to be barred, 255, 256; another confidence from Chase, 258; prospects of trip to Garden of the Gods, 258, 259; walking with Booth in Garden of the Gods, 261, 262; at Denver Club, 263–65; complained of to Booth, 266; one of the 'Beggars on Horseback,' to be tried by Booth, 267, 268; the trial, 269,

270; cleared, 270; confidential news of next season, 272; not to be reëngaged, 272; watches Booth's last Iago of season, 274; entertains him with Frank Mayo's criticism of his inartistic Iago, 279, 280; told of Mrs. Irving's letter to Booth asking for tickets, 281, 282; suggests Booth play *Richelieu* on one-night stands, 283; his approval rouses suspicion of manager against her, 284, 285; gasps at hearing Booth called 'Uncle,' 286; might-have-been visit to Newport, 288; Booth makes faces at her on closing night, 290; grateful for Barrett's training, 290; watches Booth burlesque Richelieu, 291, 292; last drive with him, 293; asked by Chase to guard against scenes at good-bye, 294, 295; sobs at parting, 297, 298; in *Partners*, 299; calls on Booth and Barrett during New York engagement, 300, 301; to Detroit to visit Booth, 301–04; invited to The Players when in New York, 305; an afternoon with him in Detroit, 306–10; warned by him against marrying a careless man, 309, 310; many reunions, 311; absorbed in Booth's Shylock, 312, 313; the last good-bye — forever, 314, 315; mementoes and memories, 316, 317

Monterey, 225, 226, 239, 241, 258, 301, 302
Monterey Hotel, burned, 224
Mormon Temple, concert in honor of Booth, 242; acoustics, 242, 243
'Mother's gratitude, a,' 168
My Sweetheart, 193

Nabob Hill, 206
Napoleon, Booth's desire for a play on him, 117, 118
New Orleans, 3, 4, 104, 105, 110, 140, 237, 259
New Way to Pay Old Debts, A, 12, 197, 198
New York, 67, 68, 69, 70, 71, 72, 91, 92, 97, 98, 134, 243, 273
Niblo's (New York), 286

Oakland, Cal., 148, 162, 163
Omaha, 266
Oneida, yacht, 255
'One-Night Stands,' 86, 283; *note*, 288
Oswego, N.Y., 86
Othello, 12, 33, 268, 301. *See also under* Characters
Owens, John E., 124

Palace Hotel, 164, 167, 205, 216, 225
Palmer, A. M., 299
Palmer, Minnie, 193
Partners, 299
Peacock feathers an omen, 218–20
Philadelphia, 86, 88, 89, 98
Pittsburgh, 99

INDEX

'Players, The,' club, genesis, 254, 255; aims discussed, 255, 256; room of hallowed memory, 299; Booth's pride, 305; life berth for Magonigle, 306; invitation to Miss Molony to call on Booth there, 310; promise — unfulfilled, 314, 315; a memory, and imagination, 316
'Popper,' see Magonigle, J. H.
Programmes of satin, 243
Prompt Books (Booth), 17, 20, 21, 176

'Quality of Mercy' speech, 312

Ranch Ten, 248
Rankin, McKee, 74
Richard II, 108; III, 5, 12, 14, 49, 57, 58, 61, 64, 80. See also under Characters
Richelieu, 9, 11, 12, 13, 14, 19, 22, 33, 89, 242, 273, 283, 284, 285, 286, 289, 293
Rienzi, 91
Rochester, N.Y., 86
Rock, Ida, 12, 13; rôles, 14; 37; 'in love' with Booth, 38; a lone Court Lady, 39; excursion to Minnehaha Falls, 45–47; nicknamed Ido, 100; prepares to play Regan, 100–02; name left off programme, 103; Booth's guest in 'David Garrick,' 105; helps darn his socks, 126–28; 144, 167, 184, 188, 218; hanging from brass rods, 237; difference of future, 239; pleased at brass band prospect, 247; breakfast at Manitou Springs, 261; causes stage-wait, 265; apologizes, 266; one of the 'Beggars on Horseback,' 269; on stage with Booth as he burlesques Richelieu, 291; remembered affectionately by Booth, 306
Rocky Mountains, crossing the, 253, 305
Royle, Edwin Milton, of the company, 13; rôles, 14; in Merchant of Venice, 82; his acting as Guildenstern, 244; as Tubal, 244; home in Salt Lake City, 244; his Squaw Man, 245
Royle, Mattie, 243
Royle family, 244
Russell House, 301, 313

Saenger Saal, 248
Saginaw, Mich., 36
St. Louis, 55
St. Paul, 48
Salaries paid for lost performances and travelling, 19, 72, 145
Salt Lake City, 242; concert in Booth's honor at Mormon Temple, its acoustics, 242, 243; young Mormon prima donna, 243; home of Edwin Milton Royle, 244
Salvini, Tommaso, as Othello, 166, 199, 200, 201, 203, 209, 210, 215
San Antonio, 136, 137, 139, 145, 146, 154
San Francisco, 61, 97, 104, 132, 138, 140,

143, 146, 149, 156, 160, 163, 164, 165, 167, 173, 174, 176, 178, 179, 183, 184, 198, 199 205, 218, 222, 224, 302
San Francisco Fire Boy, The, 146, 149, 163, 291
Saunders, Mrs., 174, 182
Schiller Theatre, 65
Scranton, Pa., 86
Seal Rocks, 234
Shaw's Gardens in St. Louis, 56
Sherman, Gen. William T., 4
Skinner, Otis, 311
Sophie of the Baldwin Theatre, 301, 302, 303, 310, 312
'Springes to catch woodcocks,' 290
Squaw Man, The, 245
Staats, Johanna, 313
Stage-wait, 90, 265
Star system, 275
Star Theatre, New York, 3, 7, 68; opening night, 69; closed on Booth's illness, 71; reopens, 72; 134, 155
Streamer, Volney, of the company, 13; rôles, 14
Sturgeon, Mr., of Barrett's company, 31, 32
Sullivan, Barry, controversy with orchestra leader Lothian, 78, 79
Sullivan, John T., of the company, rôles, 13; wants 'She,' 189; association with Minnie Maddern, 190, 191
Syracuse, N.Y., 86, 87, 241

Tabor Opera House, 260
Tannhäuser, 248
Terry, Ellen, gift to Miss Molony, 15; helps on her Jessica dress, 15, 16, 43, 44; her grace, 155; ranged with Minnie Maddern, 196; her tours, 220; compares Irving's Iago with Booth's, 278, 279
Thomas, Walter, of the company, 13; rôles, 14
Those Bells, 74
Tudor Hall, Bellair, Booth homestead, 97

Utica, N.Y., 86

Vaders, Emma, leading lady with Booth, 13; rôles, 14; makes one of group, 18; jumpy, 30; at supper with Booth, 34–36; one of the 'Chickens,' 37; nicknamed Amo, 37; 'in love' with Booth, 37–39; excursion to Minnehaha Falls, 45; suspected of wanting to play Jessica, 53; visits Shaw's Gardens in St. Louis, 56; Magonigle becomes 'Papa' to her, 56; reproved for changing speech, 64; how she might appear to Booth, 85; leaving Boston in good spirits, 87; guest in 'David Garrick,' 105; envious over darning of Booth's socks, 126; in San Francisco, 164; first appearance there, 167;

INDEX